Gorkhaland Movement

About the Author

Swatahsiddha Sarkar (b. 1975) is an Assistant Professor in the Department of Sociology, University of North Bengal (Darjeeling, India). Besides having a handful of published research articles in academic journals and edited volumes, he keeps up keen interest in the field of Identity Politics and Ethnicity. He has been associated with Gorkha Ethnicity and Politics for more than a decade. The author is an M.Phil. in Himalayan Studies and recently awarded the Ph.D. Degree (Delhi School of Economics, Delhi University) for his Doctoral Thesis on Gorkha Ethnicity and Movement in the Darjeeling Hills. He has co-edited a volume on *Ethnicity in India* (Levant, 2013).

Gorkhaland Movement

Ethnic Conflict and State Response

Swatahsiddha Sarkar

CONCEPT PUBLISHING COMPANY PVT. LTD.,
NEW DELHI-110059

ISBN-13 : 978-93-5125-007-4

First Published 2013

Published and Printed by

Concept Since 1974

Concept Publishing Company Pvt. Ltd.
A/15-16, Commercial Block, Mohan Garden
New Delhi-110059 (India)
T: 25351460, 25351794, *F*: 091-11-25357109
E: publishing@conceptpub.com, W: www.conceptpub.com
Editorial Office: H-13, Bali Nagar, New Delhi-110 015, India.

Cataloging in Publication Data--Courtesy: D.K. Agencies (P) Ltd. <docinfo@dkagencies.com>

Sarkar, Swatahsiddha, 1975-
Gorkhaland movement : ethnic conflict and state response / Swatahsiddha Sarkar.
p. cm.
Includes bibliographical references (p.) and index.
ISBN 9789351250074

1. Nepali people—India—Darjeeling (District)—Politics and government. 2. Gurkhas—India—Darjeeling (District)—Politics and government. 3. Darjeeling (India : District)—Politics and government. 4. Darjeeling (India : District)—History Autonomy and independence movements. 5. Darjeeling (India : District)—Ethnic relations. 6. Gorkhaland Territorial Administration. I. Title.

DDC 954.1400491495 23

Dedicated
to my parents

Acknowledgements

The idea of the present book grew up out of my association with the CCRHS, New Delhi as a Fellow for the period 2010-11. Not to mention that the necessary funds needed for the completion of the present study were generously allocated by the CCRHS, New Delhi. I am thankful to the entire CCRHS fraternity, especially to Ms. Varsha Gewali, Ms. Meha Dixit, Mr. Faizan Ahmed and Mr. Sunil Gupta who took keen interest in the present work. The book came out initially as a project report of the CCRHS and I am thankful to the entire CCRHS team for allowing me publish the reworked version of the project report. Although, the work is financially assisted by the CCRHS, it does not reflect the viewpoint of the organization in anyway.

My departmental colleagues have helped me a lot by raising several critical points whenever I discussed issues with them. Prof. Sanjay K. Roy's contributions deserve special mention, who identified several debatable points raised in the present study and offered valuable suggestions to rework them. I am indebted to him. Field assistants like Kumar, Sophia, Karma, Smriti, and Pooja have taken the pains to complete the interviews of the informants and in collecting relevant data from the field. I am extremely thankful to them. Mr. Pintu Majumdar and Mr. Gour Gopal Barman have helped in data processing while Mr. Subir Das Mohanta gave the present effort a printable shape. I am grateful to all of them. I am also indebted to Dr. Madhumita Sen, Dr. Debaprasad Chatterjee and Dr. Jyotiprasad Chatterjee for their enriching comments and constructive criticisms offered on the occasion of one of my presentations held at Maulana Azad College, Kolkata in the recent past.

No word of thankfulness can be sufficient for the contribution that Mrs. Basnet of Darjeeling has made by giving me the opportunity to consult some of the rarest Government documents which have been profitably used in the present study. Satyadeep, Dibyendu and Anjan have stimulated critical nods in my thought as always. I am obliged to them. Last but not the least in the list of acknowledgement my respondents are there to whom I am immensely obliged. It is they who have given me time, even amidst their busy schedule, to discuss on issues of my purpose. It is because of their cooperation and help I have been able to incorporate the 'field view' in the present study.

I am also grateful to Mr. Ashok Kumar Mittal of Concept Publishing Co. Pvt. Ltd., New Delhi-110059, who took keen interest in my work and even patiently allowed me to incorporate the postscript and some necessary reworking in the text.

However, for analytical inconsistency, thematical guilt or incorrect data, if any, none other than me is responsible.

Siliguri, Darjeeling **Swatahsiddha Sarkar**
August 28, 2012

Contents

List of Tables

List of Figures

1
Introduction

The issues of ethnic consciousness, ethnic conflict, and ethnic violence until recently were being overlooked, underestimated, if not essentialised by the social scientists, who were engulfed mainly by any of the two overpowering ideological strands prevalent in social science scholarship, i.e. either modernisation or Marxism. The modernisation school denies the existence of the issues like ethnic consciousness or conflict (since, it presumes that, the very term 'ethnic' reflects the idea of tradition, hence needs to be negated) at the cost of legitimising the hegemonic 'melting pot thesis'. The Marxist tradition, on the other hand, nullifies the ethnic issues by branding them as 'false consciousness' and as remnants of capitalism to be replaced by proletarian internationalism.

However, the experience of our everyday life disproved the strength of such theoretical deductions. Instead of evaporating the religious, linguistic, and ethnic differences, the process of modernisation provoked them. People started valuing more the cultural traits they have, rather than their class position, to raise their voice. On the whole, the so-called grand narratives have largely failed to grasp the emerging global social issues in any meaningful way. Attempts were thus being made to think beyond the meta-narratives of 'class' as primary conceptual and organisational category and to focus instead on those moments and processes produced in the articulation of cultural differences (Bhaba, 1994:1).

Discarding the assimilationist assumption as well as the epiphenomenal tag, ethnic conflicts have become a global issue of concern. While the newly independent countries continue to experience the effects of ethnic polarisation, ethnic passions have now proliferated in those regions of the world, which remained largely outside the purview of ethnic upsurge earlier. Ethnic identity issues now stirred not only the so-called developed countries like Canada, United Kingdom, Spain, France, and the United States but also in the former Communist countries too. Ethnic and racial cleavages have now become a part of the global political landscape (Jalali & Lipset. 1992-93:586). Indeed, there has been an ethnic revival throughout the globe, which showed that the clashes the modern political systems are experiencing with, are more cultural and civilizational rather than economic, political or ideological (Huntington, 1997: 21).

Besides being a global issue of concern, ethnic conflicts and movements are gaining momentous growth in South Asian political landscape in general and in countries like India, in particular. It is no exaggeration to put that post-independent Indian politics is torn between politics of identity and politics of culture. Gorkha bid for a homeland, among others articulated on the pretext of language, culture, community, and region within Indian union has been a recurrent theme of India's national politics for quite some time now. However, Gorkha ethnicity in India is not of recent origin. It did maintain a colonial pedigree too. In that Gorkha movement appears as a historic occurrence having more than hundred years' legacy. On the contrary the conflict resolution initiatives taken so far in Indian subcontinent, in general and in case of Darjeeling hills, in particular are not many but practically few in number.

The attempts to resolve the growing ethno-regional conflicts in India remain by and large amenable to a single approach that presupposes the conflicts principally as political problems and hence attempts were made to resolve the same politically. Consequently, the several measures adopted so far to bring in ceasefire and peace in conflicting zones in India fall back upon such initiatives like political intervention and negotiating political power-sharing agreements, or initiation of new political structures. The recommendations of the States Reorganisation Commission (SRC), Constitutional recognition of language, the regional autonomy proposals, Sixth Schedule status, or the sub-state level autonomous district councils are some such strategies used so far to dissipate tensions and resolve issues effectively whenever conflicts have arisen in the wake of ethno-regional claims within the larger body polity of India. However, on certain particular occasions, the Indian state took resort to direct military intervention to dismantle domestic conflict permanently (Kashmir, Nagaland etc.). In a certain sense, the experience of conflict resolution measures in India does suggest that as if the ethno-regional conflicts and movements are more a law and order problem and hence the recurrent need is to discipline the unruly subjects according to the pedagogic substance of an archetypical nation state, which disapproves by and large the social and cultural plurality of individual minds and souls. The ethnic conflict resolution measures undertaken by the government attempted to function more as an apparatus of power by virtue of the field of visibility in which communities were to be located, each in their respective places for a centralised and unseen observer.

The experience of Gorkha movement throughout its more than hundred years' history has been reflective of two major claims: firstly, an aspiration to govern themselves without jeopardizing the sovereignty of the nation-state (i.e. 'self-determination without secession'); and secondly, the urge to recognize collective rights and almost all salient cultural and social issues that earmarked their distinctions and distinctiveness from an inescapable 'other' (i.e. 'politics of culture', 'identity' and 'recognition'). Although the conflict resolution measures have been able to fulfil, at least initially, the aspiration of self-government of the contending parties, they fail to meet the challenges posed by politics of identity and recognition. Consequently, conflict resolution measures in deeply divided societies like India fail to usher in peace and tranquillity in a sustainable manner.

The Government, however, has remained engaged in settling down Darjeeling imbroglio not only when it turned violent but also in such situations when the movement was more or less peaceful. It is interesting to note in this context that available studies on Darjeeling [like those of Subba (1992), Timsina (1992), Kar (1999), Samanta (2000) among others] despite having made significant contribution in understanding ethnic phenomena in Darjeeling hills have avoided making any assessment regarding the peace keeping initiatives. Available narratives of Gorkhaland have documented the track record of violence (e.g. Samanta, 2000) and the historical development of the movement with enough detail (e.g. Subba, 1992). Undoubtedly, such analyses pinpointed the strength of Gorkhaland as a specific case of an ethnic movement. Nevertheless, the issue of conflict resolution or for that matter such crucial questions like what were the definite strands (i.e. approaches) and steps (i.e. the strategies of conflict resolution) the state has taken recourse to while dealing with the overall dynamics of Gorkha ethnicity and movement of Darjeeling hills, are completely glossed over, if not ignored. More particularly such issues like: did the state responded to the Gorkha movement in equal terms especially when we do know that the movement has been continuing for more than a century and obviously followed both a violent and a non-violent warpath? What was the overall treatment Gorkhaland movement received from the part of the state? How to conceptualise it? How to theorise relationship between ethnicity and the state? All these are significant areas of inquiry particularly in the treatment of Gorkha problem not merely as a case of ethnicity but as a significant example that could well set the tune of the study of ethnic conflict resolution in a micro perspective in deeply divided societies like India. This is not to claim that the present study has drawn attention to a virgin field. Rather what is novel is its approach towards an issue that has already been considered in some detail. Precisely, the present effort is but an attempt to fulfil the above posed academic void (in relation to Gorkha ethnicity) by analysing the pros and cons of peace initiatives and conflict resolution measures adopted and exercised by the state in the context of Darjeeling hills and thereby to arrive at a micro-level understanding of ethnic conflict resolution and peace keeping measures in Indian situation.

Although scholarly works with particular reference to Darjeeling's ethnic conflict and conflict resolution measures are rarely available, there is no dearth of literature on the conceptual and theoretical aspects of conflict and peace resolution initiatives with reference to Indian situation. It would not be out of place to pay attention to some of the recent works of this genre.

Baruah (2010) in his recently edited *Ethnonationalism* collective poses the question: "How is India doing *vis-à-vis* the challenge of managing its exceptional diversity?" The essays presented in the volume have answered differently to the problem posed by the editor. For example, Kanti Bajpai suggested that a mix of state violence and political compromise with militant groups has been successful at least in the sense that India has not splintered. Gurharpal Singh questioned the conventional wisdom about India's successful record in managing diversity. Sumit Ganguly warned of the dangers of using the army against particular ethnic groups in poly-ethnic states like

India. Ganguly further argued that insurgency in India, in general and Kashmir, in particular, arose out of a process of political mobilisation that was juxtaposed with steady institutional decay. Atul Kohli while analysing the trend of ethno-nationalist movements in India has argued that such movements followed an inverse 'U' curve: heightened mobilisation of group identities are followed by negotiations, and eventually such movements decline as exhaustion sets in, some leaders are repressed, others are co-opted, and a modicum of genuine power-sharing and mutual accommodation between the movement and the Central and State authorities is reached. The inverted 'U' curve explains Tamil Nadu situation rather well and even Sikh ethnonationalism can be explained through this model, argues Kohli. However, there is doubt whether the inverse 'U' curve model can help us appreciate Darjeeling situation, which in fact, showed a curvilinear pattern of growth.

J.S. Chima (2010) in his book on Sikh separatism attempted to develop a coherent and consistent theory for explaining the rise and decline of Sikh insurgency in India. The central argument of Chima's thesis is that internal disunity and competition between state elites often contribute to the rise of violent ethno-nationalism, and their internal unity and coordinated action can conversely help dampen violent ethno-nationalist movements.

What would be the possible answer to the recurrent dilemma faced by the policy-makers over the ideal mix up of development and military approaches to contain insurgency is the central theme of another major collective on counter-insurgency edited by Barauh (2009). While one of the contributors of the collective pointed out that development in north-eastern India means a little more than externally delivered economic packages which can be translated through various backdoor means and leakages, at the soonest possible into hard cash, another contributor argues that neither development nor a military fix can achieve peace in north-eastern region. Only concerted efforts to establish the rule of law, a system of accountability, and faith in the institutions of government can break the cycle of violence, the authors say. Bethany Lacina, one of the contributors, suggested that the influence and endurance of insurgency in the north-eastern region are because of the fact that armed groups are embedded in the workings of the north-eastern civilian politics which makes it difficult for politicians or bureaucrats to act independently of the rebels. This finding seems to be the case in Darjeeling hills too.

Benedikter (2009) has produced a useful short guide on autonomy movements in South Asia and attempted to show, through various case studies, how such ethnic conflicts were solved through self-government measures. Although the guide includes a separate chapter (Chapter 23) on Darjeeling situation (written by the editor himself) and covers the recent eventualities of Gorkhaland movement but it hardly maintains any conclusive statement regarding the effective step to promulgate peace in future Darjeeling. However, elsewhere the book did count on the potentiality of autonomy as a device for regional democratic self-government and minority rights protection. The case studies available in this book help gain a synoptic view on the contemporaneous problems of ethnic conflicts in South Asia and the possible ways to resolve such conflicts amicably through autonomy measures of different sorts.

The Context

The Gorkhas are spread all over the subcontinent; however, the present study is concerned precisely with the Gorkhas located in the Darjeeling hills and their claims to have separate state of their own. Darjeeling is the northern most district of the State of West Bengal containing hills and plains regions. Three hill subdivisions (namely Darjeeling *Sadar,* Kurseong and Kalimpong) constitute the hill portion of the district while Siliguri subdivision represents the plains part of the district. Until recently the demand for a separate state in the name of Gorkhaland covered uphill portion of the district only. With the passage of time the territorial jurisdiction of the much hyped Gorkhaland State went on increasing. Along with the hills the proposed territorial limits of the Gorkhaland movement in contemporary days claims to cover the areas of Teari (located in the plains areas of the district of Darjeeling) and Dooars (located in adjacent district of Jalpaiguri). The following map (Fig. 1.1) indicates the territorial limits of the proposed State of Gorkhaland.

The Gorkhaland agitation was built, as its name indicates around Gorkha ethnic identity. Its perception of the problems of the ethnic Nepalis in India differs from that of the leadership in Sikkim, and so do their political strategies (Dube, 1997: 194). However, it would be erroneous to conceive of the demand for a separate state called

Fig. 1.1: Proposed Map of Gorkhaland

Source: Available at: http://upload.wikimedia.org/wikipedia/commons/5/50/Proposed_Gorkhaland_Map.jpg(Accessed on 8.1.12)

Gorkhaland as an abrupt upsurge of 1980s. In fact, the demand for a separate statehood has its seeds rooted deeply in the developments of colonial rule of the early 20th century. The first recorded instance of the demand for separation of Darjeeling hills from the then Bengal on the grounds of ethnic difference can be traced back in the year of 1907[1]. Since then the demand for a separate arrangement for Darjeeling hills has been raised time and again. Moreover, the same demand still remains unabated and the movement is still continuing with added vigour and vitality. Within this long stretched time frame (i.e. from 1907 to 2012) Gorkhaland movement has had harped not only on statehood alone but on several issues like constitutionalisation of Nepali language, citizenship issue, political status of the territory, abrogation of Indo-Nepal peace treaty of 1950, tribal status, sixth schedule status, Darjeeling-Sikkim merger, inclusion of more areas within the purview of the proposed state of Gorkhaland, Gorkha Adivasi Pradesh, Gorkhaland Territorial Administration (GTA), and finally, Gorkha Adivasi Territorial Administration (GATA).

There is no gainsaying the truth that in any analysis of ethnic movement emphasis on the domain of state is obvious. Since it is around the institution called the state the question of ethnicity or for that matter ethnic movements revolve. In ethnic situations, such as in Darjeeling hills, the state in fact, plays a dual role. It can instigate and aggravate the ethnic problem and at the same time it has the capacity of containing the conflict that it provoked. In case of Darjeeling hills the relationship between the State and Gorkha/Nepali ethnicity has been found to be intimate from the very beginning. The Colonial State structure has well maintained the difference of the hills from the plains for politico-economic reasons. The administrative arrangements of different sorts were implemented so as to fulfil their own imperial interest in the hills. The people of Darjeeling hills from the very beginning were thus trained in the logic of difference but hardly realised the hidden colonial design of exploitation camouflaged as differential administrative arrangements. In a certain sense, the British had left Darjeeling by successfully invoking the idea into minds of the hill people that Darjeeling has been a segregated tract from the mainstream of Bengal.

The hill masses have actively participated in the democratic governance (there were exceptions too in this regard) of the country since Independence. However, this hardly implies that they have left their claims for separating their tract from the rest of West Bengal. Even though the post-colonial state structure is different from its colonial predecessor on the ground that it discontinued the colonial designs of exclusion and hence exploitation, the contending groups have often charged the post-colonial State as 'neo-colonial' on the pretext that it hardly takes heed of their claims. State run welfare and developmental activities on the one hand and the percolation of political power through the different democratic institutions of governance in post-independent era, on the other hand have made the ethnically conscious groups aware regarding the strength of ethnicity. Ethnicity thus has been continuously written and re-written within these processual arrangements of state welfarism and political power. Gorkhaland movement is no exception to this trend. The different demands the movement has raised over the years can be understood within these processual linkages of state and power.

Methodological Concerns

Dwelling upon interviews, observations, and secondary data analysis the present study attempted to arrive at a critical understanding of conflict resolution initiatives taken place with respect to the question of Gorkhaland movement. The in-depth understanding of the peace building efforts initiated by the State and the responses of the people towards the same requires a thorough knowledge of the internal dynamics of the local society and culture. This has been undertaken through repeated visits to the hills and also gleaned out of the experience of the present researcher's decade long association with the problem and the area.

In fact, the question of methodology depends much upon the conceptual frame one intends to pursue while analysing the problem at hand. The conceptual framework tells us much about how to approach and contextualise the problem of study, what to investigate, how to investigate, and how to design the whole fact finding programme. Thus the question how we should approach the issues of conflict, peace and conflict resolution initiatives constituted the very first step to work out a methodological stand for the present study.

Peace is a normal condition of human society characterised by a relatively high degree of interpersonal harmony that renders a commitment to avoid violence of any short. Conflict similarly is also a normal aspect of all societies although it implies incompatible needs, deeds and desires leading towards interpersonal/group antagonism, rivalry and often hostile encounters too. The point is that no society can remain all the time peaceful or conflict ridden. Both peace and conflict are relative social condition and stability in either term is neither feasible nor even desirable. Conflict resolution measures in this sense involve such strategies which aim at maintaining the relativity of both conflict and peace in a desirable manner. Peace initiatives thus do not suggest the complete dismissal of conflict in order to achieve eternal peace. The study has not considered the terms like peace or conflict in any fundamental sense. Ethnic conflicts do involve fierce battle, and often hostile manner of group rivalry figured out in violent terms but even in such situations too peace is not desirable if it attempts to eliminate any of the contending parties. This means peace could be gained and conflicts would be resolved in a meaningful sense if the measures protect the interests of the either party and provide the scope for the full blown growth of human capacities without any barrier or hindrance.

Having said all these, the methodological stand for the present study becomes clear enough. That is to say in other words, the relevance of both the ideas of peace and conflict needs to be judged from the vantage point of the state and government and at the same time from the vantage point of the people's perception regarding the same. Both the perspectives are necessary in the sense that both reveal different predilections regarding the same issue. And through a proper sociological analysis of these differential viewpoints a workable solution to the problem of peace building could be well founded. In an attempt to grasp the modalities of the differential perceptions of both the state and the people, fieldwork and secondary data analysis have been made.

For collecting primary data a detailed questionnaire was prepared and circulated among more than fifty individuals (fifty-seven in actual number). The respondents were purposively selected using the criteria of sex (out of 57 respondents 37 were males and 20 were females) and occupation (17 male teachers, 8 employed males, 12 male students, 5 employed females and 15 female students constituted the universe of 57 respondents). The questionnaire was specially designed for the educated persons alone and in majority of the cases the respondents were found to be tied up with some variety of associations available in the local society. In a certain sense sincere efforts were thus made to cover the viewpoints of civil society members and as a matter of fact all of the respondents were having at least graduation as minimum educational background. All the respondents did maintain close connection with the hills (either because the hills is their native place, or that they do have close relatives in the hills and make frequent movement to the hills and feel concerned regarding what happens there in the hills). Covering the viewpoint of the hill people through the questionnaire was made personally by spending the month of June 2011. However, field assistants were engaged in collecting data particularly from the plains region. Collection of questionnaire was completed by the end of July 2011. As such the field trip was significant in the sense that it was completed during that phase of time when the recent conflict containment strategy Gorkhaland Territorial Administration (GTA) was just on its offing and the issue has been made so popular that even a child would have known that something was going on in the name of GTA. For consulting Government documents visits in District Collector's office have been made. Besides libraries of North Bengal University, Centre for Himalayan Studies, Ratan Tata Library of Delhi School of Economics, Delhi University have been visited for the purpose of collecting secondary data on the issues of peace, conflict and conflict resolution. Close scrutiny of everyday eventualities has also been made through content analysis of available news reports published in local and national news dailies.

There are three principal modes of narration popular in social science research, viz. 'ethnography', 'thick description', and 'stylised facts'. Ethnography is a preferred mode for anthropological research providing the every detail of the life cycle of a tribe, or a community. Thick description is also preferred by those who attempt to narrate the research problem in splendid detail but is sceptical of cross-case theorisation. Concentrating on the 'essentials', stylised facts as a mode of narration tends to present a disembodied and linear narrative. That is to say, it presents a selection of facts first and present the analysis later (Varshney, 2002: 21). The present study intends to follow neither the methods of ethnographic detail, or 'thick description', nor even the format called 'stylised facts'. However, the endeavour throughout the whole study would be rather to use the various sources of data more in the form of narration that aimed at amalgamating the facts with interpretations. In true sense the format of narration for the present study would stand in between the three principal methodological strands (as discussed above) popular in social science research.

In the present study an attempt has been made to arrive at a critical understanding of the peace keeping measures undertaken so far to mitigate the problem of Gorkha ethnicity and movement in Darjeeling Hills, West Bengal. This has been done by probing into the pros and cons of the movement *vis-à-vis* the response of the State as manifested in its deep seeded history and as emerged in the contemporaneous past. To put the matter in other words, the movement in its long drawn history has raised several issues and that the State also responded variously towards such burgeoning claims. The book contains six chapters and in the following pages the issue of conflict resolution has been critically estimated both with analytical rigour and with empirical data culled out from the biography of the Gorkha Movement. Finally, the study attempted to raise the plea for an alternative approach while thinking in terms of peace and conflict containment in liberal democracies like that of our own.

With the help of a detailed analysis of the event structure of Gorkhaland Movement further efforts were made to answer the grave question that: why ethnic conflicts do survive in Darjeeling hills despite several efforts to resolve the same have been made time to time? In the course of analysis the present study also attempted to throw some light on the possibility of developing an alternative approach grounded on sociological reasoning towards the issue of conflict resolution. This has been done against the backdrop of a detailed analysis of Darjeeling's Gorkhaland Movement which served the purpose of being a pointer to the fault lines involved in the path of settling the rather emotive issue covering community sentiments, regional consciousness, and cultural-historical lineages all at once. The study has shown in clear terms that conflict resolution strategies worked out to resolve Gorkha imbroglio were out and out political in nature and piecemeal in approach. The study ends up with a rather pessimistic prognosis and arrived at a conclusion that the way Gorkha Movement has been handled so far by the State can hardly foster sustainable peace and tranquillity. However, it is also proposed that there is scope for working out strategies with due emphasis on the social concerns that the movement has upheld but somehow got delinked in the process of devising strategies to resolve the problem. The study strongly argues against the tendency of the liberal nation state to view ethnic loyalty in contradistinction to national loyalty. The study also raises the argument that the missing link between ethnic loyalty and national loyalty can be established by a different approach that, in fact, poses a challenge both towards the liberal expectancy of peace and tranquillity on the one hand and the very foundational logic of liberal bourgeois democratic state, on the other. It is proposed that the real threat lies neither in the conflicting claims nor even in the violent gestures that the Gorkhas have shown but perhaps in the attempt that nullifies the significance of 'us-them' divide in the name of forging a universal 'we'. Instead of 'forceful assimilation' due recognition of claims raised by different stakeholders of the movement may help us derive policies/measures directed towards 'integrative peace'.

Chapter Outline

The present study throughout its six chapters has elaborated different aspects of conflict containment keeping in view Gorkhaland movement as a test case. The second chapter deals with the conceptual issues involved in the understanding and analysis of peace work. Global as well as national level experience of conflict resolution measures have been critically estimated in order to pinpoint the necessity of devising an alternative analytical framework. From third chapter onwards specific attention was put towards tracing out the genealogy of state response towards Gorkha ethnicity starting from the colonial days. The fourth chapter specifically locates the violent turn of the movement and change of stand of the State towards handling the situation in Darjeeling hills. The chapter covers up the eventualities leading towards the formation of Darjeeling Gorkha Hill Council (DGHC) as the first such experiment initiated by the State outside Sixth Schedule areas. Fifth chapter emphasizes on the twists and turns taken place in the response of the State and the development of the movement during post-DGHC phase. Sixth chapter hinges on the contemporary experience of conflict resolution taken shape in the form of the new tripartite agreement called Gorkhaland Territorial Administration (GTA). A social forecasting has been made on the possible outcome of the new treaty signed recently to resolve Darjeeling problem once again. Chapter seven in lieu of arriving at a conclusion attempts to expand such arguments which may lead towards developing further courses of fresh analysis. In order to make the study thoroughly updated the Postscript has been included. The Postscript has been prepared keeping in view the very recent developments taken place in the area under study.

In fact, the critical analysis of conflict resolution measures with particular reference to Darjeeling situation is overdue. Since Darjeeling hills has not only experienced the continuation of an ethnic movement for more than a century but also the region experienced war of nerves, severe tension, violence, enough bloodsheds, loss of life and resources in the wake of Gorkhaland Movement that turned violent in the 1980s. Again a new arrangement has recently been agreed upon by the conflicting parties on the one hand and the State and Central Government on the other, which have finally led towards the formation of the new set up called the GTA. The Gorkhaland Territorial Administration (GTA) has started its march with the expectations of all-round peace and development in the Darjeeling hills. Within such a crucial juncture the significance of the present study could hardly be brushed aside.

NOTES

1. *Vide* Appendix I for a detailed chronology of the movement.

2

Towards Sociology of Conflict Resolution: Themes and Perspectives

Politics of ethnicity by and large is based on a linkage between political movement and ethnic identity and involves a subjective belief of having enemies, intruders or invaders (this results into the powerful desire to protect what the contending groups see as common to 'them' from 'others'). Despite the significance of a dyadic framework of ethnic 'we' *versus* outsider 'they' as most studies put stress on, a triadic framework of analysis as proposed by Dipankar Gupta is indeed a valuable contribution towards this end of understanding the linkage between ethnicity, state and politics. Gupta's insistence on the triadic framework (which he developed out of his studies on Sikh ethnicity) stresses not only upon the ethnic 'self' and outsider 'other' components but also takes into consideration those relational frameworks which were mediated through a third party in the process. The third 'party' in Gupta's analytical framework is simply mediated by the government or the state (Gupta, 1996:11). Viewed in the light of these arguments ethnicity by definition involve the domain of the state, which (according to our already proposed framework) falls within the domain maintained by the 'macro-structure' and helps articulate the micro-realities to become a socially significant and politically countervailing force to be reckoned with.

Keeping in view the above posed analytical proclivities it may be argued that ethnic movements are invariably political in nature and is rather bound to develop a political project in order to sustain its efficacy in the long run. The proposition that ethnic movements are essentially political reveals two senses of politicization. Firstly, it does mean the increasing tendency to politicize the existing issues at hand and also to bring in a wide variety of issues and social relations within the fold of politics. Secondly, they are political in the sense of entering the political and institutional arena, and engaging in strategic interaction with the State. Hence, ethnic movements are political in both the senses: that their 'content' eventually get politicized and their 'form' gradually come under the grip of institutionalized domain of politics run at the behest of the State. There is in fact, no apparent hostility towards formal politics and increasingly it becomes clear that ethnic movements, like all other social movements, tend frequently to rely on the state or other outside sources of material support. It is true, argues Foweraker, that such support only comes at a price; and that negotiation with the state has to be conducted in a context that may often include clientalism, patrimonialism, co-option, and electoral fraud (Foweraker, 1995:63).

Ending Ethnic Conflict: Options for Negotiation

The argument that the sustenance of ethnic conflict and movements in present day world increases the propensity to become confined within the institutionalized political domain maintained by the state, also invite the attention of both, the state and the conflicting parties, towards arriving at a mutually agreeable stand leading towards containment of conflict. In a certain sense, this is an obvious outcome in any long-drawn conflicting situation. As we are aware that neither conflict nor even peace could be a stable social condition, although both are normal social phenomena. However, this is not to suggest that we have nothing to do towards regulating conflict but to wait for auto-generated normalcy. In fact, rational minds and rational organizations have been engaged in this field and were suggestive of several such strategies, methods, policies, programmes and approaches aimed at pacifying the conflicting tendencies or to mitigate the problem from the root in order to bring forth peace and tranquillity. No wonder such a programmatic view of conflict negotiation brought forth numerous success stories as also stories of failure and frustration. Despite having gained a mixed rate of achievement the issue of conflict containment developed plethora of arguments, analysis, concepts, conceptual paths, theoretical frameworks to such an extent that these efforts ultimately created a separate branch of social scientific knowledge itself.

The specific ways through which peace study programmes attempt to approach the issue of conflict containment are an amalgamation of several models, policies and concepts amongst these the concepts of conflict prevention, management and resolution are significant. When viewed loosely these three concepts may appear as similar especially in view of the outcome they are desirous to attain. This is why quite often we come across with their interchangeable use or it may seem that they involve overlapping issues in them. Before we move further in discussing other intriguing issues involved in the process, it is necessary to put stress on the basic assumptions, objectives, processes, methods/strategies and the application of these three conceptual modules of our reference. The point is that the three concepts are different in the sense of how they view conflict and what is prescribed as containment strategies but there exists hardly any theoretical or ideological difference so far as the outcomes are concerned. In essence the concepts of conflict prevention, management, and resolution do differ from each other with reference to the question of the 'means' to be devised and employed. However, in respect of the 'end' all of them share some degree of mutual agreement in that all of them aimed at containing conflict in some form or the other. Keeping in view the basic analytical threads that these concepts employ and which could also help one have a succinct overview of the issues involved in them, a table is presented in the following (Table 2.1).

The various conceptual categories involved in the analysis of conflict containment are indicative of several measures, strategies and recommendations. Hazleton is of the view that "in response to such question: 'how to end violent ethnic conflict?' all such measures tend to fall within two broad categories: (a) conflict management strategies; and (b) conflict resolution approaches" (Hazleton, 1998: 109). Both of these categories maintain a fair degree of commonality in that both reflect a pronounced bias towards power sharing as the most viable strategy. In other words, they overemphasize on mutual co-existence, which they believe to be the ready outcome of the institutional innovations and safeguards that they propose as the most viable strategy towards finding out a solution in conflict torn social situations.

Table 2.1: Basic Concepts of Conflict Containment

Concepts	*Basic Assumption*	*Objective*	*Process*	*Method/Strategy*	*Application*
Conflict Prevention	Anticipating conflicts as potentially violent events	Prevent conflict escalation towards attaining violent manifestation Establishing accountable government	Institutional change Power sharing	Incentives for peaceful accommodation Cooperation of civil society organizations and business communities	Theory and model building
Conflict Management	Conflicts are inevitable and normal social phenomena Conflicts are rational and organizational forms of behaviour	Reducing the intensity of conflict Containment of conflict	Interventionist efforts Reorientation of contentious issues Reconstitution of divisions among conflicting parties Emphasis on past issues of grievances	Emphasis on new initiatives, programmes, institutional structures Government intervention Strategies of manipulation	Applied in practice
Conflict Resolution	Conflicts are not necessarily negative Awareness of conflict parties regarding their mutual interests, needs and perspectives	Resolve conflict in a constructive manner	Recognition of contending issues in order to arrive at mutually satisfactory solutions Institutional framework for interest accommodation	Cooperation Non-confrontation Non-competition Balance of power Government intervention	Both theoretical and applied

Conflict Settlement: Approaches and Strategies

Ethnic conflict management refers to those theories and policies that seek to make it possible for conflicting parties to pursue their aims without recourse to violence (Woods *et al.*, 2011: 155). Conflict containment strategies generally aim at adjudicating conflicting interests of contending parties. As such the number and variety of conflict containment strategies do vary spatially and temporally. The different sets of strategies and measures suggested by peace researchers and scholars are distinctive in the sense that each variety provides concrete realities about individual cases. However, this does not debar them enjoy overlapping significance on many occasions.

To begin with Lijphart (1968b) and Nordlinger's (1972) studies may be considered as the two major classics in the field of peace and conflict resolution studies. Being heavily influenced by Lijphart's thesis of consociationalism (which will be taken up separately for analysis in the course of the study) Nordlinger has provided a general framework of identifying the ways of regulating successfully ethnonational and communal conflicts in deeply divided societies. He outlined six such practices: a stable governing coalition, the principle of proportionality, the mutual veto, purposive depoliticisation, compromise, unilateral concessions. What is worth noting in all these practices is that the issues like active role of the elites and the preparedness of the mass public to accept them are emphasized (Nordlinger, 1972:119). Despite such conclusiveness in the approach Nordlinger's findings set the tune of future research activities in this field.

Another noted scholar Horowitz, who was very critical about the elitist model of conflict containment, identified five ways through which ethnic conflicts can be reduced: dispersion, emphasis on intra-ethnic conflict, incentives for inter-ethnic cooperation, encouragement for non-ethnic alliances, reduction of disparity between groups. Horowitz further suggested three policy frameworks that may address these strategies effectively: federalism or devolution, electoral arrangement, and preferential policies or affirmative action (Horowitz, 1985: 628-651). Considering ethnic conflict management as the handling of grievances Black (1984) has charted out five types of conflict management strategies: self-help, avoidance, negotiation, settlement and toleration.

While developing a policy analysis and outlining the choices the African state had in settling ethnic conflicts, Donald Rothchild (1986) presented a nine-fold schema of conflict regulation. Rothchild was of the view that these strategies involved intersecting and overlapping features. The nine-fold strategies of conflict containment move generally from the most explicitly coercive to the least: subjection, isolation, cultural assimilation, avoidance, displacement, buffering, protection, redistribution, and power sharing. Considering ethnic conflicts more as the resultant effect of fear and insecurity than anything else, Rothchild in another study (co-authored with Lake) further admitted that ethnic conflicts can hardly be resolved entirely but can be suitably contained. Characterizing ethnic conflict management strategies more as 'confidence building mechanism' Rothchild and Lake pointed out some such measures, which seek to reassure minority groups both of their physical security and cultural safety. The conflict containment measures as suggested by Lake and Rothchild are: demonstration of respect, power sharing, electoral engineering, regional autonomy, and federalism (Lake & Rothchild, 1996).

Based on the experience of ethnic conflict situations of the Middle East, Heraclides (1987) has noted that the classical modes by which states strive to resolve revolutionary ethnic conflicts include policies such as: extermination, population expulsion, coercion-domination, institutionalized discrimination, assimilation, democratic majority rule, and individual human rights, minority protection, integration, system of disproportional power sharing, autonomy, federal arrangement and territorial separation. This long list of policy options were further categorized into 'policies of denial' and 'policies of acceptance'. 'Denial' policies include all those modes of resolution that directly or indirectly deny the existence of insurgent in-group as a separate group or as a nation. The 'acceptance' solutions on the other hand (a) admit the existence of the other side as a separate group or as a distinctive nation, and (b) acknowledge the existence of the insurgents as the other party to the conflict whose grievances are to be considered in the process of reconciliation (Heraclides, 1987: 198-199).

Similar efforts to categorise conflict resolution measures were also made by others. McGarry and O'Leary (1994), for example, have provided eight distinctive macro methods of conflict regulation. While some of the methods (like genocide, mass population transfer, partition/secession, and integration/assimilation) were categorized by them as the methods for eliminating differences, the other set of methods (like hegemonic control, arbitration, cantonisation/ federalism, and consociation) were branded as methods for managing differences. McGarry and O'Leary also highlighted the effectiveness of such methods as was evident in the courses of European and African history. However, it would be erroneous to treat these two categories of strategies as distinctive. Nor even one is superposed hierarchically against the other. All these strategies are having overlapping significance and can even be employed in unison to handle a particular situation (McGarry and O'Leary, 1994: 94-95). McGarry and O'Leary's 'taxonomy' of eight macro methods of conflict resolution were applied by other studies as well (e.g. Todosijević 2001).

Smoha and Harf (1992) while dealing with the diverse modes of conflict resolution in deeply divided societies came to the conclusion that possible solutions to ethnic conflicts contain four main alternative strategies: suppression, reconstruction of ethnic identities, power sharing and state building. Coakley (1992) listed up a number of ethnic conflict management strategies like: indigenization, accommodation, assimilation, acculturation, population transfer, frontier arrangement, genocide, ethnic suicide. He further subdivided accomodationist ethnic management strategies in two domains: the political and cultural. Within the political domain the ethnic conflict management strategies do vary according to the regime type. If the political system is centralised then political strategy takes the shape of consociation. If the political domain is having decentralized form of governance then federalism comes up as a strategy to handle with the fierce battles those aimed at securing autonomy and self-governance.

It is interesting to note that in majority of the cases depicted so far there is an innate tendency to rely upon the territorial arrangement as the most suited practice for ethnic conflict containment. Be it in the mode of power sharing, state building, cantonisation, federal arrangement, territorial separation, or autonomy in every case territorial management of conflict is invoked. The concern for a territorial approach in the field of conflict resolution studies has been a widely discussed issue. Gurr, one the chief proponents of territorial self-governance approach, suggests that the 'recent historical track record shows that, on balance, autonomy arrangements (in territorial terms) can be an effective means for managing regional conflicts' (Gurr, 1993: 301, parenthesis added). Following Gurr and his influential MAR (Minorities at Risk) project data several studies (Cohen, 1997, Saideman *et al.,* 2002; Bermeo, 2002; Schneckener, 2002) have pinpointed the efficacy of territorial self-governance approach as the most viable measure for containing ethnic conflicts. Harff and Gurr (2004: 186) gone to that extreme in claiming that 'if no autonomy options are open to regionally concentrated groups, armed conflict may occur.' The wide range of studies available on the area of territorial self-governance, however, fail to suggest in clear terms what form of territorial arrangement is suitable for accommodating ethnic grievances. Territorially based autonomy arrangements accordingly were offered several epithets, qualifications and criteria. Stefan Wolff gives us a clue in this regard. He defined territorial self-governance both as a tool of statecraft and as a mechanism of conflict resolution in divided societies and encompasses five distinct governance arrangements—confederation, federation, autonomy, devolution, and decentralization (Wolff, 2010: 9).

Literatures that focus on the non-territorial arrangement of ethnic conflict are few but constitute a burgeoning field research. Academic works of this genre are promoted mainly by those who were highly skeptical of territorial approaches to resolve ethnic conflicts. They are of the opinion that instead of being a cure, territorial approaches induce conflict. Scholars like John Coakley (1994), Marc Howard Ross (2010) endorse that ethnic conflicts can be well managed by such strategies which may not have a direct concern for territorial settlement. Ross (2010) has drawn attention to what he preferred to label as 'less formal procedures' those intended to get the parties to where they can negotiate effectively, not on the substantive, constitutional and territorial proposals for ongoing management of ethnic conflict. He instead proposes six different approaches which neither focus on territory nor even consider territorial arrangement as necessary. Ross has considered that the effort to establish conditions for effective intergroup peacemaking is a significant step as well as a departure with regard to the question of conflict containment and offered six such ways: community relations, principled negotiation, human needs, psychoanalytically rooted identity, intercultural miscommunications, and conflict transformation.

All said and done, methods of conflict resolution depend generally upon the ways of defining the problem of ethnic conflict. This is indeed a fascinating proposition in that viewing the issue of ethnic conflict management in this manner one can appreciate the very fact that conflict containment strategies do not evolve from without. Neither they are piecemeal or haphazard nor even do they result just from the whimsical wishes of statecraft. For analytical precision the several strategies and methods elaborated so far can be well categorized under a few concrete approaches. These approaches do reveal the standpoint of the state with regard to the question of ethnic conflict. There exists a variety of arguments pinpointing the causes of ethnic conflict. With the risks of being too generalized an endeavour, the present study proposes that the different interpretations regarding why do ethnic conflicts occur a four-fold classification can be made. This is done mainly to appreciate how the state approaches the problem of ethnic conflict. Needless to mention that each of these approaches involve certain particular perspectives in them which lead towards a definite pattern of policy formulation and finally towards a set of methods and strategies of conflict resolution. Following Oberschall (2007) four such approaches are elaborated in the subsequent sections and the necessary link of these approaches with the perspectives, policies and measures of conflict resolution are also being shown.

Ancient Hatred (AH)

Ancient hatred is not a theory regarding the origin of ethnic conflict but a notion derived out of primordial theory of ethnicity. AH assumes that ethnic identities are primordial, unchangeable and ascribed that is why they involve high risk for repeated conflict. According to this viewpoint ethnic relations are overburdened with collective myths, cultural distinctiveness, and hostile emotions. AH approach attributes ethnic conflicts to the 'natural' strains and stresses of ethnic communities, which are unsolvable unless a radical step is taken. AH approach is, therefore, pessimistic about ethnic conflict management and about establishing lasting peace through policies of accommodation and adjustment. Complete separation is the usual way through which ethnic groups could feel at home. The significance of AH approach from the part of the state turns the story upside down. When the state looks at ethnic conflict under

AH lens it considers ethnic conflicts as dangerous for the stability and sovereignty of the nation itself and readily refers to such procedures like elimination or denial as most suitable policy options. AH approach in this manner acquires a reactionary stance for contending parties of both sides. While the ethnic communities go all-round for complete separation or secession, the state urges not to waste time with social, political, economic, and administrative engineering but to go for eliminating ethnic conflict by promulgating such stringent measures like repression, suppression, hegemonic control, extermination (including ethnic suicide, genocide etc.), forced assimilation or by expulsion of the conflicting population itself.

Manipulative Elites (ME)

The notion of manipulative elite is drawn from instrumentalist interpretation of ethnic conflict. ME approach as such denies the primordial cause and does treat ethnic conflicts as situational creations and thus solvable. Ethnic elites contend for power by manipulating ethnic divisions and by using people's emotional attachments for personal gratification. Conciliation in such situations is possible if the ethnic activists are made satisfied. It is in this way ME approach comes closer to liberal perspective and believes that accommodative strategies can definitely play fruitful role in conflict containment. ME approach is thus suggestive of such policies which aim at managing differences instead of eliminating them. Power sharing arrangements, cantonisation, decentralization, electoral engineering, territorial self-governance, autonomy measures etc. are typical examples of ME approach based strategies and methods of conflict resolution.

Security Dilemma (SD)

Security dilemma (also referred to as 'spiral of insecurity') holds that ethnic conflicts arise under conditions of state failure and breakdown. When state authority declines, ethnic groups become anxious for their survival. They invest in and prepare for violence, and thereby make actual violence possible. This has particularly been the case in Eastern Europe and Soviet Union soon after the collapse of communism. SD approach proposes that ethnic conflicts are neither the result of 'ancient hatred' nor even they are created by the manipulative elites. Ethnic conflicts are most often caused by collective fears of the future. As groups begin to fear for their safety, dangerous and difficult-to-resolve strategic dilemmas arise that contain within them the potential for tremendous violence. Ethnic activists and political entrepreneurs, operating within groups, build upon these fears of insecurity and polarize society. Political memories and emotions also magnify these anxieties, driving groups further apart (Lake and Rothchild, 1996: 41). The notion of security involves an urge to look beyond the present political equipoise to alternative futures—a future that seems to be capable of reinstating the present and past aspirations. SD approach hence can be labelled as conservative. It is conservative in the sense that the perception of insecurity is not aimed at total transformation of the existing social arrangement nor even it can be reduced through the mix and fix strategies of interest accommodation. Rather, the urge is to transform the society so that the past and present of community living can be restored. The conflict, therefore, is not about securing an unknown future but about a future that is drawn out of the contingencies of past and present group living. The policy perspective that revolves around SD approach stresses on the need of the policies of accepting differences. As such SD approach relies upon strategies like indigenization, minority protection, individual human rights, institutionalized discrimination, demonstration of respect, reconstruction of ethnic identity, psychologically rooted identity, buffering, isolation, community relations, acculturation etc. Precisely by accepting differences and by providing necessary space for the realization of such differences SD approach looks forward in the direction of conflict containment.

Economic Roots (ER)

Economic roots approach emphasizes on poverty, economic stagnancy, unemployment, development disparity as the root cause of ethnic conflict. Unlike the earlier three approaches ER approach poses the problem of ethnicity in pragmatic terms and tries to build up a thesis that looks into real social and economic positioning of the ethnic groups. For them deprivation is not merely a metaphorical notion that exists in historical memories, or in psychological appeals. Deprivation is more a felt-in-experience having direct bearing upon everyday life. Therefore, the thesis that ethnic conflicts are rooted economically is worked out more in pragmatic terms. In this sense the ER approach falls within, what may be called, a pragmatist perspective. ER approach advocates pragmatic ways of reducing the grievances. Mainly focusing on the confidence building policy measures ER approach advocates several strategies of conflict resolution like: principled negotiation, human needs, affirmative action, redistribution, inter-ethnic cooperative incentives, state building, devolution and reduction of disparity.

The different strategies, policies, perspectives and approaches of conflict resolution elaborated so far can be well grasped through the following Table 2.2.

Table 2.2: Conflict Resolution: Conceptual Framework

Approaches	*Perspective*	*Policies*	*Methods/Strategies*
Ancient Hatred (AH)	Reactionary	Denial	Repression, suppression, hegemonic control, extermination, ethnic suicide, genocide, coercion-domination, forced assimilation, population expulsion, secession, and partition
Managing Elite (ME)	Liberal	Acceptance	Power sharing, autonomy measures, proportionality, electoral engineering, cantonisation, decentralization, federalism, consociation, confederation, territorial self-governance, and autonomy measures
Security Dilemma (SD)	Conservative	Acceptance	Indigenization, minority protection, individual human rights, institutionalized discrimination, demonstration of respect, reconstruction of ethnic identity, psychologically rooted identity, buffering, isolation, community relations, and acculturation
Economic Roots (ER)	Pragmatist	Confidence building	Principled negotiation, affirmative action, human needs, inter-ethnic cooperation, redistribution, state building, devolution and reduction of disparity

It deserves mention that the proposed four-fold categorization of the different conflict resolution measures as outlined in the above table should not be considered as an exclusive model. There could be overlapping significance of all the four approaches, perspectives, policies and measures. Moreover, it is almost impossible to determine when the state will take recourse to one particular set of strategies over the other. More often than not the shape of the modern state of contemporary period in matters of settling ethnic disputes does appear as an elemental square having four strategic qualities of being reactionary, liberal, conservative, and pragmatist. In other words, the four-fold analytical model as suggested above accepts the position that all the four sets of approaches, perspectives, policies and measures can be made use of by a single state in unison or in part. The approach of the state towards ethnic conflicts does vary according to the form and substance of the conflict itself. Similarly, the conflict containment measures were adopted rather calculably by the state in accordance with the situational requirement. They do capacitate the state to become strategic enough in handling conflict situations. As in most cases strategies defy any set pattern and vary according to the situational contingencies, ethnic conflict strategies, policies, perspectives or approaches likewise can hardly be exclusively categorised as such. Hence, the worth of the present classificatory model, if any, is based on its heuristic value and not for its exclusive theoretical underpinning. The four-fold categorization as such may be treated more in the Weberian sense of an 'ideal type classification' which may help understand the different measures of conflict containment with some analytical precision.

Conflict Settlement: Theories

The experience of settling ethnic conflicts and movements across national borders typically assumes that such conflicts can be addressed through institutional bargains that establish macro-level structures through which micro-level incentives are disseminated towards the conflict parties. Existing theories of conflict management generally acknowledge the importance and usefulness of institutional design in conflict resolution, but offer rather different prescriptions about how the most appropriate models are to achieve stable conflict settlement. In one of his recent publications, Wolf maintained that 'from an institutional design perspective three theoretical approaches have dominated the conflict management literature: consociationalism, centripetalism, and power dividing (Wolf, 2011: 164). These issues deserve a brief elaboration since they were applied in most cases in divided societies and that they have already generated huge academic and policy debates besides theoretically rich literatures in the field of peace and conflict resolution studies.

Consociationalism

Although the term consociationalism is generally associated with Arend Lijphart's who developed it during late 1960 (out of his studies on the political systems of Scandinavian countries, Netherlands and Belgium) soon consociationalism gained a variety of admirers and critics too. Initially Lijphart made use of consociationalism as a variety of democratic system (Lijphart 1968a). Later on, however, consociationalism has been viewed by him more as a strategy in the politics of accommodation (Lijphart 1968b) and also as a common denominator for plural democracies (Lijphart, 1977).

Consociationalism suggests that decision-making, and consensus through accommodation among elites regulates conflict and provides stable democracy in divided societies (Lijphart, 1984, 1996a). The politics of accommodation at the elite level can be a substitute for cross-cutting affiliations at the mass level (Lijphart, 1968b). Consociational model is best suited for plural democracies. Lijphart's model did not, however, go unchallenged. Critics have pointed out that while focusing on institutional, constitutional and legal characteristics of accommodation, Lijphart put little emphasis on such issues like how external powers, the socio-economic process, and policy outputs impose themselves on social relations between communities and on the decision-making process itself (McGarry and O'Leary, 2004). Many others argue that stability in divided societies may be due to other factors besides the consociational model, factors such as attitudes of the citizens, the socio-economic system, citizen participation, the perception of civil rights, the influence or lack of citizenry power on policy and government, and government responsiveness to citizens preference do play favourable role towards stabilizing the deeply divided societies (Byrne, 2001: 333-34). Serious questions were raised from other directions as well. It is argued that Lijphart's theory ignores completely the propensities of intra-group conflict, particularly in those situations where other leaders mobilize people within that ethnic group against its own leader. Critics like Wright maintained that leaders of different blocks in a consociational system are often more extreme than mass of the people they represent (Wright, 1987:275). Despite criticisms consociationalism has developed from being a description of conflict resolution in Western Europe into an influential set of prescriptions about how best to reduce ethnic conflict throughout the world. It deserves mention that in an attempt to enlarge the verifiability and generality of his model Lijphart gone even to depict India, besides other non-Western countries, as a consociational form of democracy and argued that India—the largest democracy in the world—also shares the basic tenets of his theory, which lie behind the proverbial resilience of Indian democracy even amidst all possible odds (Lijphart, 1996b).

Centripetalism

Developed out of the works of such scholars like Horowitz (1985, 1990, 2000, 2003), Sisk (1996), Reilly (2001), and Wimmer (2003) the perspective of centripetalism grew more as a reaction of Lijphart's formal power sharing thesis. It emphasizes that, rather than designing rigid institutions in which elected representatives have to work together after elections, inter-group political accommodation is achieved by electoral systems that provide incentives for parties to form coalitions across group lines or in other ways moderate their ethnocentric political behaviour (Horowitz 2004: 507-8). Reilly (2001: 11) in attempt to develop the major threads of centripetalism as a theory argues that in practice centripetalism tries to encourage three major issues: (i) electoral incentives for campaigning politicians, (ii) emphasis on arenas of bargaining under which political actors of different groups have an incentive to come together to negotiate and bargain, and (iii) centrist, aggregative political parties or coalitions which seek multi-ethnic support. Among other things the principal tool of centripetalism is the provision of electoral incentives through which, it is assumed, the ethnically based parties would be in an advantageous position to appeal to fellow partners of other ethnic groups and also to members other than their own and thereby contribute towards the formation of multi-ethnic political aggregation. Needless to mention such an approach considers the individuals primarily as a rational political actor and projects ethnicity or for that matter ethnic conflict essentially as an elite phenomenon.

Power Dividing

Power dividing is the latest approach in the debate over the utility of the different models contribution towards ushering in peace in deeply divided societies. Roeder and Rothchild (2005) are the one who contributed towards this end of suggesting power dividing as a strategy of peace building in ethnic conflict situations of divided societies. Instead of Lijphart's power sharing model (which they believe would appear as detrimental to peace and stability in the long-run) they recommend power dividing as an alternative strategy to manage conflict. Power dividing is seen as the outcome of three principal strategies—civil liberties, multiple majorities, and checks and balances.

Roeder and Rothchild offer nine policy recommendations for the strategy of nation-state stewardship (Roeder & Rothchild, 2005: 337-345): (i) creating or holding together only those states in which constituent groups share a sense of nationhood and agree to live together; (ii) limiting government to minimize contentious issues that are decided centrally; (iii) delaying intervention until a clear victor emerges; (iv) lengthening protectorates to give moderates a chance to emerge; (v) building institutions from the ground up so that local institutions of self-governance can emerge before central ones; (vi) phasing withdrawal in accordance with the build-up local capacity; (vii) dividing power between different institutions and arenas such that ethnic stakes in politics are lowered; (viii) broadening negotiations for long-term arrangements to include other than just ethnically defined interest groups in the decision-making process; and (ix) limiting power sharing in favour of direct rule by the international community.

Critics have pointed out many fault lines within these propositions. Among other things it was mentioned that the model and the recommendations may satisfy any liberal mind but it is doubtful whether they could claim universality. Primarily because the issues were raised on the pretext of US model of democracy, and the model bears little resemblance with the socio-political realities of conflict-torn social systems of the rest of the world

Table 2.3: Synoptic view of the Models of Conflict Settlement

Models	*Proponents*	*Major Tenets*	*Conducive Factors*
Consociationalism	Lijphart	Grand Coalition Government Segmental Autonomy Proportional Representation Minority Veto	Consensual institutions and practices Balanced bi-cameralism Multi-party system Territorial Federalism Decentralized system Rigid Constitution Tradition of compromise
Centripetalism	Horowitz, Sisk, Reilly, Wimmer	Electoral incentive for cross-community coalition Encouragement of cross-partisan and cross-ethnic bargaining Aggregative political parties or coalitions	Preferential majoritarian electoral system Flexible federal structure Strong minority rights regime Powerful judiciary system and effective enforcement mechanism
Power Dividing	Roeder and Rothchild	Strong enforceable civil liberties Multiple majorities Checks and balances	Emphasis on human rights Separation of power in different branches of government Specialized agencies to involve multiple and changing majorities in policy issues Commitment to resolve dispute through bargaining and reciprocity

(Cordell & Wolff, 2010: 153). In a certain sense, the model in general and the nine-fold recommendations in particular are aimed at mitigating the problem merely by transforming the same. It hardly stresses on the root cause of conflict and renders little hope regarding how to handle the basic issues of grievances. Manipulating the political process and accommodating the leaders in the same in some form or the other hardly guarantee the sudden evaporation of ethnic passions in real sense of the term. Major arguments of these three models as elaborated by their respective proponents are elaborated in Table 2.3.

Conflict Settlement in Practice: Indian Scenario

Post-independent India did not start its march amidst peace and tranquillity. Nor even the long cherished goal of independence did help India remain scot-free from the virulent conflicts of myriad sorts. Amidst the irreparable agonies of partition conflicts based on language, region, and ethnicity either in Punjab, Andhra or in the North East started cropping up since the early days of India's independence. The forces of centrifugality, however, dangerous they may be, are viewed more as the reflections of governability crisis than as revealatory forces of alienating nationhood that remain germane to the idea of a politically cultivated nation state structure. However, a political audit of independent India, no matter how hurriedly made, is capable of showing the Indian nation state as a remarkable success story that succeeded in containing the disintegrating forces and thereby to maintain its so-called resilient structure. The point is that the biography of post-independent India could serve the purpose of being the treasure house of rich quantitative and qualitative data that could help us verify the validity of the different conflict settlement models and approaches on the one hand and can also lead us develop newer bases of fresh analysis, critical perspectives, and innovative arguments, on the other.

The principal assumption behind any analysis within the field of conflict settlement is based on the premise that how the state responds towards conflict situations. However, it deserves mention that all varieties of conflict situate themselves within a milieu that is being shaped both by the state and the society in some fashion. Contending parties in the name of conflict or movement either attempt to affect the ideology of the state or the value premises of the society in some form or the other. The response of the state or of the society, by and large, towards any conflict or movement gets affected in turn by the type of the authority structure and/or the value system that it maintains. But what we find in issues elaborated so far that the focus of analysis with regard to such questions like peace, conflict and conflict resolution are surprisingly concerned with the perspective of the state. Consequently, the numerous models, concepts and strategies we talked about so far are all putting stress on the vexed question: 'how the state, rather than the society, responds towards ethnic situations?' It is no wonder that the analyses of conflict settlement issues in India, as elsewhere have been struggling with this statist perspective, ignoring the significance of the value premises of the society, and is less committed towards developing newer models, concepts or strategies, which could have reasonably been done by illuminating the 'societal perspective'. In this section we would summarize the scholarly efforts made by the Indian social scientists in the field of conflict resolution and try to locate how state centric their arguments were.

To initiate analysis in this direction T.K. Oommen's analytical framework would be helpful. Although his framework of analysis is aimed at analyzing the broader issues of social movements in Indian situation in general, but it seems to be quite useful in case of apprehending the issues involved in the process of ethnic movement *vis-à-vis* the response of the state. Oommen is of the view that the response of the state towards movement situation does not occur in a unilinear manner rather it is dictated by the nature of mobilization of the conflicting parties on the one hand and by the very character of those who hold state power on the other (Oommen, 1990: 185-87).

Conceptualizing the issues in this manner Oommen outlined four such possible ways through which the state usually responds to conflict situations (including ethnic conflicts as well). These are of facilitation, toleration, discredition, and repression. It deserves mention that Oommen foresaw the strengths of a societal perspective and indicated that analyzing the issue of conflict containment from the perspective of value premises of the respective society can reveal an entirely different discourse on the issues at hand. Conspicuously, however, he avoided elaborate the same any further and ultimately concentrated on the statist perspective alone. An elaborate understanding of the patterns of state response, that Oommen chalked out, may be gained from the following Table 2.4.

Instead of a general analytical framework Mitra (1997: 37) attempted to develop a dynamic model of governance in the fashion of a dynamic equilibrium. Mitra's model of dynamic equilibrium involves four sets of independent variable, which alone or in combination, account for the variation in governance. These are: (a) Law and order management (methods of conflict adjudication at local, district, regional and national levels are taken into consideration at this stage); (b) Redistributive policies (of interest here are the issues like: labour laws, agrarian reforms, tenancy legislation, minimum wages laws, welfare legislation, positive

Table 2.4: Oommen's framework of state response to social movement

Dimensions of Movement		*State Response*
Ideology	*Means*	
Same as that of the State	Defined as legitimate by the State	Facilitation
Different from that of the State	Defined as legitimate by the State	Toleration
Same as that of the State	Defined as illegitimate by the State	Discredition
Different from that of the State	Defined as illegitimate by the State	Repression

discrimination, and methods of minimizing rent-seeking behaviour); (c) Constitutional sanction for 'sacred beliefs' (stress here is on non-negotiable values such as group identity, ethnicity, shared religious ideals and on communal accommodation as the basis of constitutional solution of confessional politics in divided societies); and (d) Rules of succession, recruitment of new elites and political order (the variables would include elections as a method of elite recruitment and the effectiveness of election commissions in maintaining free and fair competition, and creation of new political arenas which create more effective intermediate institutions).

In an attempt to answer a self-posed question: can democracies accommodate ethnic nationalism? Kohli (1997: 325-6) maintains that the fate of these movements largely reflect the nature of the political context, though group characteristics around which movements emerge and the resources these groups control are also consequential. More specifically, two dimensions of the political context appear to be especially relevant, namely how well central authority is institutionalized within the multicultural democracy and the willingness of the ruling groups to share some power and resources with the mobilized groups. Within such political pretext where well established central authority is run by firm but accommodative political elites Kohli envisages that ethnic movements would follow an inverse 'U' pattern of growth. In other words, initially such movements would have a spiralling effect and in the long run, particularly when they confront state authority, they would decline. Understood in this manner, ethnic conflicts constitute a political process whereby the central state and a variety of ethnic groups discover their relative power balances in developing country democracies. Kohli reminds us that the strategies which lead the ethnic movements follow an inverse 'U' pattern of growth are: prolonged process of power negotiation, repression or cooption of leadership, power sharing and mutual accommodation between conflict parties and the state.

In a recent article Lacina (2009) has made a critical comparative analysis of the way the so-called local autonomy institutions function in the entire North East India including Darjeeling hills. The idea of autonomous councils as operationalized either in the North East or in Darjeeling hills emerged basically as a coping strategy based on the notion of redistributive political power and were activated particularly when conflicts proved to be beyond the control of the respective state governments. Lacina equated the functioning of autonomous councils in the local context as local autocracies and argues that these localized autocracies limit peaceful political competition. In the absence of institutionalized and rule based means of politics, changes to the local distribution of power lead to violence by challengers looking to seize control of resources or leaders seeking to reconsolidate dominance. Lacina is of the opinion that much like the North East contemporary Darjeeling especially demonstrates these dynamics.

Somewhat less ambitious attempts were made by several other scholars, who instead of developing any model, framework or argument theoretical, conceptual or otherwise preferred to assess the empirical situations and the exact strategies through which India nation state so far attempted to challenge or settle the janus faced ethnic conflicts took place in the subcontinent. In order to cut the long story short the major findings of the scholars engaged in such academic exercises are presented in a tabular form in Table 2.5.

Assessment of the Statist Approach and the Need for a Societal Perspective

Keeping in view the literatures cited above specific comments can be made. In most cases the analytical models, approaches, and frameworks whatever was developed in Indian context by Indian scholars or by others there is a tendency to accept the Western theories rather uncritically. For example, while consociationalism occupies a favourable position in Kohli's otherwise excellent analysis,

Table 2.5: Ethnic Conflicts and State Response: Empirical Findings

Scholars	*Findings*
Partha S. Ghosh (1998)	i. *Military Response* (as applied in Kashmir, Punjab, and parts of North East India) ii. *Politico-Constitutional Response* including such strategies like creation of new states, intra-state-centric model (viz. DGHC, BAC, JAAC, LAHDC), regional council (NEC), Tribal autonomy scheme (under Fifth and Sixth Schedule provisions of the Constitution), and ethnic accord (Assam accord, Punjab accord etc.)
Amalendu Misra (2001)	i. Constitutionally guaranteed preferential treatment ii. Negotiation iii. Economic incentive iv. Force and repression against the adversaries v. Moral arguments
Rajat Ganguly (2009)	i. Counter-insurgency operations involving issues like direct liquidation, elimination of outside support, border sealing and counter-infiltration operations ii. Politico-judicial legislations (like TADA, POTA etc.) iii. Peace Accords

centripetalism approach has its significant presence in Mitra's dynamic equilibrium model.

The ethnic conflict resolution measures undertaken by the government attempted to function more as an apparatus of power by virtue of the field of visibility in which communities were to be located, each in their respective places for a centralised and unseen observer. It is in this way conflict resolution measures in India acquire the characteristics of what Foucault has termed as *Panopticon*. Conceptualising the conflict resolution measures as *Panopticon* may help us appreciate how they helped produce 'homogenous effects of power' and attempted for the diffusion of disciplinary mechanisms throughout the social body as a whole occurred through the four particular processes:

(a) An expansion of disciplinary institution (this has been the case with SRC recommendations, and the grant of Sixth Schedule Status to conflict zones);

(b) The emergence of positive and productive disciplines (the measures like regional autonomy prescriptions and the constitutional recognition of language are having such potentialities);

(c) A de-institutionalisation of disciplinary mechanisms (the establishment of district councils at sub-state level exemplifies this);
(d) The organisation of a police apparatus (direct military intervention strategy is the case in point).

The point is that in considering the ethnic conflicts merely as political courses of action, the state often loses sight of the very fact that communities use politics not just to advance their political interests but also to define and redefine the social cultural whole in which they live in. This is why the conflict resolution measures, by and large, have been articulated in India according to the technologies of power inscribed in the body of a post-colonial nation state and remained largely insensitive to the social cultural appeals warring groups raise often couched in conflicting terms.

The basic presumption in the process of conflict settlement is to treat the state as the major stakeholder whose sanctity and interest has to be maintained at any cost. The perspective of the society or for that matter the very fact that conflicts could also be generated out of societal impulse is glossed over, if not nullified completely. Remarkably this appears to be invariably true in case of all the scholarly exercises we have referred to. This possibly explains why studies on conflict settlement are overloaded in most cases by the scholars having political science as academic background. Having said all this let us now proceed further to understand the phenomena of ethnic conflict and conflict resolution measures rather sociologically.

Towards a Sociological Perspective of Ethnic Conflict and Conflict Resolution

It is worth mentioning a fact that the endeavour to develop a sociological approach towards understanding the processes of ethnic conflict and conflict containment strategies is having two distinctive advantages. First, it views both ethnic conflict and conflict resolution measures as social processes and not just as structural constructs. It treats both conflict and conflict resolution measures with a degree of methodological elasticity and portrays them at various levels of their functioning in a dynamic interactional setting. Second, a sociological approach is always aimed at examining a social process in terms of both its intrinsic character and also in respect of the dynamic forces of social transformation in society to which the process itself remains amenable. Viewed in this way, sociological approach offers an opportunity to blend micro-realities with that of macro-history of the issues at hand and helps thereby to develop an engaged understanding and a reasoned explanation of the processes in broad historical and cultural specific terms. Sociologists in India have been engaged in intensive assessment and analysis of diverse social processes in society, particularly those related to value, culture, and social structure, which might offer new insights in the analysis of conflict and conflict resolution measures related to ethnic phenomena.

We have already come across several distinctive conceptual formulations and strategies of conflict resolution measures in relation to ethnic movement situations in India and dominant among such views are those held by the political scientists who while looking at the problem from a macro perspective emphasized on the points of view of the state. In such perspectives the study of the relationship between social structure, culture, and ethnic aspiration appears to have rather weaker link. The basic tensions between national loyalty and ethnic loyalty are often misconceived in dialectical terms. The linkages of ethnic solidarity with that of economy (i.e. the class question), culture (viz. issues like language), ideology (viz. self-respect and self-determination), or societal filiations (like community ties, kinship bond, migration pool etc.) are analyzed at a very general level. Such endeavours do not, however, examine the issues the way sociologists or for that matter the social anthropologists do, in the context of micro-historical processes and their given normative framework in the social structures, such as caste, community, family, kinship, locality, region, belief system etc. The local cultural traditions, in which local cultural aspirations remain embedded, are not examined closely while formulating policy perspectives for mitigating ethnic conflict situations. In the absence of such an approach we really do not know how ethnic conflicts sustain for a longer period of time and how they establish linkages between the top and subterranean levels of mobilizations, and involve fissures and tensions in-between. Without having a comprehensive understanding of the interplay of these intricate issues and processes any effort towards developing a sociologically grounded understanding of peace and security against the backdrop of ethnic conflicts, violent or otherwise, will surely prove to be inadequate.

Sociology of Ethnic Conflict: Beyond Elitist Perspective

The macro-historical analyses of ethnicity and ethnic movement by and large project an elitist viewpoint. Analysis of this genre treat ethnic phenomenon as a construct of the political elites. Ethnic movements were thus seen more as a phenomenon engineered by the elites who harped on the ethnic cleavages just to mobilize the masses in order to fulfil their self-designed goals and aspirations. The general mass in such discourses hence appears to be silent and are represented merely as those direction less lots who were always ready to carry out the decisions and dictates of the elites. As a result the formulation of conflict resolution measures derived out of such one-sided understanding of the whole process excessively put stress on the prominence of the elites generally at the cost of the masses. Consequently we find measures and strategies to handle with ethnic conflict situations were developed just to appease the elites only. In other words conflict resolution measures undertaken in ethnic conflict situations in India took care of the elites' interests and aspirations (mis)conceiving the same as the true reflection of the masses. There is no reason to believe, neither empirical or epistemological, that in ethnic movement situations all the aspirations of the general mass are reflected nor it would be proper to hold that what the elites project as mass appeal in the movement agenda common people are always supportive of all such claims. In fact, there exists a very thin but sharp dividing line between what is called as "populism" and what is referred to as "people's perspective". It is, however, possible and is often the case may be that on several occasions the fad of populism is fed through essentials derived from people's perspective. Ethnic movement merely as populism may direct attention towards the mass hype, passion and obsession with ethnic claims. Even in such situations one cannot be very sure that 'ethnic populism' is reflective of ethnic aspirations of the general mass in its entirety. The present effort is to stress on this departure of analytic focus that is needed to be worked out if durable solutions against the burgeoning ethnic claims are to be devised.

Besides the important role played by the elites in the articulation of ethnic movements, there exist other issues, processes and forces, which are no less significant in both sharpening and sustaining the ethnic cause. Despite having made considerable amount of contribution in deriving an epistemology of ethnic phenomena, instrumentalist arguments (those emphasize on the role of the elites as the single most important determining factor of ethnicity) put less emphasis on the spontaneous aspects of the conflict articulation those occur through 'horizontal' or mass level mobilizations rather than through 'vertical' or elite level of social political mobilizations. However, the distinction between horizontal and vertical mobilizational domains of ethnicity is far from being clear cut. Nor even it is proposed here that 'horizontal' ethnic mobilization is superposed over the 'vertical' one. In fact, the operation of social institutions and ethnie at the local level is a 'relatively' autonomous phenomenon.

Yogendra Singh's proposition is worth recalling here, who emphasized on the historical role played by inter-structural autonomy of basic social institutions in Indian society. Singh is of the opinion that the institutions of social stratification, political administration and values and beliefs in their relative autonomy provided flexibility of responses to forces encroaching upon from outside (Singh, 1988: 7). These could be forces of colonialism, alien cultural contacts, a new political culture, development, new economic relations, market forces and the like processes of change.

What is argued here is that if 'vertical' domain of ethnic mobilization (as the instrumentalists argue) is involved in the analysis of elitist perspective, the 'horizontal' domain of ethnic mobilization (the emphasis the subaltern historians dwell upon) emphasizes on segmentation and autonomy. In essence, however, both the perspectives, in a certain sense, suffer from conceptual reductionism. While the former looks at ethnic phenomena from above the latter views it from an isolated bottom. But in reality ethnic phenomena is fed with the elemental forces and processes emanating from both the directions. That is, it involves both macro and micro realities in a definite fashion of an organic causality. Argued in this manner, the category of 'mass' is not to be conceived of as that contingent lacking agency and creativity and hence need to have a corresponding reliance over a higher order contagion of political elites all the time, nor even the 'mass' is a completely isolated and autonomous whole and need not be thought of in a segmented manner devoid of the impact the macro-historical processes could bring forth. What is proposed instead, is that a comprehensive understanding of ethnicity could be arrived at if one is able to fuse both the perspectives in some fashion of an organically linked process.

Issues like ethnic loyalty and national loyalty, according to our proposed model of sociological analysis, are to be viewed as social processes in continual interaction in all societies those have passed the stage of segmentary social organization. In such societies ethnicity crops up from amongst the linkages with local and mass level institutions, communities and cultures to sustain itself as a socially appealing and politically compelling force. Ethnicity or ethnic movement is basically a process, a product of historical conjuncture of social forces through which the linkages are not only established or expanded but also qualitatively strengthened. Ethnicity in this sense is neither a finished social event, nor even it maintains a formal structure but is constituted of a normative model and is linked with organic historical process through which ethnic groups strengthen themselves by qualitative differentiation from within and their superior integration organically, within a territorial boundary (Singh, 1988: 9). Hence, ethnicity refers to the ethnic group as a tendency inspired by its existence or as the aspiration to build up its own existence.

The emphasis on the pros and cons of a sociological approach of ethnicity and ethnic conflict continued so far is but an attempt to illustrate ethnic conflict and movement as a process in which counter pulls of antagonistic tendencies remain active in accordance with the conjuncture of historical and societal forces. In fact, these counter pulls establish our argument that ethnic phenomenon is not entirely an instrumental affair nor even it is an isolated and autonomous event. Its strength—more latent than manifest—lies in the interlinkages and interplay that takes place in between the micro-realities and macro-historical structures at various levels in a fashion of constituting an organic whole, which is dynamic and plastic and that is why ethnic movements lasts long.

3

Movement and State Response: Colonial and Post-Colonial Arrangement in Darjeeling Hills

Contrary to the conventional mode of social theorization that attempts to explain society along the line of those convergences that bring people together, the present chapter intends to understand the Nepali society in India, in general and of Darjeeling hills, in particular through the principle of exclusion. Recognition of Indian Nepalis as citizens of India, or the urge to have a separate state of their own within Indian body polity are some such crucial political claims that need to be understood not through the inclusive aspects social living but through the exclusive and sequential relations that the Nepalis in India have maintained in relation to the mainstream. The argument is that the sub-text of Gorkha ethnicity in India has been written and re-written through a series of exclusions maintained by the state structure as a whole. There might be several other courses of exclusion (direct/indirect or active/passive in nature) meted out by the Nepalis in everyday life, however, we will illuminate only the political treats of the problem. In that the chapter explores the notion of exclusion more as a discourse rather than as a concept. That is, the idea has been used and articulated in the present chapter through the language of politics as revealed in the paradigms of governance.

Colonial Governmentality and the Exclusion of Nepalis

As pointed out earlier that the craving for Gorkhaland is indeed a historic occurrence. The idea of a separate administrative arrangement for Darjeeling hills was mooted during the early years of the twentieth century and then onwards the demand of segregation went on unabated. The issue remains alive still today and never died out even amidst the forces of state repression too. The colonial roots of the segregationist politics in Darjeeling hills are well founded. In order to enjoy the hills for bodily comfort and to exploit the hill resources for fulfilling mercantile interest the colonial rulers attempted to invest the idea of 'difference' through all possible channels of social engineering. The 'natural' difference between the hills and the plains were articulated through the different vices of colonial governmentality[1] as categorical expressions that distinguished Darjeeling as a separate administrative unit, as distinctive linguistic zone, as a unique economic formation, a separate culture area and finally as a separate region as a whole.

Not to mention that the exposure towards colonial governmentality enabled the people of Darjeeling hills have an early experience of the art of being governed differently. Administrative epithets and measures like 'Backward Tract', 'Scheduled Area', 'Excluded Area', 'Partially Excluded Area', and 'Waste Land' were basically the ploys meaningfully devised by the 'rational modern father' (i.e. the colonial state) not only to demarcate its offspring but also to draw boundaries among the siblings and finally to prohibit and exclude them from having a greater familial interaction with the mainstream society so that the scope for nation building could be narrowed down to a large extent. The discourse of exclusion as it occurred through colonial governmentality was rooted in and routed through the activation of such discursive practices like security, surveillance, control and progress couched in a fashion of racially founded 'paternalism'. All these, in fact, constituted the core of the modern notions of state craft that the imperial state apparatus employed as and when the question of administering the border areas or newly acquired territories came in.

The efforts towards 'walling off' of the others in locales such as Darjeeling hills ultimately generated 'walling in' of the feelings regarding the art of being governed differently. The communities living in such spaces with clear cut borders and boundaries of their own achieve a self-definition, no matter how paranoiac it may be compared to the great cause of mainstream nationalism. This self-definition was an act of everyday life hence it varied according to the contingencies of mundane life courses. With the passage of time the resources of this self-definition kept on varying but that did not, however, help it move out of the discourse of exclusion. Resources such as citizenship, self-rule, cultural right, difference, and backwardness widely define the trajectory of self-definition as it passes on from colonial situation to a post colony. The discourse of exclusion changes its *modus operandi* in the transition that took place in Indian body polity at large. Though the genealogy of the structure of exclusion was laden with the colonial project of othering the society from the state, in the post colonial situation the same otherization went on but in the name forging nationalism. This self-definition argues Selma K. Sonntag increasingly assumed liberal character and was conflated against the veneer of Nehruvian liberalism and nationalism applied to the British Raj's excluded and partially excluded areas to exclude them from normal post-independence legislative and political processes (Sonntag, 1999: 418-419).

To cut the long story short it may be maintained that the demands of separate arrangement for Darjeeling hills raised during colonial period were by and large the by-products of the discourse of exclusion wherein the colonial governmentality augured itself to dissociate state from the society. There had been several such attempts raised by the indigenous acculturated elites to 'wall off' the hills from the vicissitudes of the plains on the grounds of preserving the 'in-group' (hill people as a whole) from the superior Bengali society and culture. The idiosyncratic cultural insularity of the hill society had gained patronage, if not a tacit approval of the ruling class cohort (represented by the assemblage of the planters, bankers, missionaries, and above all the colonial state apparatus) who were delighted to have the natives differentiated on the grounds of culture, language, region but never fulfilled the demand of carving out the frontier region completely from Bengal and encouraged instead the 'walling in' mentality of the hill people.

This has been repeated time and again throughout the colonial period particularly since 1907 when the urge to have a separate administrative arrangement outside Bengal was raised for the first time in the name of the hill people. Such demands of segregation was raised more in a continuous fashion and fascinatingly all demands were raised in anticipation of significant changes that have already taken place or were likely to take place in the local context due to the introduction of new rules, orders, acts etc. in the larger context. It is rather pointless to debate over the issue whether such segregationist gestures did involve spontaneous mass aspirations or were manufactured by the elites for fulfilling their limited self-interest. The issue is that they reflect an urge to be governed differently and that the genealogy of this urge in the context of Darjeeling hills is to be located in the particular fashion of colonial governmentality. The notion of colonial governmentality tells us how the making of the rebel self of the Gorkhas was tremendously obfuscated and was forcibly altered as an accommodative self directed towards attaining recognition through privileges, rewards, and protection. The question of outright restructuring of the given arrangement or the initiation of a fundamentally new structural arrangement in which the desires of self-rule could successfully be met was shelved rather permanently. The hue and cry of self-rule was cut down to size to facilitate the processes of governance and to secure the path of progress that involved a self denying aspiration for modernity. This can be termed as the 'aporia of self-rule' whose origin was rooted in colonial governmentality and did maintain significantly its post-colonial incarnations too.

Locating the Nepalis in Post-Colonial Nation State: 'Exclusionary Logic' of Nationalism

To initiate the discussion let us consider that why some particular national communities needed to be represented in a decolonized nation, like that of our own, in a hyphenated manner when many others are simple treated as a non-hyphenated national. For example, an 'Indian Bengali', or say an 'Indian Oriya' is rather a meaningless provenance, while an 'Indian Nepali' is always deemed to be a meaningful category not only for the non-Nepali Indians but also for those who belong to such categorization. The crux of the matter is that while the former group is treated more or less as an axiomatic natural citizen, the latter is always at our nationalist edge, if not under the sign of a question mark, even though both of them share a similar pattern of colonial past and a post-colonial presence. Viewing the problem of Nepali identity in this way one may become apprehensive of another take: that how the construction of a non-hyphenated national as opposed to its hyphenated other is made possible.

Every nationality has had to define itself as the sacred heritage of the ancestors, a power of assimilation and civilization—and therefore, of domination and exclusion (Balibar, 1988:726). The unambiguous loyalty of a genuine nationality hence remains historically immersed to the conception of civilizational core typified by a definite and definitive territorial limit. This possibly explains why the 'Nepalis are after all the Nepalis'. Nevertheless they might have a recorded history of their presence within India for the past several centuries, and Nepal did maintain a heritage of cultural reciprocity with India from time immemorial.

The formulation of a more sharper kind of identity came with the Westphalian formulation that equated the nation with that of the state in a unique fashion of singularity to give way to the assertion that the nation = the state, or the corresponding catch that one state = one nation. The presumed shift of the nation state towards the discursive notion of 'one nation one state' predicated political structures towards an exclusionary logic of nationalism, citizenship and belongingness to the true nation. The sub-text of post-colonial Indian nation state inheres this inbuilt contradiction (read crisis) of approving a pedagogy of homogeneity (of 'one nation, one state' variety) amidst the inescapable presence of performative heterogeneities of myriad sorts. In other words, it is the pedagogy that tells us that the nation and the people are what they are and performativity keeps reminding us that the nation and the people are always generating a non-identical excess over and above what we think we are. The 'other' of the nation state emerges out of the oscillation that takes place repetitiously between what Bhaba calls the 'pedagogy' and the 'performative' (Bhaba, 1994:145). The Nepali identity question is, in this sense, caught between the shreds and patches of cultural signification and the certainties of a nationalist pedagogy.

The case of the Nepalis in India unfolds a double edged character of national identity, more as an obvious sequel of Bhaba's double narrative movement of pedagogy and performative, exemplified through the capacity of defining who is a member of the national community and who is an 'other'/'alien'/'foreigner'. To put the matter in simple terms, it is proposed that the existence of a national community presupposes the existence of other nations. The nation thus has to be understood more as a part of dual relationship than as an autonomous self-contained unit. Such dual relationships become vivid even in the attempts of the settled Indian Nepalis themselves who strived hard to popularize Gorkha identity as a replica of Indian identity for the Nepalis of Indian origin and such categorization would separate them, as they believe, from the Nepalis of Nepal (i.e. the 'other'). Those who are opposing the Nepalis' claim of being a true Indian, or are ready to tarnish and invalidate their claim of Indian citizenship are equally amenable to the same plot lines of double identification.

Immediately after independence the Gorkhas of Darjeeling hills were relentlessly vocal in raising the urge of self-government. The aporia of self-rule took a new turn, not a qualitative shift altogether, more as a matter of right and hence amenable towards constitutionalism. The post-colonial state apparatus although unsuccessful in replicating all the vices of its colonial predecessor, has attained success at least in one respect in creating its 'subject' population alongside a system of canonical protocols to be followed by the 'subject' population, which would facilitate them emerge as 'normal', 'legitimate' and 'disciplined' (instead of emerging as 'pathological', 'illegitimate' and 'unruly' entities) offspring of the mother nation, on the one hand and of the paternalistic state structure, on the other. Soon after independence the major problem that Indian nation state had to face, much in a similar vein like that of all liberal democracies, was the challenge of multiculturalism. In other words, the question as to how the state would accommodate the incessant fissure between the national and ethnic differences in a stable and morally defensible way constituted the crux of the problem of Indian nation building from the very beginning. It is not out of place to mention that Nehru and Nehruvian liberals were successful in persuading the assimilationists and thereby to incorporate liberal constitutionalism in Indian body polity as the handiest technique to accommodate the burgeoning claims raised from the margins of the nation state. The crucial questions of autonomy and self-rule were left open to a variety of Constitutional provisions like Article 370 (granting special status to Kashmir), Article 371 (containing special provisions for Nagaland, Assam, Manipur, Mizoram, and Arunchal Pradesh in sub-clauses A, B, C, G and H respectively), Article 244 (administration of scheduled areas and tribal areas, i.e. the provisions for Fifth and Sixth Schedule). Governmentalization of poly-ethnic rights and special representative rights also find the proper expression in the body of the Constitution itself. Articles 14-16 (containing provisions for positive discrimination), Articles 29-30 (provisions for protecting minority interests), Articles 46-47 (Directive Principles laying down the constitutional basis for welfare of the marginalized), Eighth Schedule (providing space for linguistic recognition) are the cases in point. Post colonial Indian nation state thus envisages the protection of civil and political rights of the individuals and their growing constitutionalism as the major political mechanism for accommodating contentious issues like cultural differences, claims of autonomy, and the recognition of self-government.

Techniques of Inclusion: Post-Colonial Indian Nation State and Darjeeling

Having stressed out the structures of exclusion that gave Gorkha ethnicity a definite shape and articulation since the colonial days let us now deal with the techniques of inclusion invested by the post independent state that attempted to redress amicably the Gorkha aspiration for self-rule in Darjeeling hills. First such effort came up in the Constituent Assembly debates where threadbare analyses of such crucial issue like: 'what would be the policy of administration regarding the 'excluded' and 'partially excluded areas?' was held. Series of similar efforts had also taken place like the recommendations of the States Reorganization Commission, regional autonomy question, issue of election and electoral politics. Not to mention that Gorkha ethnicity had encountered all these policy prescriptions in the process of its evolution over the years. However, it needs to be pointed out that neither of these strategies and policy measures were worked out to pacify any particular conflict situation of Darjeeling hills. This was so simply because of the fact that Gorkha ethnicity of Darjeeling has not reached a volatile situation by then. It was only in the 1980s that Gorkha ethnicity had resorted to violence and mass killing which urgently called for direct intervention of the state to normalize the situation. In short, prior to the late 1980s Gorkha ethnicity has been in a phase of latency and Darjeeling hills was yet to occupy a distinct position in the eyes of the State that would have instigated direct intervention of the administrative machinery. Consequently, the policy measures whatever were worked out was meant for the entire nation and partly they have constituted the institutional measures which fall under the gamut of the so-called project of nation building. Gorkha ethnicity of Darjeeling hills had nibbled out the required resources for its survival out of the project of nation building and throughout its latency phase it amicably adjusted itself to the requirements of such issues and processes. Let us have some elaboration on these issues.

Constituent Assembly Debates and the Concern for Darjeeling

Soon after independence Government of India in making recommendations for 'partially excluded areas' of the provinces other than Assam (particularly of Madras, Bombay, Bengal, Central Provinces, Bihar and United Provinces) has formed a sub-committee. The sub-committee of the Advisory Committee of the Constituent Assembly had been constituted of seven members and five co-opted members and among the five co-opted members Dambar Singh Gurung[2] of Darjeeling was the sole representative of the 30 lakh of permanently domiciled Gorkhas spread throughout the length and breadth of the country, beside Darjeeling and Assam where they did have fairly large concentration. In determining the areas to be classified as 'excluded' or 'partially excluded', the Secretary of State for India issued instructions as per the Government of India (Provincial Legislative Assemblies) Order, 1936, which shows the different tribes classed as backward, and among these tribes are to be found the inhabitants of the excluded and partially excluded areas. The excluded and partially excluded areas were well defined areas populated either predominantly or to a considerable extent by aboriginals. The excluded and partially excluded areas, however, do not by any means covered the entire population of tribal origin, and in many cases represented only a comparatively small proportion of the aboriginal population, the rest of them being scattered over non-excluded areas. The District of Darjeeling was such an area which has maintained the status of 'partially excluded area' since the last days Raj even though the non-tribal population of the area was fairly high.

The main feature of the Partially Excluded Areas was that they were not altogether excluded from the scope of the Provincial Ministries like the excluded areas nor was the expenditure on them fell outside the scope of the respective state legislature. In fact the administration of the areas had not been appreciably different from the rest of the province and the Provincial Governments were in greater or lesser degree opposed to their exclusion. The sub-committee report on the excluded and partially areas (other than Assam) emphatically maintained that:

> The partially excluded areas of Bengal consist of the District of Darjeeling and certain police station areas in the Mymensingh district which border on the Garo Hills of Assam. The Darjeeling District is shown to contain 141,301 (37.54%) tribes out of a total population of 376,369 in 1941. The tribal population of the district seems to consist largely of labour employed in the tea gardens and some Lepcha and Bhotia. Actually, the latter are only about 20,000 in number. The prominent community in Darjeeling is the Gurkha or Nepalese community which numbers about 2.5 lakh. A good many are employed in the tea gardens and the local police force also contains a high proportion of them. The Gurkha are not regarded as a backward tribe and the thirteenth schedule to the Government of India (Legislative Assemblies) Order does not include Gurkha.
>
> They feel, however, neglected so far as other ranks of Government service are concerned and in the trade and business of the place, the Marwari has the upper hand. On the other hand, the small community of Lepcha (12,000) finds itself dominated by the Gurkha and one of the complaints is that their land (the Lepcha claim to be the original inhabitants) has been gradually taken away from them by Nepalese immigrants. The partial exclusion of Darjeeling was recommended by the Government of Bengal not because it was considered as backward area but because it was felt that safeguards were necessary in the interests of the hill people. The fact that Darjeeling was the summer capital of the Government of Bengal and the existence of European tea-planters may have played some little part. The 1941 census shows that even among the tribals (mostly tea garden coolies) there was 16,450 literates out of a total population of 141,301 and 2,571 of these were women. The local bodies (Municipality and District Board) are not wholly elected bodies and the Deputy Commissioner is the President of the Municipality. Undoubtedly the land the

> hill tribes need to be protected from the maw of money lenders but there is little case otherwise for continuing partial exclusion or special administration [Sub-Committee Report 1947: Annexure III (Appendix D)].

It is apparent from the excerpt of the Sub-Committee Report that the concern of the Government regarding administration of the partially excluded areas, in general and of Darjeeling hills, in particular was not either of isolation or of complete exclusion. Nevertheless the apex body was aware regarding the segregationist aspirations of the acculturated elites of the region among whom Dambar Singh Gurung was the one. The Government instead opted for not recommending the continuation of the special administrative statuses that the area might have experienced during colonial rule and considered it as an integral part of the State of West Bengal and as a district of the same state. The urge for separation of the Gorkhas from Bengal was stalemated on the basis of the ground realities wherein the apex body did not find any justification for isolating the district from the rest of the State of West Bengal.

It is worth noting a point that Dambar Singh Gurung, the first ever Gorkha who dared to raise the Gorkha bid for power in the apex level national body like that of Constituent Assembly, came back to Darjeeling with an exposure towards the inclusionist fervour of politics that the Government was encouraging in independent India. Such a change of stand, basically an understanding Gurung has gained out of his active participation in the Constituent Assembly Debates, has made its expected reflection in the hill politics. On the occasion of the Annual Conference of the League in 1948 at Siliguri Dambar Singh Gurung had insisted on his moderate stand and declared that "(I)t would not be of any benefit for a little nationality like ours to go against the Congress, the party in power. Since Congress has taken over the responsibility to rule over the country we should remain close to the Congress leadership with good faith" (Gurung, 1971:17). The loadstar of inclusionist politics that the nation building project has imparted in Gurung's mind had its transient significance in the hill politics. Soon exclusionist politics was insisted by a new brand of leadership represented by such personalities like Rup Narayan Sinha and Randhir Subba among others who consistently harped on the segregationist stand.

States Reorganisation Commission (SRC) and Darjeeling District

Immediately after the first Assembly election Bidhan Chandra Roy, the first Chief Minister of West Bengal, and his Ministry had to face two crucial issues of immense political significance. One was the burning question of how to sort out the refugee problem and the second one was the issue of merger of the northern part of West Bengal consisting of the three districts, namely Darjeeling, Jalpaiguri, and Cooch Behar with the mainland of West Bengal. The northern part of West Bengal was physically separated from the rest of the West Bengal mainland as a result of the propositions of Radcliffe Boundary Commission which drew the boundary line between West Bengal and East Pakistan (now Bangladesh). Initially there was a political hue and cry both in Bihar and West Bengal regarding the issue of merger of some portions of the Purnea District, having a sizeable section of Bengali speaking population, with West Bengal. Maya Devi Chetri, in her capacity of being the sole Member of the Rajya Sabha from West Bengal, had hard pressed the demand of Bengal-Bihar merger while delivering her speech in the Upper House of the Indian Parliament on December 21, 1955 (Lama 1996:97). Finally, as a result of the reorganisation of the states, Islampur subdivision of Purnea district in Bihar was added to West Bengal. Islampur's addition provided a connecting link to Darjeeling, Jalpaiguri, and Cooch Behar districts with the rest of West Bengal and thereby ending the enclave status of these three Districts (Sengupta, 2007:232).

Although initially the INC had taken a soft stand[3] towards both the issues of language and linguistic reorganisation of the state more as a policy, if not as a promise. However, with the independence of the country the INC had shown an attitude of no-compromise towards these linguistic claims of regional specificity and characterised them more as an inhibitor towards the process of nation building. As early as in 1947 Jawaharlal Nehru, in his capacity of being the first Prime Minister of the country, had opposed the formation of states based on linguistic lines[4]. Hence, the INC had taken recourse to a policy in the name of nation building that equated nationalism with *status quo* (Majeed, 2003:85). The National Government, however, with much reluctance had decided to appoint the SRC in December 1953 which came out with its recommendations in 1956.

M.N. Srinivas well reminded us way back in 1957[5] that the Report of the States' Reorganisation Commission had been a whole new event in Indian history since it was based on a principle which explicitly recognised, contrary to the idea of the political system that existed in pre-British India, a principle which tacitly approve the coincidence of the cultural and political frontiers (Srinivas, 1998:15). The SRC has provided an altogether new political impetus in independent India. It has transformed language—a cultural substance—into a resource for political burgeoning and encouraged regional political outfits to clamour for separate territorial arrangement on the basis of linguistic principles. In fact, the decision to allow the Andhras to separate from Madras was the signal for linguistic groups all over India to raise similar claims. In North India, linguistic groups which had not previously expressed a desire for separate status began to agitate with extraordinary vigour. New organizations and pressure groups dedicated to the linguistic idea sprang up all over the country. Needless to mention that since the late 1950s the whole gamut of sub-state level political process in India centred on the issue of language and Darjeeling was not an exception in this trend.

Nepali Language Movement and the Response of the State

The issue of language movement in case of Darjeeling hills deserves special mention. Historically there has existed a very intimate relationship between Nepali language and Gorkha ethnicity in Darjeeling hills. On many occasions Gorkha ethnic conflict did project the recognition of Nepali language as the bone of contention. History suggests that Nepali language in Darjeeling hills has appeared as a marker of ethnic identity, a vehicle for expressing cultural distinctiveness, a source of national cohesion, and most importantly an instrument for building up a political community.

In fact, the use of Nepali language as a politically viable component of the movement has been a post-colonial strategy. Nepali language politics has received an implicit encouragement soon after the realisation that the post-colonial Indian political process had ultimately accepted, despite several ifs and buts, the linguistic principle of state reorganisation. However, it would be erroneous to apprehend that Nepali language issue had no vitality of its own during the pre-independence phase of the movement. Rather, it may be argued, in a certain sense that Nepali language issue was able to bring forth community solidarity among the heterogeneous hill mass on the one hand and energised the common people to participate more vigorously in the local political scenario on the other. Although Nepali language issue was successful in developing the sense of a distinctive Nepali linguistic identity among the hill folk but the same had failed to make any headway that might have led towards a parallel movement for securing the political aspiration of the Gorkhas during colonial period. However, the linguistic solidarity movement that went on under the banner of the *Nepali Sahitya Sammellan* (established in 1924) had given birth to a fresh stock of leadership (Dambar Singh Gurung was certainly one such leader) that directed the later courses of the history of the movement.

Besides providing a fillip to the incipient Nepali nationalism in Darjeeling hills Nepali language issue has been used meaningfully in the post-independence period by all major political parties. For example, the All India Gorkha League (AIGL) since its inception in Darjeeling hills (1943) has had harped on the language issue. The language issue has also caught the attention of the undivided Communist Party of India (CPI), which submitted a memorial on 6th April, 1947 stressing the need of using Nepali language as medium of instruction in schools, colleges and that Nepali must replace English and other languages in the Court, Government Offices and other Public Institutions (WG, 1986:35).

The language demand was intensified in the mid-fifties with the appointment of Official Language Commission with B.G. Kher as Chairman in 1955 and that of the States Reorganization Commission (SRC) in 1953. Nar Bahadur Gurung, the MLA (Independent) from Darjeeling, made a critical estimation of the stand undertaken by both the Congress and the Communists regarding the issue of the Report of the SRC in his deliberations in the West Bengal State Assembly in 1955. In his speech Nar Bahadur Gurung hard pressed the demand for the implementation of SRC's recommendations in Darjeeling taking it as a District of minority linguistic group. Upholding the provisions of the Report of the SRC Gurung had claimed that "The SRC has recommended on page 212, paragraph 784—'If seventy per cent or more of the total population of a district is constituted by a group, which is a minority in the State, the language of the minority group and not the State language, should be the official language in that district.' This can be applied in the case of Darjeeling District" (Gurung, 1971:30).

Immediately after Independence, Nepali ethnicity became politically prominent by upholding the claim of Official Language Recognition. Demands were raised not only in the floors of Assembly by the political representatives of the hills, but an all-round public uproar started fomenting as well. During such a situation the Government of West Bengal under the Chief Ministership of Dr. Bidhan Chandra Roy, had ruled out the *locus standi* of such a claim. The West Bengal Provincial Congress Committee (WBPCC) in their supplementary note (submitted to the members of the SRC when they visited Darjeeling) pointed out that the Nepali speaking population of the District was only 20 per cent (Gurung, 1971:29). Dr. B.C. Roy while ruling out the claim of Nepali language to be designated as the Official Language of the District made use of the Census data and upheld the view (in his speech delivered in the Assembly on 23rd February, 1961) that "The number of people speaking Nepali in the Hill District, according to 1951 Census, is only 19.98 per cent; even if we leave out Siliguri subdivision and take Darjeeling, Kurseong, and Kalimpong, it is 25.92 per cent. Therefore, Government felt that it would be better to wait for the 1961 Census which would be coming within a few months and then we may be able to decide whether Nepali language should be either in a District or a municipality recognised as an additional language of the area" (Gurung, 1971: 53-54).

The Government's stand on the issue of including Nepali language as the Official Language for the district of Darjeeling was disciplinary as well as pedagogical and was based on the notions of what Appadurai would call as *statist imaginaire* of a modern nation state, which India had inherited from its experience of the colonial state craft. It is rather obvious that a state founded upon the art and science of colonial political imagination, would be considering such demands as 'dysfunctional' for the whole body and spirit of a nascent nation state. The recommendations of SRC on the one hand and the relevance of the census data in determining the status of Nepali as the official language of the State on the other had provided the ground for reviving the linguistic nationalism of the early 1920s once again. All the major political and cultural platforms and the intelligentsia in the hills initiated the linguistic movement anew this time with an implicit message of enumerating Nepali as the mother-tongue especially by those who had enumerated their own dialects (*Kura*) as their mother-tongue during previous Census operations. All these undoubtedly had provided a new impetus within hill politics unleashed through the cultural appeals of an invigorated linguistic movement. Consequently, we find the 1961 Census figure for Nepali language in Darjeeling District has shown a sharp increase than the earlier census decades. The corresponding figure for the Nepali language in Darjeeling District was 369130 (59.09% of the total population of the District and secured a decadal variation of +314.95%) [Census 1961: 39-41].

It is interesting to note that the Chief Minister and for that matter the State has paid excessive attention to the issues of numbers and quantification as revealed in the Census figures while responding towards the demands of the hill people. This indeed, has had a specific effect of linking linguistic identity towards a distinctive logic of enumeration that produced a new '*colonial imaginaire*' within the post-colonial body polity of India whose role was more justificatory, pedagogical, and disciplinary. Numbers thus gradually became the part of the illusion of bureaucratic control and a key to *statist imaginaire* in which countable abstractions, both of people and their languages created the sense of a controllable indigenous reality even within the post-colonial situation (Appadurai, 1993: 317). The validity of the arguments posed here can be well judged by analyzing Table 3.1.

Table 3.1: Showing the change of Nepali language speakers (%) in different Census decades (1911-61)

Mother Tongue (Nepali)	*1911*	*1921*	*1931*	*1951*	*1961*
Absolute figure	56,768	63,936	92,970	88,958	369,130
Percentage variation	—	+12.68	+45.41	– 4.32	+314.95
% to total hill population	29.37	30.89	38.84	27.06	91.19

Source: Compiled from Census 1961, Darjeeling District Handbook: p. 40.

It appears from the above Table 3.1 that although Nepali language happened to be the lingua franca of Darjeeling hills, 1951 Census data has recorded Nepali as mother-tongue for only 27.06 per cent of the total hill population. The Census data, had represented an administrative reality in which Nepali language was neither being shown as the language of the majority of the population of the hills nor even any rising trend of population speaking Nepali language was visible (upto 1951). This led the Government not to recognize Nepali as an Official Language of the State and Dr. B.C. Roy thus had persuasively suggested the hill people to wait till the 1961 Census data become public.

Perhaps the most dramatic turn in the language movement had taken place instantaneously. Series of politico-cultural activities, programmes, mobilizations, strike, meetings, and rallies were organized to ameliorate the status of Nepali quantitatively. Increasingly it has been felt by the hill population that Nepali language should be enumerated as their mother-tongue during the time of forthcoming Census operations so as to enhance the number of Nepali language speakers, in lips and bounds, from the hills itself. It is needless to mention that such mass mobilizations regarding Nepali language issue became successful and ultimately the demand had been accepted by the Government as the 1961 Census data proved the preponderance of Nepali language speakers in the hills. In an attempt to pinpoint the significance of the issue of enumeration and Census data in the case of Nepali language movement it may be said that the Census has appeared more than a bureaucratic and/or administrative text; it did have social implications for the Nepali speech community, besides its administrative significance for the state. To say it in other words, Census as a social text does not simply describe how the State perceives the different sections of people, their mother-tongues, or the like resources; it is also an exercise that influences the way people perceive themselves and in doing so contributes to the construction of identities through the distinctive logic of enumeration. This is what has happened in Darjeeling hills during the late 1950s when the entire hill folk had become obsessed with the appeal of Nepali language as their mother-tongue. Being capacitated with the energies harnessed by language, Nepali/Gorkha ethnicity in Darjeeling hills has transcended towards broader political questions like regional autonomy and the demand for a separate state which led towards the full blown growth of a state-hood movement based on the premises of self-determination, cultural distinctiveness, and ethnic exclusivity.

Regional Autonomy in Darjeeling Hills

Although in 1988 Darjeeling hills did experience for the first time the institutionalization of regional autonomy in the form of Hill Council, the very idea of regional autonomy had been on the edge of hill political scenario since the 1950s. In fact, the idea of regional autonomy for the District of Darjeeling was mooted by the communists more as a matter of amended party stand regarding the issue of self-determination. In fact, the Darjeeling branch of CPI and later the CPI (M) has harped on the principle of regional autonomy so consistently that it brought forth political mileage in the local context. It is no wonder then to trace out the fact that Darjeeling District Committee of the Communist Party of India (undivided) had submitted a memorandum to the then Chief Minister Dr. B.C. Roy during his visit to Darjeeling on October 11, 1953. The memorandum represented a charter of 27 demands to the Chief Minister and the charter of demands included the issues related with education, unemployment, public health, local self-government, cottage and small scale industries, reduction of land rents of *Khas Mahal* and agricultural lands, the implementation of Plantation Labour Act of 1951, and the plantation labour's non-wage benefits, besides the claim of "extending benefits of the new Constitution by granting 'Regional Autonomy' to the people of Darjeeling District" (for detail *vide* WBLAP, 1954:271-276).

The Darjeeling District Committee of the CPI had also submitted its proposals for regional autonomy for the District to the members of the SRC when they had visited Darjeeling in the month of May 1955. The Communist leader Ranen Sen hard pressed the demand of regional autonomy for Darjeeling District in the Assembly during the month of December 1955. Upholding the party position Ranen Sen declared in his speech in the Assembly: "(...) For these Nepali brethren we demand Regional Autonomy within the State of West Bengal—within the State of West Bengal. I repeat the expression within the State of West Bengal, because there has been a good deal of misunderstanding over the matter. Atulya Ghosh, President of West Bengal Congress, who understood it quite well, gave it out that we want the exclusion of Darjeeling from West Bengal" (Gurung, 1971:25). While discussing over the issue the opposition leader Mr. Jyoti Basu (of CPI who later also became the Chief Minister of West Bengal) reiterated the same position of regional autonomy status for the District of Darjeeling in his speech delivered in the Assembly on 9th December, 1955 (Sarkar, 2004: 135). Again, Ananda Pathak, in his capacity of being the CPI (M) MP of the Lok Sabha has raised the issue of creating an Autonomous District Council for the district of Darjeeling and neighbouring district where the Nepali speaking population is in a majority as per the provisions laid down in Article 244C of the Constitution of India. He proposed a Constitutional Amendment Bill (Bill No. 122 of 1985) on March 7, 1986 in this regard in Lok Sabha, which was, however, rejected outrightly.

While the communists were the harbinger of the idea of regional autonomy as a matter of political principle to settle the decade long urge of the hill people for self-rule within the limits multicultural constitutionalism, the other political parties like the All India Gorkha League (AIGL) and the Congress were not far away from playing out this newer brand of politics—the politics of autonomy. As a matter of fact, AIGL during the late 1950s and the District Committee of the Congress during the late 1960s have accepted the principle of regional autonomy as a viable political strategy, if not as the formal official party standpoint. In fact, the political implication of the issue of regional autonomy was so far reaching that the political movement of self-rule was shelved temporarily and instead all the major political parties of the District became busy in finding out their respective political advantages in the process of political bargaining related with the issues of regional autonomy and its inbuilt constitutionalism. In a certain sense, the movement for a separate territorial arrangement or for that matter of self-rule was reduced to a movement for 'regional autonomy' during these decades.

Election and Electoral Politics

The history of the movement during the three decades ranging from 1950s to 1970s has shown some interesting developments. The movement during this period of time was more or less peaceful and democratic, if not pro-State. Barring a few occasion[6] strikes were hardly called on, elections were never boycotted, no incidence of genocide or of mass killing have ever happened. AIGL, Congress, and CPI/CPI (M) evolved as the major political platforms of Darjeeling hills although they did have their District Committees established in pre-Independence phase. All the Assembly and Parliamentary elections were held at regular intervals in which all the above mentioned political parties and also some independent candidates have participated. It deserves mention that while the AIGL was the only indigenous political platform during this period of time, the other political parties [like the INC or the CPI (M)] have also thoroughly depended upon the hill people while distributing the party portfolio or nominating the candidates for elections, for obvious reasons. It is also interesting to note that the prominent leaders of the Congress during this period of time were either the dismissed AIGL members or had an erstwhile linkage with the League. For example, N.B. Gurung who happened to be the District Congress Committee President of Darjeeling during 1963-1967, Member of All India Congress Committee in 1972 besides being the Deputy Minister of Labour in B.C. Roy's Ministry for two times was the younger brother of Dambar Singh Gurung who founded the AIGL. Although N.B. Gurung himself was incharge of the Labour wing of the League since its inception, he resigned from the League in 1962. With N.B. Gurung's resignation not only the dominance of Gurung family over the League was ended but also the prominence of Kalimpong as the base area of AIGL activity had diminished. Soon Deo Prakash Rai came up as the undisputable leader of the League who never lost in the Assembly elections during his lifetime and always contested the election from Darjeeling constituency and thereby made Darjeeling the epicentre for AIGL activities. However, the Gurung dynasty, even after switching over to Congress, still remained politically significant in Kalimpong. N.B. Gurung failed to win over the Assembly election of 1962 which he contested as a Congress candidate from Kalimpong but his cousin brother Krishna Bahdur Gurung won the 1967 election as a Congress candidate from the same constituency. Krishna Bahadur Gurung also became the President of Kalimpong Congress Committee in 1967. N.B. Gurung's son Gajendra Gurung also won the 1972 Assembly election from Kalimpong on Congress ticket and on January 31, 1975 he became the State Minister of Bengal (Rawat, 1996: 248).

As far as the Assembly election results were concerned it may be said that from the very beginning Darjeeling hills had its representation in the West Bengal Assembly and many of the MLAs of the District also sworn in as Deputy Ministers, and Cabinet Ministers too like Shiv Kumar Rai and N.B. Gurung (who served as Deputy Minister of Labour), Deo Prakash Rai (served as Cabinet Minister). Interestingly enough all of them belonged to AIGL when they became Ministers. In the fifteen Assembly elections held so far (during the period 1952-2011), maximum number of seats within the three Assembly constituencies of the hills were won by the AIGL (18 out of 45, i.e. 40%), followed by GNLF (11 out of 45, i.e. 24.44%), CPI (M) (8 out of 45, i.e. 17.78%), Congress (3 out of 45, i.e. 6.67%), GJM (3 out of 45, i.e. 6.67%), Independent (1 out of 45, i.e. 2.22%), and CPI (1 out of 45, i.e. 2.22%). This is revealed in the following diagram (Fig. 3.1).

Although Electoral systems represent perhaps the most powerful instrument available for institutional engineering, with far-reaching consequences for party systems, the composition of legislatures, and the durability of democratic arrangements, the experience of Darjeeling hills suggests that electoral process has hardly served the purpose of either being a process of 'constitutional engineering' or an 'institutional design' that could have led towards the peaceful amelioration of ethnic antagonism. Electoral politics has instead sharpened the ethnic cause leading towards political valence. Initially AIGL, the first ethnic political party of the hills, almost singlehandedly captured all the Assembly seats while GNLF, since its inception in the 1980s, have predominated the Assembly election results. Again in the recent past the same phenomenon was repeated. The Gorkha Janmukti Morcha, which emerged just in 2007 after displacing Ghising and his GNLF, has attained sweeping victory with huge margin in all the three Assembly seats in the hills.

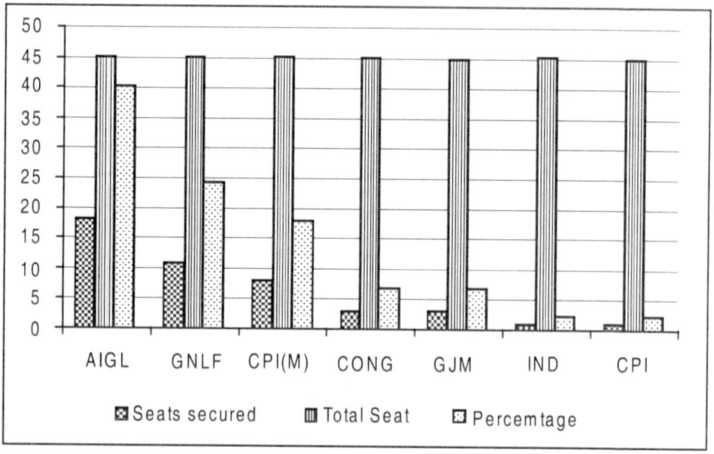

Fig. 3.1: Assembly Election Performance of Political Parties in Darjeeling Hills (1952-2011)

The point is that the ethnic political parties did consider election and electoral politics as an 'opportunity structure' rather than as the 'institutional design' to promote democratic durability. Perhaps that is why they either prefer for aligning with an established political party after having made the self-assessment regarding their own strength. If they find the ethnic cleavage gets truly reflected through the political activism that their respective political parties have spearheaded, they compete the election without forming coalition with other political parties (this has been the case with AIGL, GNLF and GJM's sweeping electoral victory) and in other situations they find it more calculative to support others just to win over others (this is how GNLF has supported the Independent candidate N.T. Moktan who won the Kalimpong Assembly seat in 1991 Assembly election). In exceptional situations when the ethnic parties do find the election as an event that is not going to yield political opportunities but rather will dismantle the tempo of ethnic struggle they simply go for boycotting the election (this has been particularly the case during 1982 and 1987 Assembly elections when Gorkhaland movement has reached its zenith and GNLF boycotted the Assembly election twice).

Consideration of electoral process as an 'opportunity structure' appeared to be far more precarious in case of Parliamentary elections, although Darjeeling has been allotted with a single seat for the entire district. If we consider the election results of Lok Sabha polls we will find that out of the fourteen Parliamentary elections (held during 1957-2009) Congress and CPI (M) has won most of the times (Congress for five terms and CPI (M) for six terms) while ethnic parties like GNLF won only once and an Independent candidate and BJP has also won the Lok Sabha seat of the district only for once. However, the poll results as reflected through the quantitative data hardly yields the significance of ethnic politics that has played a very significant role in electoral match making particularly in case of Lok Sabha seat. It is also significant to note that the Parliamentary election results are hardly comparable with the trend of Assembly election since the single seat offered for Darjeeling was meant for the entire district (including both the hills and plains areas of the district). Even then it may be said that while the victory of Congress in the initial phase (particularly the victory of Theodore Menon who won twice in 1957 and 1962) was having the tacit support of the AIGL the victory of Congress candidate Inderjit in 1991 and Dawa Narbula in 2004 was the result of GNLF's

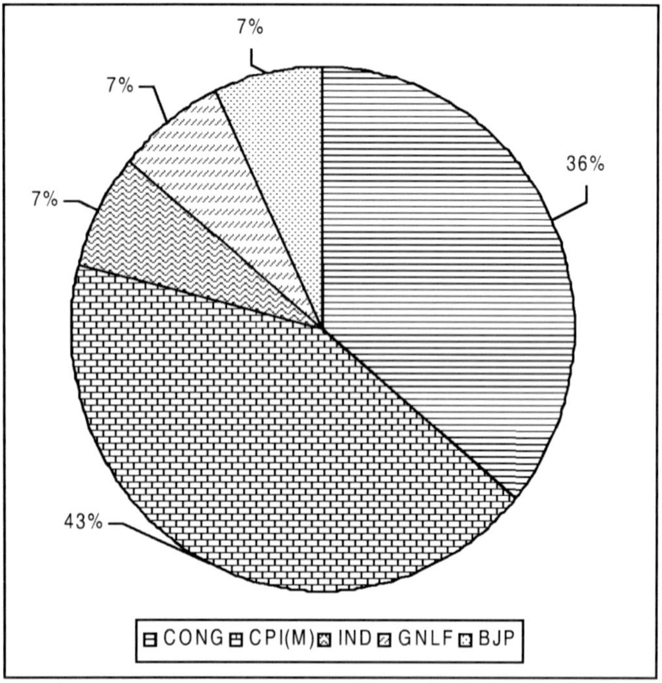

Fig. 3.2: Lok Sabha seats won by different political parties during 1957-2009

backing. GNLF only once filed its own candidate Inderjit, a Delhi based journalist and neither a Gorkha nor a hill man, and secured sweeping victory. Similar is also the case of the last year's success story of the BJP. In the political history of the district BJP has never been considered as a significant political party in terms of its support base nevertheless it participated in both assembly and Lok Sabha elections and all the time shown a very poor performance in terms of its share in the electoral turnouts. Even then it secured a sudden victory with heavy margin in the last parliamentary election held in 2009. It would seem to be very unusual if we do not consider the pretext of BJP's electoral strategy this time. It needs to be pointed out that it is not the Hinduvta ideology that secured BJP's success but the electoral alliance of BJP and GJM that played the match making role. The GJM has backed the BJP candidate Jaswant Singh—again an outsider—and campaigned in his favour with the hope that if BJP comes in power it will sympathetically look into the long cherished demand of a separate state[7].

The point is that the insistence of the ethnic parties (be it AIGL, GNLF or the GJM) in case of Parliamentary election in Darjeeling district all the time considered the electoral process as the short cut route for achieving their demands fulfilled and satisfied. In the process the real essence of election as the pillars of successful democracy gets sty-mied. At times when the ethnic parties did not find any of the political parties as helpful in fulfilling their aspirations they have no other options left for them but to go for boycotting the election. Not to mention that the ambivalent attitude of the GNLF regarding the Parliamentary elections held during 1996, 1998 and 1999 has enabled the CPI (M) attain a smooth sailing. This would have also been the case if the GJM has not acceded to the BJP as an election partner in the last Parliamentary election held in 2009.

The Darjeeling situation is suggestive of the very fact that the political leaders typically find the election as the sphere wherein the rewards of outbidding on ethnic lines can surely be gained. Aspiring politicians greedy for attaining electoral victory at any cost have strong incentives to harness these identities as a political force since ethnic identities tend to be invested with a great deal of symbolic and emotional feelings that constituted its potentiality of being a weapon much stronger than a politics based on issues or ideologies. Scholars are apprehensive of potential dangers involved in these processes. Such mobilization of ethnic identities for political purposes can create a 'divided society' argues Rabushka and Shepsle (1972:21) while Sisk is of the view that politics in such situations can quickly come to be characterized by centrifugal forces, in which moderate political centre is overwhelmed by extremist forces. The failure of democratic politics is often the end result of these processes (Sisk, 1995:23). As issues of ethnic politics becomes an increasingly central part of the electoral process cycle of ethnic hostility and conflict unwinds which undermines the prospect of peaceful democratic politics taking root (Reilly, 2004:4-5). In fact, the open competitive election in Darjeeling hills has facilitated the politicization of ethnic communities which in turn add to the consequent danger of ethnic extremism and violent destabilization of the political order. Instead of developing a deep democratic culture the issues of election and electoral politics has offered a highly politicised path in which only ethnic cleavage has gained prominence rather than politics of issues or of ideology. Instead of enlarging the scope of democratic inclusion of the ethnic entrepreneurs in the larger body polity and providing the ethnic political parties a scope to become a partner in the overall governance process of the region, election and electoral politics strengthened the capacity of ethnic cleavage to fix up the goals and directions of local politics. This possibly explains why the democratically elected members of the Assembly from the hills, quite often in the past, did not even hesitate to resign from their posts of being the MLAs of the region. The point is that the procedural norms of a democratic system have been well maintained in the hills ever since India's independence but the idea of 'substantial democracy' is yet to be realized.

Democratic Aptitude of the Hills: The Field View

However, the field data give a different direction in the overall analysis. That the prospect of democracy is not that bleak as was revealed in the analysis of electoral data. The practice of democracy is still having its roots well founded in the hills even though that often gets stymied particularly at the time of elections. As far as the opinion of a minuscule section of the hill literati is concerned it has been found that people in general have faith in democracy as the best political system. Out of the 57 respondents 31 (i.e. 54.37%) favoured democracy as the best political system. However, dictatorship is favoured by a small section of respondents 9 out of 57 (15.80%) while one respondent (1.75%) escape commenting on the issue. It is interesting to note that a sizeable section of the respondents registered their bewilderment regarding what is going on the hills in the name democratic governance. 16 out of 57 respondents (28.08%) were of the view that whether it is democracy or dictatorship that does not make any difference in what people think of the political system. This in fact led me investigate another domain of people's perception regarding what they think of their society *vis-à-vis* their capacity to change the same. Interestingly enough 77.20% (44 out of 57) of the respondents believe that people like them can make a difference while 12.28% (7 out of 57) of the respondents believe that the system does not offer much room for the individual to bring forth change, while five respondents (8.77%) are not very sure regarding their capacity or regarding the nature of society that would have encouraged the individual to usher in change.

Only one respondent (1.75%) avoided registering any comment in this regard.

Respondents were asked to submit their opinion regarding the need and justification of the political parties. The responses gathered were fact revealing. Majority of the respondents (40 out of 57, i.e. 70.18%) considered political parties as the most important instrument for a stable democratic order that prevents political stagnancy and usher in democratic change in the store house of power. 8.77 per cent of the respondents (5 out of 57) estimated political parties as the short-cut route to enjoy control and hegemony over the masses while nine respondents (15.79%) considered political parties as the significant vehicle to exert the political prominence of the community in the realm of wider politics. Three respondents (5.26%), however, avoided commenting anything.

It is always very significant to consider the viewpoints of the civil society members in order to have a grip over the issues of peace and conflict. Backed by such an understanding the present study attempted to cover up the viewpoints of more than fifty civil society members (57 in actual number) on a pertinent issue: as to how they assess the significance of the election in an ethnically ripe political environment that Darjeeling hills has historically maintained? While 22.81 per cent of the respondents (13 in actual number) considered election as the lifeline of democracy 77.19 per cent of the respondents (44 in actual number) have assessed the same differently. Among the 44 respondents seven (15.91%) considered election as the best process to assert agitational voice in a democratic mode, sixteen respondents (36.36%) estimated elections as that platform in which people do not merely cast their vote as a matter of right but take the opportunity to address their aspiration at the national level, and 21 respondents (47.73%) weighed up election as the manifestation of both (i.e. to assert agitational voice democratically and to address the voice of the community at a broader level).

It is often alleged that in ethnic situations elections are often manipulated and the experience of the Darjeeling hills is not free from such allegations. In order to assess what people think regarding the issue of electoral manipulation all the fifty-seven respondents were asked: whether they think it justified to manipulate election on the pretext of ethnic emancipation? Interestingly enough almost all the respondents (56 out of 57, i.e. 98.25%) were of the view that 'manipulation of electoral process election is not justified on any ground whatsoever' while only one respondent (1.75%) favoured electoral manipulation with the intention of achieving ethnic emancipation.

As pointed out earlier the event of recently held Assembly election of 2011 was very significant in Darjeeling hills since it was at this juncture the GJM has tried to achieve people's mandate rather straightforwardly by putting its own henchmen as candidates to fight for Assembly seats under its own banner. GJM has attained a sweeping victory but what the civil society members think on the issue of electoral politics that provided scope, at least apparently, to all the major political parties to file their respective candidates from the hill constituencies. How people assess the sliding victory of the GJM? Responses on these issues were very crucial in the sense that they could help us have an understanding of what happened in reality and how people used to assess the same. While 19 respondents (33.33%) were of the view that this year's assembly election reflected democratic culture of the hills in a meaningful way 29 respondents (50.88%) opined that although multiple parties participated in the recently held assembly election but in actual reality the entire process has in fact indicated single party dominance. It is interesting to note that 5 respondents (8.77%) believed that it would have been better if there was a single agenda electoral politics this year. However, by 'single agenda politics' what they actually meant was the need for a single political claim (of Gorkhaland) by a single political claimant (whatever might be its name who ever might be its leader that does not matter) harping on the same single issue for people's mandate. Four respondents (7.02%), however, avoided putting any comment in this regard.

Responses gathered regarding the overwhelming victory of the GJM in the Assembly election were of mixed variety. While 25 respondents (43.86%) felt that people voted the GJM most since they considered the party as the most capable to direct the Gorkhaland movement towards success, 13 respondents (22.81%) were of the view that people voted the GJM out of their perception of fear, threat and danger. Nine respondents (15.79%) considered that the lack of a suitable alternative many a time led people cast vote in favour of the GJM. Equal number of respondents were of the view that people favoured the GJM because of its declared electoral strategy to support the Trinamool Congress. As per people's understanding, as the nine respondents reasoned, the electoral alliance was a right strategy which may provide the GJM an opportunity in the post election period to secure a fair political deal towards self rule. However, one respondent abstained registering any comment in this regard.

Pondering upon the field view it may be argued that while democracy is not having a very smooth sailing in the hills nevertheless the road towards a healthy democratic system is not blocked either. This becomes far clearer when one considers the opinion of the hill people regarding the issues like: justification of political parties, significance of election, and the assessment of the recently held assembly election in the state. However, it needs to be stressed out that that the significance of the inclusive arrangements—be it the electoral system, regional autonomy question or even the linguistic principles of states reorganisation—have been evaluated by the hill people grossly on the plane of the desire of self-rule. It would be an utter mistake if one considers that a politics of segregation ran parallel with the politics of inclusion in the Darjeeling hills. Nor even it would be proper to hold that the mechanisms of inclusion were worked out in Darjeeling hills not as a counter discourse to the already existing politics of segregation. The point is that the relationship between the segregationist politics and inclusionary measures are very intimate. Hence, it seems quite appropriate to argue that the politics of segregation in the hills is rather fed by and articulated through the mechanisms of inclusion. The modalities of inclusive measures as a whole have brought new resources, which in fact, helped the discourse of self rule attain new vigour and vitality played out by the emerging ethnic leadership in the dynamic field of identity politics.

NOTES

1. The notion of governmentality, a portmanteau word, widely used by Foucault and the term is used in the present study in the Foucaultian sense. To elaborate the idea Foucault suggests that to govern means to govern things or by the same token to govern human beings by turning them into 'things'. To fulfil this task the governmental rationalities embark upon an assemblage of institutions, procedures, calculations, tactics, strategies etc. which

are being used for governance and thereby to transform the ruled into 'things'. This complex institutional processes backed by knowledge of science of governing constitute in essence what is called as governmentality.

2. Dambar Singh Gurung was also the founding President of the first indigenous political platform of Darjeeling hills known as All India Gorkha League (AIGL) established in 1943.
3. For example INC in its Nagpur Session 1920 had accepted the principle of linguistic reorganization of the State and reiterated the same position in the election manifesto of the party during 1945-46 which "stood for the freedom of each group and territorial area within the nation to develop its own life and culture within the larger framework, and it has stated that for this purpose such territorial areas or provinces should be constituted, as far as possible, on a linguistic and cultural basis" (Zaid & Zaid, 1981:531).
4. Nehru's approach towards the issues of language and linguistic state formation has been discussed at length by R.D. King (King, 1997).
5. This observation was made by Srinivas in his Presidential Address to the Anthropology and Archaeology Section of the 44th Session of the Indian Science Congress held in Calcutta in January 1957 which latter was reproduced in his book *Caste in Modern India and Other Essays* first published in 1962.
6. Strikes became a handy political tool for the Communists, in particular, who used this strategy in matters of settling the labour related issues in the tea gardens during the 1950s. However, peaceful strikes were also called on in reaction to the negative response of the state towards the language movement of 1960s.
7. BJP in its election manifesto has emphasised its favourable stand on the formation of small states like Gorkhaland, Telengana etc. That perhaps persuaded the GJM to consider BJP in confidence and go for alliance with it according to the codes of the so-called 'opportunity structure'.

4

Movement and State Response: Gorkhaland in the 1980s

Desire for self-rule in the form of demands for the creation of separate *Uttarakhand Pradesh*, inclusion of Darjeeling in the State of Assam, or a separate State of Darjeeling kept on rolling until the 1970s. During the early 1980s the stagnated political undercurrents of the hills were transformed into a vibrant and volatile bloody struggle for attaining a separate state for the Indian Gorkhas to be carved out from the State of West Bengal. Subhas Ghising and his newly formed political platform Gorkha National Liberation Front (GNLF)[1] took the lead and spearheaded the Gorkhaland movement in the region. Throughout the early 1980s Ghising was busy in preparing the ground work for his newly formed Party. By 1985 Ghising was able to establish the required mass base for his party which helped him unleash the violent struggle of Gorkhaland. By 1985 Subhas Ghising had been successful to establish six frontal organisations, namely Gorkha National Women's Organisation (GNWO), Gorkha National Youth Front (GNYF), Gorkha National Students' Front (GNSF), Gorkha Volunteers' Cell (GVC), Gorkhaland Welfare Organisation (GWO), and Gorkha National Ex-Servicemen Organisation (GNEO). All these organisations as their names suggest had different categories of followers and different spheres of activities although they were guided by a single thread, i.e. the demand of Gorkhaland.

Through his provocative speeches and capitalising on the organizational strength of the GNLF Ghising had been successful to make people dream about his dreamland of Gorkhaland. The ethnic cleavage was so firmly activated that people became ready to sacrifice their life by a single call of their undisputed leader. Thus the preparation on all sides for a violent and aggressive movement was almost over by 1985. The Darjeeling Government College incidence of August 1985 had added fuel to the smouldering state of the movement. On August 28, 1985 Assistant Professor B.K. Chatterjee of Darjeeling Government College had passed a sarcastic remark (Go back to Nepal!) referring to a group of agitating students who failed to secure an admission in the College. GNSF took several political programmes (including processions and strike) against such a comment made by a senior Bengali College teacher. Darjeeling Government College remained closed from August 28, 1985 to September 10, 1985 as a result of the strike called by the GNSF. The Government of West Bengal instead of calling upon an Enquiry Commission, as was demanded by the GNSF, had promulgated Section 144 Cr.P.C. in Darjeeling town (SMB, 1985: 6-7).

The Turbulent Phase of the Movement

During 1986 the movement reached the do or die phase. In a meeting at Ghoom the GNLF President had formally launched the movement with the declaration of 11-point programme of action[2] on March 13, 1986. This meeting was attended by a huge gathering perhaps because of the Meghalay incidence of March 1986 which created grave concern among the hill people regarding the fate of the Nepalis in India, an issue that Ghising did emphasize consistently since his emergence. Thus the coincidence of Meghalya event, in which a sizeable section of the Nepali population was evicted, has brought the rather complex issues of citizenship and identity crisis, the building blocks of Ghising's Gorkhaland movement, to the level everyday understanding. The able leadership of Ghising, enabled GNLF capitalise on the situation. In order to disseminate the 11-point programme and other political activities of the GNLF throughout the three hill subdivisions several magazines and journals mushroomed under the auspices of the party like *Swatantra Manch Ko Bulletin, Jana-Paksh, Voice of Gorkhaland, Radio Gorkhaland, Gorkhaland Ko Jankari, Gorkhaland Ko Sankalp, Gorkha Sandesh* and others.

In pursuance of the 11-point programme of action a Black Flag protest successfully began on April 13, 1986 when a huge body of mass (more than 15,000 souls according to newspaper reports) assembled in Darjeeling despite the imposition of Section 144 and road blockade by the police. Once begun in April the movement gained momentum and spread like a rapid fire. The second step of the movement started with the declaration of the 72-hour *bandh* (strike) call which started, according to the 11-point programme, on May 12, 1986. The *bandh* call was marked by a series of incidents leading to death and mass imprisonment of the movement supporters. This was followed by a road blockade by the GNLF in demand of unconditional release of their party members arrested during the course of 72-hour *bandh*. Another *bandh* was called in Kurseong the next day which turn out to be total and curfew was declared all over the hills. More BSF and Eastern Frontier Rifles platoons were added to the already deployed three companies of the CRPF and other armed personnel (Statesman: May 26, 1986).

Mr. Ghising addressed a 10-day (July 12-21, 1986) non-stop meeting in Darjeeling and its neighbourhood to mobilise support for the movement in Kalimpong area. In courses of these meetings he gave an ultimatum to the Prime Minister for a verdict on his demand for a separate state before it was too late to save Darjeeling hills to go up in flames. July 27, 1986 was decided to be the day when the clause 7 of the Indo-Nepal Peace Treaty of 1950 would be burnt in every towns and villages of Darjeeling hills (Telegraph: July 16, 1986). Copies of the said clause were burnt on the scheduled date followed by a mass procession at 8th Mile, Kalimpong. Police took resort to *lathi* charge and ultimately fired indiscriminately at the agitating mob that claimed fifteen lives among whom women and children were in majority (Telegraph: July 28, 1986). As a reaction to these atrocities Subhas Ghising declared a 108 hours *bandh* bringing life in the hills to a standstill. The GNLF had also called off the Independence Day celebration in the hills as a measure to protest against the police firing in Kalimpong. However, the decision was withdrawn by the Party President himself just at the eve of the Independence Day.

In a certain sense, the Kalimpong killing did mark a point of no return from the demand of Gorkhaland. The movement which hardly had much support base in Kalimpong gained popular support and created mass excitement over the issue of Gorkhaland overnight. Mr. Prem Kumar Alley, the President of AINBS had sent a Telegram to the Prime Minister in protest against the incidence of mass killing in Kalimpong (Emergency Meeting of the AINBS dated July 28, 1986). Mr. Yonzon from Singi in Kalimpong resigned as a member of Darjeeling Zilla Parishad in protest against the police atrocities. The event of police firing in Kalimpong had resulted into a mass resignation of the hill people from the different platforms of governance which they represented. Eight Commissioners (out of 15) from Darjeeling Municipality, one (out of 12) from Kurseong Municipality, several others from the Panchayat Samitis, Darjeeling Hill Areas Development Council, ABTA and other bodies have resigned (ABP: November 21, 1986). Towards the end of the year several incidences of violence, blood shedding, and destruction of public and private properties were reported. Inter-party clashes [between GNLF and CPI (M)], clash with the army personnel took place at Singhtham tea estate, Pool Bazar, Rambuk tea estate and at Sonada (ABP: December 3, 1986 and Telegraph: December 14, 1986). In short, throughout the 1986 Darjeeling hills remained fierce, tensed, and was blazing.

In the year 1987 the movement still remained to be a violent one. In an effort to show their grievances against the State the GNLF has adopted the political programme to observe 'Anti-Bengal Day' from January 23-25, 1987. Wide publicity had been made through the circulation of leaflets, in which it was mentioned that the agitators should not indulge into confrontation with the Police or the CRPF and that no provocative slogans should be raised except '*Gorkhaland Jindabad*', '*Hamro Mato Farkai Deo*' (return back our native soil/ motherland), 'We Want Gorkhaland', and 'Long live Gorkhaland.' However, under the pressure of Central Government the 'Anti-Bengal Day' programme was withdrawn on January 22, 1987. The Assembly election of 1987 has added new dimension in the movement. The GNLF as usual had boycotted the Assembly election to be held in the month of March but had assured the Chief Election Commission that this time they would ensure peace during the election. However, the GNLF had three dummy candidates one (Diamong Mothay) in Darjeeling, one (Bhim Kumar Rai) in Kalimpong, and one (Tularam Rai) in Kurseong. Though the administration had anticipated violence and preparation was thus made accordingly for the election, the instances of violence and confrontation hardly took place. With an average of 7 per cent of polling out of a total 3,32,818 voter in the three hill constituencies the CPI (M) had won all the three seats. This mass apathy towards the Assembly election once again proved the stronghold of GNLF over Darjeeling hills although CPI (M) won all the seats. Experiencing this massive support towards its claim of election boycott the GNLF unleashed the movement with more vigour and violence. The GNLF started following the path of an all-round aggression not only against the CPI (M) activists but also with the military personnel. This helped the state to exercise more stringent punitive measures to pacify the situation. TADA was thus promulgated in the troubled zones of Darjeeling hills on June 23, 1987. However, the TADA was withdrawn, when negotiations were underway for the formation of Hill Council, on July 25, 1988 (Samanta, 2000:148).

The Track Record of Violence: Gorkhaland Movement in the Mid 1980s

In an attempt to provide a brief overview of the violence and atrocities cropped up during the mid 1980s in the hills either in the name of spearheading the Gorkha movement or to counter the same by the State authorities we can notice at least three distinctive phases. The first phase (April-October 1986) is marked by inter-party clashes. Violence erupted out of a strategy that projected those whoever had opposed the idea of Gorkhaland. All the non-hill political parties and their hill representatives too were made the direct enemy to the great Gorkha cause, these political parties and their henchmen were increasingly being viewed as those who corroborate to the very idea of 'prison administration' of the State of West Bengal. This has become a popular saying in those days that 'one can be merciful with a snake but not with those who opposes Gorkhaland' (*"Saplai kshama dinu sakincha tar Gorkhaland birodhilai kshama dinu sakindaina"*) Provocative slogans like the following used to ignite the mass sentiment:

> *"Afno Mato bhanda Sddharta Sankar Roy thulo hoina!!*
> *Afno Mato bhanda Anada Pathak thulo hoina!!*
> *Afno Mato bhanda Dawa Narbula thulo hoina!!*
> *Bangalbato hamro Mato pharkaunu parcha!!"*

("Neither Siddharta Shankar Roy, nor Anada Pathak, nor even Dawa Narbula—no one is having a greater cause than our own motherland/homeland!! Our native soil/motherland needs to be separated from Bengal" Translation mine).

Although the bone of contention was worked out against all the major political parties and their leaders in actuality CPI (M) men and CPI (M) party offices were made ready targets. Anada Pathak and his relatives and other party cadres' houses were gutted besides numerous CPI (M) party offices were burnt down. Hundreds of CPI (M) followers were killed while thousands came down to the low lands of Siliguri.

The second phase (November 1986-April 1987) started with the countermovement spearheaded by the CPI (M) men to combat the armed attack of the GNLF with similar counter offensive measures. Killing and counter killing marred hill politics for some moment. In the process of maintaining peace in the region state armed police were engaged and several police men were also killed in the mayhem. Not to mention that within these series of instances of inter-party violence and police intervention uncounted innocent civilians had been slain. The following Table 4.1 can give us a minuscule idea of the human casualties occurred during this turbulent phase. However, human casualties were much more than what this rather official statistics reveal.

Table 4.1: Official statement regarding human casualties occurred during Gorkhaland movement

Categories	*1986*		*1987*		*1988 (Jan.-Sept.)*		*Total*	
	Killed	*Injured*	*Killed*	*Injured*	*Killed*	*Injured*	*Killed*	*Injured*
CPI (M)	10	31	17	20	20	25	47	76
GNLF	37	118	31	52	72	61	140	231
Police	02	26	14	56	13	78	29	160
Others	06	–	14	31	56	111	76	142
Total	**55**	**175**	**76**	**159**	**161**	**275**	**292**	**609**

Source: Compilation from official sources as quoted in Samanta (2000: 149).

It was the turn of the State that characterised the third phase (June 1987-till the signing of the accord in August 1988). Besides the State armed police and BSF the State Government deployed huge contingent of paramilitary forces to normalize the violent situation by force and repression. Besides killing and counter-killing the GNLF went on plundering State property and resources. Huge amount of Government property in the form of offices, buildings, vehicles, and even culverts were destroyed as a measure to retaliate against the State repression on the one hand and symbolically representing the erasure of West Bengal Government from all possible corners of the hills, on the other. The following Table 4.2 can help assume the devastation caused by the Gorkha wrath during the mid 1980s.

Table 4.2: Official statement regarding the plundering of property happened during Gorkhaland movement

Categories of Property	*1986*	*1987*	*1988 (Jan.-Sept.)*	*Total*
	Private Property			
GNLF members' houses	226	33	54	313
CPI (M) members' houses	254	164	19	437
Cong-I members' houses	28	—	—	28
CPI members' houses	01	—	—	01
	Government Property			
Vehicles	04	40	—	44
Police vehicles	05	—	—	05
Offices, buildings, culverts etc.	01	217	313	531
Total	**519**	**454**	**386**	**1359**

Source: Compilation from official sources as quoted in Samanta (2000: 150-51).

Towards Settlement

The search for a solution towards the 'loss of nerve' created by the violent movement spearheaded by the GNLF began from the very beginning of 1987. The efforts towards this end were initiated at the behest of the Central Government. A common line of action regarding Darjeeling problem did not emerge even after the completion of two successive meetings held on January 8, and January 14, 1987 in which both the Central and State Government authorities have participated. After several rounds of talks between the State and the Centre a common approach was developed for normalising Darjeeling situation and ultimately the decision was finalised by the month of June 1987 in favour of a Development Council with required amount of autonomy for Darjeeling hills. Accordingly a tripartite meeting was scheduled to be held on July 22, 1987 in Delhi, to be participated by the State and Central Government authorities besides the GNLF delegation. A delegation of 49 GNLF members have met the Prime Minister on the scheduled date and submitted a memorandum of four fold demands: (i) to create a separate state of Gorkhaland under Art. 3(A) of Constitution of India; (ii) to grant citizenship; (iii) to establish a separate Indian Gorkha Regiment; and (iv) to include Nepali language in the 8th Schedule of Constitution of India (ABP and Statesman, July 24, 1987). Although nothing concrete came out of the meeting except the dissension among the GNLF members themselves, which also embarrassed the hill politics of subsequent period. The Government (both the Centre and the State) on the other hand insisted its firmness to the decision of Hill Council instead of a separate state. However, the GNLF delegation returned back to Darjeeling with the two-fold assurances that the Central Government has been planning to work out a solution to the issue of citizenship and that Nepali language would be soon included in the 8th Schedule of the Constitution. Amidst the disagreement raised by the claims of the party hardliners who were in favour of nothing except the separate state of Gorkhaland, the proposition of Hill Council did not materialise till the middle of 1987. Party factionalism grew up; new platforms started championing the cause of Gorkhaland instead of the status of District Council; all these ultimately affected the earlier strength of the movement on the one hand and also the erstwhile command of Subhas Ghising over the masses on the other.

The movement went on the warpath once again in 1988. Destruction of government properties, killing and counter-killing of individuals belonging to GNLF and CPI (M) were continued in and around Kalimpong subdivision and in the tea gardens. State repression kept on increasing with the deployment of more CRPF men and other military and Paramilitary forces. More than thousand people were detained under the TADA; several others were killed and injured or had left Darjeeling hills. *Bandhs* were declared several times in protest against state repression. The Hill Employees' Association launched an indefinite strike on December 21, 1987 which, however, was withdrawn on the 17th day (Telegraph,

January 7, 1988). The GNWO unit of Kalimpong had also given a 24-hour *bandh* call on January 2, 1988 in protest against the indiscriminate arrests in Kalimpong subdivision (ABP, January 3, 1988). The GNLF declared a 40-day *bandh* call in the three hill subdivisions and the Dooars region from February 10, 1988 in protest against the genocide, terrorism, and mass killing, arson and indiscriminate arrests by the State Government. However, the party hardliner C.K. Pradhan, in defiance of the Party Chief's *diktat*, had declared the extension of the *bandh* in Kalimpong for another 20 days (ABP, March 21, 1988). Side-by-side the process to arrive at a solution in the form a development council for Darjeeling hills went on. While the party hardliners had rejected the proposed Hill Council the moderates within the GNLF debated over the issues like the jurisdiction of the proposed Hill Development Council, the nomenclature of the Council, allotment of Departments, funds etc.

After several rounds of bilateral and tripartite meetings held in Delhi and Calcutta, GNLF President Subhas Ghising had agreed to sign the Accord for the formation of Darjeeling Gorkha Hill Council (DGHC). The DGHC Accord was finally signed in August 22, 1988 by Subhas Ghising, C.G. Somaiah (as the representative of the Central Government), and Rathin Sengupta, the Chief Secretary of West Bengal (as the representative of State Government). The next day another pact on citizenship was signed in Delhi between Mr. Somaiah and Subhas Ghising in the presence of the Home Minister Sri Buta Singh. As per the provisions of the said Accord Ghising willy-nilly agreed to drop the demand of a separate State of Gorkhaland but his adversaries still remained unsatisfied with the Accord and started mobilising the masses both against the leadership of Ghising and also against the operation of the newly formed DGHC. The disagreement became public when both the AIGL and the rebel leader Chhatre Subba, who earlier was entrusted with the responsibility of GVC—the militant front of the GNLF, decided to make alliance with the CPI (M) for the forthcoming election of the DGHC scheduled to be held in between December 10 and December 15, 1988 (Statesman: November 1, 1988). GNLF was accorded with the status of a political party on November 16, 1988 (Subba, 1992:156). The GNLF had a sweeping victory in the first DGHC election; out of the 28 seats it won 26 seats and the remaining two seats were won by the CPI (M).

The DGHC Accord of 1988 had settled all the demands raised

by the GNLF during the tripartite meeting held on 22nd July, 1987 in Delhi. Regarding the citizenship it was upheld that the question of the Gorkhas will be clarified through the issue of Gazette Notification by the Government of India and subsequently it was clarified through the Gazette Notification (No. 26011/6/88-IC.I) on August 23, 1988. As regards the second demand of raising a separate Gorkha Regiment it was maintained that since the Government of India did not entertain the policy of forming the regiments on class or community basis, the question of raising a new Gorkha Regiment to be composed of entirely by the Indian Gorkhas does not arise. Regarding the issue of inclusion of language in the 8th Schedule of the Constitution it was pointed out that "the Government of India is of the view that inclusion of more languages in the Eighth Schedule of the Constitution would create repercussions and reactions. It is the endeavour of the Government to develop the cultural and literary heritage of all languages irrespective of their inclusion in the Eighth Schedule". Again, as per the very first clause of the Accord GNLF had agreed to drop the demand of a separate State of Gorkhaland and accepted the Hill Development Council instead. It is interesting to note that Subhas Ghising had endorsed such a Memorandum of Settlement, which in true sense rejected almost all of his demands raised earlier, except the demand of citizenship regarding which a Notification was made accordingly. Although the DGHC Accord had been successful to bring peace and normalcy in Darjeeling hills, it certainly brought tough times for Subhas Ghising, who stood as the Chairman of the newly founded Hill Council.

Keeping in view the descriptive modalities of State response against the violent Gorkha movement of the mid 1980s it may be argued that the State and the Central Government taken recourse to different paths to attain the same destination. That is to say in other words that both the State and the Centre did not want the creation of Gorkhaland but the way things had been settled and worked out by both the hubs of power followed different routes. For example, while State Government in the name of a 'political approach' labelled the movement as 'anti-national' and 'anti-constitutional' besides alleging that the movement involved 'foreign link' and 'imperial interest' the Central Government on the contrary branded it as 'constitutional' and 'not anti-national'. While the State Government criticised such a statement by the then Prime Minister

Mr. Rajiv Gandhi that Gorkhaland movement is not 'anti-national' would add fuel to the burning state of affairs of the hills, the Central Government charged that the neglect by the state government fuelled the agitation in the hills. In fact, all these differences of opinions were merely semantic in nature and they did not, however, incorporate anything substantial in them that could have made a difference in the overall approach towards the movement. It needs to be remembered that all these allegations and counter allegations registered by the State and Central Governments against each other have taken place at that crucial moment when the tenth state assembly election was just on its offing. By alleging the State Government as responsible and by labelling the Gorkhaland movement not as 'anti-national' the Indian National Congress—the ruling party at the Centre that time—tried to enlarge its support base in the hills. On the other hand, by labelling the movement as 'anti-national' the CPI (M)—the party that ruled West Bengal then—attempted to capitalise on the situation with the hope that anti-Nepali sentiment would fetch electoral currency in the upcoming assembly election of 1987. In fact, the initial negotiations of this nature have in fact thrown the baby out of the bath tub which further unleashed new impetus for additional courses of violence and mayhem.

When it was realized that the question of resolving the problem with immediate action was indispensable there was actually no difference of opinion between the State and the Central Government. The Gorkha agitation was no longer considered to be a political problem by the government. Rather it was regarded precisely as an agitation that disrupted the law and order situation in the locality and hence needed to be resolved punitively before it was too late. Consequently both the State and the Central Government joined hands in controlling, if not suppressing the movement by force. The agencies of 'repressive state apparatus', viz. the police, the BSF and the paramilitary forces were deployed to meet the requirement of what Foucault would call *thanatopolitics*—a politics wherein the exercise of absolute power is made by or in the name of the sovereign, literally to take life. Finally, a sub-state level autonomous administrative arrangement was implemented rather hurriedly as the best mechanism for accommodating the demands of the conflicting party, a crucial decision which was duly endorsed by both the State and Central Government.

It needs to be emphasised that the autonomous council mode

of governance as institutionalised through the formation of DGHC in the war weary hills in the 1988 was the first of its kind. After Darjeeling hills the same experience of autonomous council was indiscriminately used be it the case of Jharkhand, Bodoland, or Ladakh. The point is that the response of the state to the growing and often violent group identity demands (as was the case with Gorkha agitation of Darjeeling hills) lacks a viable conceptually framed approach leading towards broader policy prescriptions which could have amicably addressed the conflicting interests of individual agitations. This form of critique is necessary—much of which would be elaborated in the course of the study—particularly because of the fact that the issues of peace and conflict resolution measures are serious enterprises in that it involves both conceptual understanding and theoretical rigour in order to arrive at policy prescriptions that would affect everyday life. It is not merely a political issue nevertheless it has to be activated by the stakeholders of political systems. Hence, working out of one sort of accommodative measure for a particular problem can hardly be hastily implemented in other situations which share very little similarity with the original problem at hand. This can neither be justified on the grounds of mere political and administrative requirement nor can even it be at all helpful in addressing the aspirations that the individual cases implicate. Conflict and conflict resolution is not a zero-sum game. It basically involves those issues and processes in which people live-in and through which human beings derive the sense of their world. That is why it needs to be understood in an empathetic and humane way rather than through the mechanically devised political and administrative policies and programmes.

NOTES

1. GNLF was established in April 5, 1980.
2. The 11-point programme of action included the issues like: (i) to observe a 'Black Flag Day' on April 13, 1986 in protest against the alleged atrocities and discrimination faced by the Indian Nepalis; (ii) to declare 72 hours strike during May 12-14, 1986 in order to invite the notice of the Central Government towards their constitutional and just demand for Gorkhaland; (iii) to burn the copy of the Article seven of the India-Nepal Peace Treaty of 1950 which

has relegated the Indian Nepalis to the status of immigrants; (iv) to burn the copy of the SRC of 1955 which had unconstitutionally merged Darjeeling along with the adjacent Nepali speaking areas with the State of West Bengal; (v) to launch movement against the Forest Department for indiscriminate felling of trees of the hill areas and sending them to the plains; (vi) to continue the vote boycott stand as a measure to declare that they no longer want to remain within the alien State of West Bengal; (vii) to boycott all the MLAs, MPs, Ministers, and political parties, who are against the demand of a separate state of Gorkhaland; (viii) to stop all the vehicles taking away the valuable boulders of Dudhia (P.S. Kurseong) to the plains as a measure to protest against the policies of the Central Government towards the demand of Gorkhaland; (ix) to launch do-or-die movement in protest against the alleged ill treatment of the Gorkhas by the Indians; (x) to boycott the observance of all national ceremonies like the Independence Day, the Republic Day, Rabindra Jayanti, Gandhi Jayanti, Netaji Jayanti until the Central Government accedes to the demand of Gorkhaland; (xi) to stop payment of taxes and repayment of the loans to the Government of West Bengal as a measure to protest against the colonial state of affairs maintained by the State of West Bengal over the Nepali speaking areas of Darjeeling hills and Dooars.

5

Movement and State Response: Gorkhaland in Post-DGHC Period

The Rise and Fall of Council Mode of Governance

After two years of mayhem, including a whole scale plundering of property and of life normalcy came in Darjeeling with the signing up of Darjeeling Gorkha Hill Council (DGHC) Accord. The DGHC came up under the State Act to guarantee the social, economic, educational and cultural advancement of the people residing in the hill areas of Darjeeling district. Although there was no such provision in the accord that would have stressed specifically on the issues of autonomy but a consensus was somehow reached that the hills would be entrusted with an autonomous Hill Council to be set up under a State Act. Several Amendments were made in the DGHC Act with the avowed goal of extending power to the Council and thereby to strengthen the basis of self-rule on the one hand and reinforce the essence of autonomy, on the other. Needless to mention that all the three Amendments made so far (during 1989, 1994 and 2001) were engaged in addressing the procedural details of how best a bureaucratically framed administrative body would function rather than to provide a framework needed for working out the principles of self-government and autonomy in actual practice.

In amending the existing DGHC Act the Amendment Act of 1989 went on substituting clauses, sections and sub-sections with better alternatives. This amendment contained some provisions related to electoral offences [except the inclusion of 'minority communities' in place of 'non-Nepali community' in sub-section (3) of Section 5 of the DGHC Act, 1988 nothing concrete came out]. The Amendment Act of 1994, the second in the series, was based on the recommendations of a high powered 18 members committee constituted by the State Government (in July 1990) to suggest new offices/departments to be handed over to the DGHC. Quite expectedly the second amendment came up as a lengthy approval fixing up terms and conditions of the rank and file of the DGHC (detailed recommendations were made over such issues like resignation, expiration, termination of the office bearers, particularly the nominated ones). The Amendment Act of 1994 did emphasize on the inclusion of new offices/departments in the existing arrangement. Among the new offices/departments it added 'public health and sanitation' with the existing 'family welfare' department, and also included the 'social, adult and mass education and non-formal education' within the existing provisions for education. Sports and youth services were, however, fresh additions. The said Amendment Act inserted a remarkable provision in the existing DGHC Act that in fact, helped the Government legitimize its stand over the issue of extending Ghising's status as a caretaker Chairman of the Council in the later years. The amended provision upholds: "Provided that pending the election of a Chairman, the Government may appoint by name one of the Councillors to be the Chairman who shall hold office as Chairman and Chief Executive Councillor, and shall exercise all the powers and discharge all the functions of the Chairman and Chief Executive Councillor, until a Chairman, elected according to the provisions of this Act and the rules made thereunder, enters upon his office" (*Vide* for details Datta, 1995: 116-141). The Amendment Act of 2001 moves a step further to add the term Autonomous in the existing arrangement in the fashion of DGAHC, without bothering about what this addition would have meant in real sense of the term. The third amendment has approved the inclusion of some *mouzas* from the Siliguri subdivision to the DGHC territory. It is not out of place to mention here that all the amendments were preceded by some kind of political pressure created upon the State by the Chairman of the erstwhile DGHC and the GNLF in the name of resurfacing the unresolved issue of Gorkhaland and the ensuing political ramifications. Within a spell of about one and half decade the hype of self-rule and autonomy faded away. The DGHC which was thought of as an administrative body that institutionalized both self-rule and autonomy emerged as a machinery of political highhandedness, a store house of corruption, and an agency of personal gratification. Since the beginning of 2001 denunciation of Ghising and his followers became commonplace, local political parties of all hue started openly criticizing DGHC and its Chairman, Ghising himself faced even an assassinating attempt during February 2001.

Within two years of its functioning DGHC's failure to cater the developmental needs of the hill people had become prominent. The new kind of politico-administrative experiment soon was charged with the allegations of political highhandedness, autocratic leadership, nepotism, corruption, misuse of funds, and utter negligence towards eradicating the problems of everyday life. In a little while anti-DGHC and anti-Ghising platforms have mushroomed and started acting, along with the already existing oppositional forces, to augment public opinion to rescind the ill operated development institution called DGHC.

Greater Nepal Fiasco

The gradual weakness of the DGHC on the one hand and the growing importance of other hill political parties on the other led Ghising to initiate new ploys to attract the masses. In an attempt to smooth out his political position as the Chairman of the DGHC, Ghising had taken recourse to series of political gimmicks. The spectre of Greater Nepal was basically one such ploy which Ghising had tried to exploit but ultimately failed to make any headway. He had submitted a memorandum to the Prime Minister of India on July 26, 1991 advocating that: "India's unity and integrity is today facing a dire threat from a deep conspiracy for the establishment of a Greater Nepal, which is proposed to include Bhutan, Sikkim, and Darjeeling" (the copy of the Memorandum is available in Pradhan, 1996:60-62). Again with language issue he has reiterated the same Greater Nepal bogey. Soon after 1992 when Nepali language was constitutionally recognised, Ghising started claiming that "Nepali is a foreign language and Government of India has made a serious mistake by not taking the case of 'Gorkhali'; as because the acceptance of Nepali will create an ethnic homogeneity in Darjeeling, Sikkim, Bhutan which will eventually lead to the formation of a greater Nepal."

Despite the repeated insistence of the Government of West Bengal that the concept of Greater Nepal is a 'bogey' pushed optimistically by Ghishing, the call of Greater Nepal is not a fiasco rather an issue of immense geo-political significance. A sense of historical Greater Nepal still looms large in the minds of some section of the Nepali across border that link it to the reign of Prithwi Narayan Shah, the great Gorkha king who stretched his country from beyond Kangra Valley in the west to Sikkim in the east. However, the treaty of Segauli truncated this historical Greater Nepal that extended from Sutlej to Tista. Since 1990s the claim of Greater Nepal started gaining ground in Nepal. A group calling itself the Greater Nepal Committee was formed in Kathmandu in July 1991 with the avowed goal to create a worldwide public opinion in favour of the 'Greater Nepal' and to achieve it (Dixit, 1993:16). Despite Ghising's efforts to make this issue a grave political problem the Government did not confirm the information regarding the move for the creation of a 'Greater Nepal'. Nevertheless, the Government did not recognise such demands coming from whatever sources (Par. Pr.: 1991). While Ghising has used this issue of Greater Nepal movement to suit his own argument, the issue itself needs serious consideration but that has never been the case in reality.

No Man's Land Thesis

After the failure of his 'Greater Nepal' hoax, Subhas Ghising was still engaged in preparing another political issue out of the treaties, and memoranda signed between the Governments of India, Nepal, Bhutan, and Great Britain. Soon he developed another political thesis known as "No-man's land". He sent a telegram to the Prime Ministers of India and Nepal on January 12, 1992 raising "doubts and full confusion regarding the legal status of Darjeeling region and its contiguous areas up to Bangladesh border as per the implication of the Article VIII of the Indo-Nepal Treaty of 1950. The telegram also warned both the Governments to take the matter seriously and clarify the legal status of the said region within sixty days (w.e.f. January 12, 1992) failing which the GNLF would admit that the real master of the said land is no one except the Gorkhas and accordingly the GNLF would be completely free and independent to take its own decision for the political destiny of the 'no man's land' and its people as a permanent solution." Again he has filed a petition in the Supreme Court of India on October 19, 1994 seeking appropriate directions to the Central Government for passing the relevant parliamentary legislation under Article 4 and/or Article 368 of the Constitution for the formal incorporation of the lease-hold territories of Kalimpong, Assam and Bengal Dooars and the ceded territories of Darjeeling (Pradhan, 1996: 4). On this ground that Darjeeling hills had been a "no man's land" Subhas Ghising boycotted the middle-tier *Panchayat Samiti* election in April 1994. He had also submitted a memorandum to the Chief Election Commissioner of India on April 18, 1996 declaring a boycott call to the forthcoming Parliamentary election of May 2, 1996 on the ground that elections could not be held in the constitutionally non-incorporated territories. However, nothing came out of these courses of action since the Government was firm in its stand that 'Darjeeling is an integral part of the country there is no room for any ambiguity about its legal status; hence no further clarification is required' (Par. Pr.: 1992).

Gorkhaland as Bottled Genie

In the meanwhile the anti-Ghising and anti-DGHC camp grew up anew with the emergence of some new rival political groups during the mid 1990s in Darjeeling hills. Soon after the declaration of the near possibility of a separate State of Uttarakhand by the then Prime Minister H.D. Deve Gowda in his Independence Day speech in 1996, political activism in Darjeeling hills once again geared up with the renewed claim of Gorkhaland. Not only Ghising but several other anti-Ghising political fronts revived the claim of Gorkhaland. Apparently girding itself for another round, the GNLF had organised a rally in Darjeeling on 23rd August, 1996 hard pressing the demand of Gorkhaland. On the same day a new front Gorkha Democratic Front (GDF) was established under the Presidentship of Madan Tamang who earlier headed the Pranta Parishad. Again on 25th August, 1996 five national and regional political parties [namely AIGL, Pranta Parishad, GDF, Congress (I), and BJP] formed a joint front, namely Gorkhaland People's Front (GPF) to fight for the statehood for the Nepali speaking population of Darjeeling hills and the contiguous regions. While the GPF had approached the GNLF President-cum-DGHC Chairman to launch a broad based movement in collaboration with other parties for achieving their long cherished demand of Gorkhaland, Ghising out rightly rejected such a proposal of joint political venture and opted for a separate warpath to be spearheaded only by his party (Chaudhuri, 1996:43). In fact, he was not ready to allow even an inch to his adversaries who were championing the same cause. The nature of the movement during the 1990s was characterised by three pertinent issues. Firstly, all the political parties including Ghising's GNLF raised the demand of a separate state; secondly, the renewed statehood movement had followed a peaceful and non-violent path; and thirdly, attempts were made to run the movement more within the corridors of power and Parliament rather than in the villages or in the tea gardens as earlier. A new phase thus have started that was not aimed at drawing the people to the battle ground and was delimited within the political criss-crosses centering around the axis of local, regional, and national level politics. This was rather a comfortable situation for the State in that there was no urgency, or possibly no need of, devising any policy measure as the hill politics was mesmerised with its inbuilt political crisis.

However, the rhetoric for a separate state has been used off and on by Subhas Ghising whenever he felt it necessary. The demand of a separate state thus once again was raised by the GNLF in May 2000 just at the eve of Gram Panchayat polls within the DGHC area. The elections to the Gram Panchayats were scheduled to be held on May 21, 2000 and on May 3, 2000 the Kalimpong GNLF leaders announced that the agitation for the separate state of Gorkhaland would start soon after the completion of the Gram Panchayat polls (Statesman: May 4, 2000). The revival of the demand of separate state more as a pre poll stunt had worked well and resulted into the sweeping victory for the GNLF in the said Gram Panchayat election. More in a manner of flexing its muscle the GNLF had declared a *bandh* call in support of the renewed demand for separate State of Gorkhaland in the three hill subdivisions on May 22, 2000 and once again it was publicly declared that the GNLF did not want to share the Gorkhaland issue with any other political platform. However, Ghising wanted the others to support the issue from their own platforms, but warned them against any contradiction (Chaudhury, 2000:42). Apparently, Ghising might have considered raising the issue of statehood as his prerogative while his dissidents considered that he has bottled the genie of Gorkhaland for ever.

Sixth Schedule Status for Darjeeling: Initial Efforts and Reactions

Despite Ghising's insistence the issue of separate state of Gorkhaland hardly remained under GNLF's custody but was taken over much dynamically by other political platforms of the hills. These groups had incessantly attempted to convince the people that their endeavours towards the call of Gorkhaland were much more genuine than that of Ghising and accused the GNLF of betraying the Gorkhaland cause. The survival of this large body of oppositional parties[1] in the Darjeeling hills thoroughly depended upon their stand over the issue of statehood and all of them had, either collectively or singularly, revived the movement in some form or the other. Anticipating a disquieting situation out of the all-round claim of Gorkhaland raised by the political platforms of all hues in the hills, the State Government as a measure to persuade the GNLF President on the one hand and to appease the renewed claim of the opposition political platforms on the other, had set in motion the process of amending the already (twice) amended DGHC Act. As pointed out earlier this new amendment was more an eyewash since nothing substantial came out of it except the insertion of the epithet 'Autonomous' in the existing arrangement of DGHC and the inclusion of a few *mouzas* from the Sukna-Siliguri area.

In an attempt to placate his adversaries Subhas Ghising in his Independence Day address in 2000 had announced the 'new political stand' of his party by saying that 'the demand for DGAHC areas within the purview of Sixth Schedule and granting the hill the status of a tribal region is more important than the Gorkhaland statehood issue' (Sikkim Express: September 3-10, 2000). It may be recalled that Ghising during the time of settling the turbulent Gorkha agitation of 1986-88 had refused the offer of Sixth Schedule on the ground that the Gorkhas were not the tribal people on any count but this time in 2000 he seemed quite satisfied with the same tribal status for his brethren and for the region as a whole. By the end of the year 2000 Ghising has made it public that a tripartite meeting would be held in the first week of February 2001 to review the DGHC Accord of 1988 and to consider GNLF's demand to include the Darjeeling hill areas within the Sixth Schedule of the Constitution of India. Political firmament of Darjeeling hills had again become tensed with the rekindling of the claim of the separate statehood by almost all the existing political platforms and by some new ones too, which joined the trail of reviving the claim of Gorkhaland. Gorkhaland Sanjukta Morcha (GSM), a new political platform, which included the CPRM and AIGL, in a memorandum sent to the then Home Minister Mr. L.K. Advani, opposed GNLF's demand to include the Darjeeling hills under the Sixth Schedule (Statesman: November 22, 2000). Fresh violence once again was unleashed by the GLO (which remained silent for quite some time) for the cause of establishing the Gorkhaland State on the one hand and abolishing the DGHC on the other. At that crucial juncture when the preparation of the said tripartite meeting (for finalising the decision regarding Sixth Schedule Status for Darjeeling hills) between the GNLF, Centre and the State Governments was almost over, the GLO had gone to that extreme of threatening all the 28 DGHC Councillors, including the Chairman (Subhas Ghising), either to resign from their posts by December 31, 2000 and join their armed struggle for statehood or face the dire consequences. It was also revealed from the publicly circulated printed pamphlets that two fledgling militant outfits, namely Gorkha Peoples' War Group (GPWG) and Himalayan Liberation Tiger (HLT), composed of the erstwhile GNLF militants, had supported the armed struggle of the GLO and vowed that they would not spare even Mr. Ghising if he comes between the militants and their political ambitions (Statesman: January 5, 2001).

Despite the threat and the ultimatum of December 31 none of the Councillors of the DGHC had resigned from their posts, although the situation remained panicky, and the Chairman Mr. Subhas Ghising left for Delhi on February 5, 2000 for attaining the said tripartite meeting in Delhi. It was on his way back to Darjeeling in February 10, 2000 assassinating attempt was made against Subhas Ghising killing two from his convoy and severely injuring him too, at Chilawney Dara, Pankhabari Road, about 50 km. away from Darjeeling. It was alleged that the mastermind behind the attempt to kill Subhas Ghising was none but the GLO Chief Mr. Chhatre Subba who soon was imprisoned[2]. GNLF also accused Mr. C.K. Pradhan, the President of the Party's Kalimpong branch, for having involvement in the attack of February 10, 2000. Six executive members including one Vice-President of Kalimpong unit of the GNLF resigned in protest of the said allegation, which once again stimulated the already existing Ghising-Pradhan rivalry within the

GNLF. C.K. Pradhan's popularity was based on his stress on the single agenda politics (i.e. the demand of Gorkhaland only) for Darjeeling hills depending on which he attempted to build up parallel support base for him particularly in and around Kalimpong. As a measure to oppose GNLF Central Committee's decision to dissolve the Kalimpong Branch Committee C.K. Pradhan along with his 60 other loyalists have formally resigned from the Party in April 9, 2001 and initiated the process to form his own political front. Even after the assassinating attempt on his life was made Mr. Ghising still remained stick to his earlier claim of Sixth Schedule status for Darjeeling hills and operated the administration of the DGHC almost single-handedly without even convening a session to bring the members together. Soon political activism around the issue of tribal status had swayed the entire hills and thereby marked the beginning of a new era of ethnic politics in Darjeeling hills.

Darjeeling-Sikkim Merger

Even as opposition parties were busy slamming the DGHC and its Chairman Subhas Ghising, demand for Darjeeling-Sikkim merger had been raised by a new political platform Gorkha Rashtriya Congress (GRC). GRC, a breakaway faction of the hill Congress branch, was officially launched in Darjeeling on January 7, 2004 with single agenda the merger of Darjeeling with Sikkim in view of the common geographical factors and similitude in culture and history. Emphasising on the utter failure of the DGHC to fulfil the aspiration of the hill people, D.K. Bomjan, the founding President of the party, has insisted that the proposal of Darjeeling-Sikkim merger would be the easiest way to effect separation of Darjeeling from West Bengal (Times of India: January 8, 2004). Expanding its base, the GRC has launched its women's wing for Kurseong subdivision. Saying that this was its first women's wing, Mr. Subhash Tamang, a GRC leader from Kurseong, claimed the organisation is gaining momentum towards the merger demand. Ms Mithu Rani Pradhan has been chosen as the convener of the women's wing (Statesman: January 31, 2006).

The GRC's claim of 'Darjeeling-Sikkim merger is based on the historical evidence of Darjeeling being part of Sikkim' the President asserted. Bomjan had even personally written to the Central Public Information Officer (CPIO) contending that after the commencement of the Constitution, these areas were amalgamated with West Bengal and termed as Darjeeling district, but it was unclear as to who were the recipients of the compensation for these excluded or partially excluded areas under Section three of the Requisition of Land (Apportionment of Compensation) Act of 1949, and the Absorbed Areas (Laws) Act, 1954 (Act 20 of 1954) (Sentinel: December 7, 2011). It is interesting to note that the new political outfit has raised serious concerns pertaining to the documentary history of Sikkim's integration with the Indian Union, the Government (both the State and even the Centre) is yet to emphasize on the issue with any seriousness. This might be because of the apprehension of the inbuilt contradiction of the claim itself. This is reflected in the overall significance of the issue in the political scenario of both Darjeeling and Sikkim. While there are both supporters and opponents of the very idea of 'merger' the mood of the general public is not favourable towards such a move. While R. Moktan, the President of Sikkim National Front, besides Sikkim Janashakti Party, has been raising the issues since few years back G.M. Rai, the President of Gorkha Prajatantrik Party of Sikkim, considered the merger issue as suicidal (Darjeeling Times.com, June 21, 2010).

Similar is also the situation in Darjeeling hills. While AIGL showed favourable leaning towards the claim of Darjeeling-Sikkim merger (Darjeeling times.com, September 21, 2010) the CPRM is dead against the very idea of Darjeeling-Sikkim merger. R.B. Rai, the General Secretary of the CPRM, was of the view that the issue would unnecessary confuse people and weaken the movement for a separate homeland of the Gorkhas in India. Keeping in view these dynamics over the rather contentious issue of 'Darjeeling-Sikkim merger' an effort has been made to gauge people's opinion in this regard. The same 57 respondents were asked to comment on the issue. Amazingly more than 70 per cent of the respondents (41 in actual number) did not favour the idea and only 11 respondents (19.30%) thought that Darjeeling-Sikkim merger could be a better alternative. It was still far more appealing when we considered the specific comments of those 41 respondents who disfavoured the idea of merger issue. 17 out of the 41 respondents (41.47%) did not at all favour the idea since they thought similar ethnic background need not necessarily result in similar aspiration. People of Darjeeling hills were groomed up in a different cultural set up, share a different worldview and maintain different threads of articulating community consciousness and politics than Sikkim, they reasoned. Eight respondents (19.51%) believed that Darjeeling-Sikkim merger is not a feasible idea since Darjeeling from the colonial period was placed as a superior region compared to Sikkim, and this sense of cultural superiority would act as the major deterrence in the politics of merger. Still further eight respondents (19.51%) viewed Darjeeling-Sikkim merger as a strategy to weaken the tempo of Gorkhaland movement. The rest eight respondents (out of 41) favoured all three factors cited above as their concern for opposing the idea of merger. Perhaps it was due to the gravity of the problem for being both an emotionally tempting and politically sensitive issue five respondents out of 57 (8.77%) did not register any comment. On the whole the viewpoints presented here, no matter how meagre the universe may be, are indicative of the opinion of the highly educated hill populace of contemporary Darjeeling. The opinions thus presented tell us why Darjeeling-Sikkim merger issue is yet to gain wide currency in hill politics. After the death of the founding President Mr. D.K. Bomjan on October 7, 2010 GRC has been weakened considerably although the outfit is still surviving in some form under the leadership of Nima Lama as the new Party President.

The response of the State towards Gorkhaland movement during this post Council phase was noteworthy. The State (neither the Centre nor even the State) has hardly taken recourse to direct confrontation with the confronting parties. However, the agitation during this phase remained more or less peaceful. Political murders did take place but not of genocide type. C.K. Pradhan, Rudra Kumar Pradhan, Prakash Thing were some of the important political personalities who were killed but no serious measure was taken from the part of the Government. Newer political parties were mushrooming and it seemed that the government is least bothered about these eventualities. So far as the status of DGHC was concerned government was often charged for delaying the fund flow but not so much about its total aloofness regarding the supervision of the overall functioning of the Council which was rather decaying with each passing day. Government felt only concerned whenever the demand of Gorkhaland was raised by any political party from the hills. Not to mention this has resulted into the not so necessary amendment of the DGHC Act. It may be said that the State has tolerated the movement in its length and breadth during the post DGHC phase. It would be perhaps more accurate to argue that the state's strategy was to follow a policy of least interference, which—it was believed—would encourage the inter-party factionalisms and the corresponding political conflicts evolved therefrom in the contentious region. During this phase of the movement the policy of least interference as the best strategy—having the potentiality of polarizing and frustrating the movement—was adopted by the state to respond to the burgeoning claims of the Gorkhas of Darjeeling hills.

NOTES

1. This body of opposition parties was composed of Gorkha Democratic Front (formed on 23.8.1996), Gorkhaland People's Front [coalition formed on 25.8.1996 out of five local (branch) of political parties namely AIGL, Pranta Parishad, GDF, Cong (I), and BJP], Communist Party of Revolutionary Marxists (a breakaway group of hill CPI(M) formed on 9.9.1996), AIGL, and Gorkha Liberation Organisation (Chhatre Subba, erstwhile rebel leader of GNLF, formed this new party in April 1989); and by the turn of the last century two more oppositional platforms, namely Gorkhaland Sanjukta Morcha (GSM) and United Democratic Front (UDF) joined the rat race of achieving the separate statehood.
2. Chhatre Subba was put behind the bars on March 24, 2001. After a pretty long gap Subba was released very recently on September 9, 2011. Soon after the return of one time war hero all political parties have become desirous of having his blessings. Earlier CPRM came out on the streets in raising the plea of early release of Chhatre Subba. However, the too aged Subba (71 years) is yet to disclose his future political plans nevertheless a recent newspaper clipping reported about a meeting taken place between Bimal Gurung and Chhatre Subba (Telegraph, January 14, 2012).

6

Movement and State Response: Gorkhaland in Contemporary Period

Since the beginning of the new millennium the tenor of hill politics clearly indicated that Ghising's leadership has failed to qualify the test of time and that the experience of DGHC as a politico-administrative arrangement could be anything but not pro-people as such. Besides there were many contenders other than Ghising and his GNLF who stick to the single agenda politics of Gorkhaland while Ghising—the one time messiah of the Gorkhas—was ready to go to any extent to keep him in power. It became fairly apparent that Ghising was under pressure so much so that he dared not to face people's mandate and went delaying the DGHC election calculatedly. Surprisingly the government was not ready to take any strong step in this regard. This was the immediate result of the state's strategy of 'least interference'.

In an attempt to persuade both the internal and external political pressure Ghising sought recourse to a new brand of politics the politics of Sixth Schedule. The urge to include DGHC under the Sixth Schedule, which has gained some currency in earlier course, was vigorously emphasised this time. Accordingly, he started pressurizing the Government for the necessary Constitutional Amendment needed for this purpose and went all-out to convince the mass regarding the benefits of Sixth Schedule and the possible hurdles in its way which could have been easily overthrown if each and every community of the hills become desirous to enlist themselves as tribes. Once again the social engineering aimed at forging tribal status for all hill communities created more dissidents than followers and the public opinion in the hills started gaining an anti-Ghising fillip, though not an anti-DGHC stance. People of all circles including local political parties hard pressed the demand for the DGHC election which was pending for a long time and the Government went on increasing Ghising's caretaker Chairmanship position in a way to appease the present leadership. Before it was too late to control the situation the Government decided to place the Constitutional Amendment Bill in the Lok Sabha on November 30, 2007 which sought to amend the Constitution to include DGHC in the Sixth Schedule. The Bill was referred to the Standing Committee of Home Affairs, with Sushma Swaraj as Chairperson, which submitted its report on February 28, 2008. By then radical transformation took place in the hill politics. What the Government considered as the timely step to pacify the Darjeeling situation (by introducing the Amendment Bill) has resulted into an early ouster of Ghising from the hills and the collapse of the DGHC in the subsequent period. A new political outfit Gorkha Janmukti Morcha (GJM) came up on October 7, 2007, which took up the leadership by ousting Subhas Ghising, almost permanently, from the hill politics. The GJM soon after its emergence in 2007 has emerged as the single most important political platform to be reckoned with and in the recent tripartite agreement the GJM men acted as the representative of the hills.

Gorkha Janmukti Morcha: The New Hope?

Before pondering upon the debate over the issue that whether July 18, 2011, the date when the new deal of Gorkhaland Territorial Administration (GTA) was signed between the State Government and the GJM leadership in the presence of the Central Government representatives, be treated as 'historic day' or be considered as a day that recorded an 'untenable political surrender' let us briefly review the dramatic rise of the GJM.

The issue is that the GJM became functional only in 2007, by capitalising on the Prashant Tamang phenomenon[1] and soon emerged as the most powerful political platform in the hills. Initially the GJM developed more as an anti-Ghising and anti-DGHC forum and gradually worked out its own programmes of action which were, however, nothing new in their nature and form. Bimal Gurung, the GJM chief now, was an erstwhile Councillor of the Ghising-led DGHC and was considered as one among the firebrand youth leaders of Ghising's cohort. Perhaps the experience of his early political socialisation led Gurung to follow similar courses of action like those of his predecessor, namely non-payment of taxes, electricity bills, telephone bills, Gorkhaland instead of Government of West Bengal in the hoardings of all government offices, GL no. in vehicles instead of WB, restricting tea and timber movement outside the hills, etc. What was new was perhaps a blend of *Gandhigiri* and non-violence on the surface with that of force, threat, and violence at the core. The movement this time remained more or less peaceful. However, cases of violence and of political murders[2] did happen but not in a similar scale as in the decade of the 1980s. A synoptic view of the rather dramatic rise of Bimal Gurung and his GJM can be ascertained from the following Table 6.1:

Table 6.1: Fact-file of the rise of Bimal Gurung and the GJM

Date	*Significant Events*
September 23, 2007	Prashant Tamang wins the Indian Idol reality show. Bimal Gurung acted as chief patron of Prashant Tamang Fan Club, played instrumental role in mobilising support for Tamang, capitalised on the anti-Ghising political sensitivity during the campaign to garner support for the Indian Idol contestant from the hills while Ghising found no time to spend even a word publicly either for Prashant or for the entire activity that went on under the banner of Prashant Tamang Fan Club.
October 1, 2007	Bimal Gurung spoke against Sixth Schedule and apparently against his political boss Ghising for the first time.
October 4, 2007	GNLF dismissed Gurung's membership on grounds of anti-party activity.
October 7, 2007	Gurung kicked off the idea of a new political outfit Gorkha Janmukti Morcha (GJM) in Darjeeling.
November 15, 2007	Ghising celebrates the inclusion of the Sixth Schedule Bill in the list of business of the winter session of the Parliament.
November 30, 2007	The Sixth Schedule Constitutional (107th Amendment) Bill, 2007 was introduced in the Parliament and was referred to Standing Committee of Home Affairs.
December 3, 2007	GJM called on a four-day general strike to protest against the demand of Sixth Schedule and its proposed constitutionalization.

(*Contd.*)

(*Contd.*)

February 18, 2008	Hundreds of GJM supporters blocked Ghising's arrival in the hills on his way back from Delhi. Ghising returned back stayed at Pintail Village in the foothills.
February 20, 2008	State Government refused to extend Ghising's caretaker Chairmanship beyond March 2008.
February 27, 2008	Chief Minister for the first time invited Gurung for talks soon after GJM intensified its move through relay hunger strike and general shutdown.
February 28, 2008	Sixth Schedule (Amendment) Bill was shelved.
March 10, 2008	Ghising resigned from the DGHC on request of Chief Minister.
April 1, 2008	Morcha initiated 'civil disobedience' move and called for a boycott on payment of taxes to the State Government.
April 9, 2008	Police *lathi*-charge on ex-servicemen's rally at Darjeeling move while approaching Siliguri; GJM called on strike in protest.
June 26, 2008	Gurung made public proclamation for the first time that Gorkhaland will be realised by March 10, 2010.
July 7, 2008	GJM issued decree to replace 'WB' with 'GL' on vehicle number plates. This drive generated tension both in the hills and in plains.
July 25, 2008	GJM activist Pramila Sharma was killed allegedly by GNLF leader Deepak Gurung. Houses of GNLF leaders were ransacked and burnt in retaliation.
September 8, 2008	Centre called on State and GJM leaders for the first time in the series of 11 tripartite meetings that followed.
October 7, 2008	GJM issued traditional dress code *diktat* for one month.
October 17, 2008	GJM asked all shopkeepers across the hills to write Gorkhaland in signboards. West Bengal was replaced by Gorkhaland in all Government Office signboards as well.
January 16, 2009	Clashes broke out in the Dooars when Gurung along with thousands of GJM supporters tried to enter the region. More than hundreds were injured in the clash. CRPF deployed.
February 7, 2009	Two died in Dooars clashes once again.
November 7, 2009	Ban on sale of liquor in the hills (ban was lifted on January 31, 2010).
May 21, 2010	AIGL Chief Madan Tamang was assassinated in open day light.
May 30, 2010	GJM floated the idea of 'Gorkha-Adivasi Pradesh' (GAP).
September 26, 2010	The then Railway Minister Ms. Mamata Banerjee for the first time since 1999 visited Darjeeling announced a host of development projects.

(*Contd.*)

(*Contd.*)

February 8, 2011	Three GJM supporters were killed in police firing at Sibchu when Gurung tried again to march to the Dooars.
March 31, 2011	GJM publicly announced its unconditional support to the Trinamool-Congress alliance across the Dooars and Terai for the forthcoming Assembly election.
May 13, 2011	GJM secured electoral victory in the Assembly polls from all the three hill constituencies.
July 18, 2011	Tripartite agreement Gorkhaland Territorial Administration (GTA) was signed between GJM, State and the Central Government.
September 2, 2011	West Bengal State Assembly passed GTA Bill with 68 Amendments.
October 30, 2011	John Barla besides other five top ranking leaders of the Dooars-Terai branch of ABAVP decided to join hands with the GJM and conjointly raises the claim of Gorkha Adivasi Territorial Administration (GATA) instead of GTA.

Source: Compiled from news reports of the *Telegraph* (Siliguri edition).

Gorkha-Adivasi Unity in Dooars: The Initial Efforts

One striking point of the GJM-led movement is that the renewed call for Gorkhaland this time very consistently emphasised on the issue of inclusion of Dooars and Terai regions within the proposed Gorkhaland territory. Besides the hills, the Terai and *Dooars* region has been made the epicentre of the GJM-led Gorkhaland movement. There are several issues involved in the political battle of the Gorkhas to include Dooars and Terai in the proposed Gorkhaland *vis-à-vis* the struggle of the *Adivasis* while the other communities of the region were also vocal to save the region from Gorkha invasion and the pernicious knot between the Gorkhas and the *Adivasis*. There is no denying that this time the stakeholders of Gorkhaland and counter-Gorkhaland platforms have been significantly visible even in the Dooars and Terai. The consciousness of separation and the need of having agencies of self rule *vis-à-vis* autonomy have gained populism in the tract besides there were issues of competition for having a space in the mainstream political power house.

The current tone of the Gorkhaland movement spearheaded by the GJM has been carried out more prudently. With regard to its insistence on the Terai-Dooars the movement leadership has hardly shown an iota of hesitation to speak for and stand by the plight of the *Adivasis* of the Terai-Dooars tract basically as a strategy to expand its support base in the region and thereby to keep the state under pressure. Initially of course, the GJM has not taken up the concern of the *Adivasis* of the region rather seriously. Soon after the realisation that exclusive ethnic line mobilisation would yield unavoidable community clashes and ethnic polarisation instead of any political mileage the GJM did not spare much time to change its stand. It started wooing the *Adivasis* of the region so as to become a viable political force to be reckoned with. It began emphasising on the common experience of colonial exploitation that the Gorkhas and the *Adivasis* have meted out while working as tea garden labourers. The necessity of launching a united movement against the plight, underdevelopment, and continued exploitation in the post independence period were also highlighted. However, the claim of a Gorkhaland was too exclusive to attract the tribal folk for a joint move. On the contrary series of Gorkha-*Adivasi* clashes cropped up in which the worst sufferers were the Gorkhas of *Adivasi* dominated plains and the *Adivasis* of Gorkha dominated pockets.

The first organizational effort to woo the *Adivasis* came with GJM's decision to form a separate body for the Dooars. In a public meeting held on June 29, 2008 at Garubathan (a block under Kalimpong subdivision), which was attended by 18 *Adivasi* leaders of Dooars, the GJM chief Bimal Gurung publicly announced the party decision that a separate body *Gorkha Janmukti Adivasi Morcha* (GJAM) will soon be formed in Dooars. The conveners for the western, central and eastern part of the Dooars of that new body were also decided in that meeting (TEL: July 3, 2008). Again in another occasion on December 22, 2008 the general secretary Roshan Giri upheld the party decision that the GJM would sponsor the education of financially weak *Adivasi* students from the Dooars in the hills and 'it will soon convene a meeting with the principals of the hill institutions to work out a plan for materialising this proposal'. The meeting was attended by *Adivasi* leaders like Rabinson Xalco, Dhanu Murmu, Bijay Tikka, Bidhan Tathi, Prakash Minz, and Philip Minz (TEL: December 22, 2008). Despite repeated attempts the GJM has gained little and the *Adivasi* political will still disfavoured the Gorkha political activism in what they considered as their own region, even though some of the *Adivasi* leaders have participated meetings organized by the GJM.

The GJM still dreamt of a Gorkha-*Adivasi* union as a reality and was aware of the local contradictions that emerged as too bitter to take any sort of reconciliatory initiative. Desperate in its zeal to have *Adivasi* political support in the Dooars GJM went all out to stand in solidarity with the *Lalgarh Adivasi* movement, which has after a long time united a major section of the indigenous population of Midnapore, West Bengal for a common cause. It is interesting to note that the *Adivasis* of Dooars-Terai region have extended their support and admiration for the *Lalgarh* movement and the GJM has shown a candid gesture, although for political convenience, possibly at the right time. In early February 2009 the GJM has called on a strike to protest the murder of three members of the *Peoples' Committee Against Police Atrocities in Lalgarh* allegedly by the CPI (M) miscreants on February 2 (De, 2009). The GJM leaders also attended an *Adivasi* rally in *Lalgarh* where they expressed their solidarity to the *Adivasi* movement. The points of similarity were of course police atrocities and the ruling party's handling of the situation by repression (Telegraph, February 19, 2009). Even as the Gorkhas met *Adivasis* of Lalgrah political circles in the Dooars became concerned with the possible political outcome of such a union. The *Adivasis* of Dooars-Terai regions were still undecided and the solidarity move with Adivasis of Lalgarh has not capacitated the GJM gain full blown support from the *Adivasis* of Dooars-Terai. In fact, until the GJM floated the idea of Gorkha Adivasi Pradesh (GAP) on May 30, 2010 nothing substantial came out.

Precisely the rigidity of the *Adivasis* towards lending support to the GJM was the result of the political activism spearheaded by the *Adivasi Vikash Parishad*, which has already gained momentum by raising the demand of Sixth Schedule status for the tribal dominated areas of Terai-Dooars region. Although *Adivasi* political assertion has had a pre-colonial legacy of its own, the recent political activism that went on in Dooars-Terai region under the flagship of *Akhil Bharatiya Adivasi Vikash Parishad* (ABAVP) can be traced back with a Delhi based NGO working for the social cultural uplift of the *Adivasis* in the country (Bhowmik, 2011:27). The organisation had its roots in *Adivasi Bikas Manch* which was founded in Delhi during 1966-67 by Mr. Kartik Oraon an engineer by profession and besides being a Congress MP, spread out activities in certain pockets of southern Bihar (now Jharkhand) and also visited Terai-Dooars tract as well to unite the *Adivasis* spread all over the country under one umbrella (Roy, 2012:89). However, the growing political ascendancy of the ABAVP in the Dooars-Terai region is a recent phenomenon. Some have linked it with the subsequent rise of the recent GJM led Gorkha political activism in the region (Bhowmik *ibid.*) while another viewpoint located in the present genre of *Adivasi* assertion of the region a critical engagement with the state and the conventional integrationist civil societies and foresaw the possibilities of a Bayartian notion of 'civil society formation' in the *Adivasi* self-hood (Roy, 2012: 100-101).

In fact, in the current fashion of politics of the region the epistemic value of the concepts like 'region' and 'community' often gets obfuscated. It is worth mentioning here that both the issues are lived in social categories and not just conceptual constructs. Such an understanding that stresses the axial existence of the region *vis-à-vis* community may help one appreciate how recent political developments took place in the region in which the dynamics of ethnicity went on often in the absence of an ethnic group. In place of a set of imageries like discrete, concrete, tangible, bounded and enduring groups it is the relational, processual, dynamic, eventful and disaggregated groupness that has been counted as the potential political force. It is to construe their reality, power, and significance in a different way *Adivasi*-Gorkha political activism has re-written the subtext of ethnicity in the region taking group not as the basic analytic category but possibly groupness as a contextually fluctuating conceptual variable. The later dynamics of *Adivasi*-Gorkha political activism, particularly after the signing of the GTA Accord, is indicative of these tendencies.

The Beginning of Another New Arrangement: Gorkhaland Territorial Administration (GTA)

The inclination towards attaining some kind of agreement with the Government in the form of an interim set-up came into vogue during 2010. By September 2010, the GJM agreed to accept the interim set-up but with qualification. The GJM proposed the name of the new arrangement as the Gorkhaland Regional Authority (GRA) and moved further despite opposition registered by the CPRM and AIGL. The State Government, that time led by the CPI-M, had even finalised a draft proposal for the formation of what it thought as the appropriate Gorkhaland Autonomous Authority (GAA). It is remarkable to note that the GAA proposal had provisions for legislative power besides executive, administrative and, financial powers over 54 subjects/departments/offices to be handed over to the new body. It may be a matter of mere coincidence but it is a fact that the recent GTA arrangement has replaced on several points the text of the earlier GAA draft. But a more serious issue is: why then did the GJM not finally accede to the earlier settlement and waited for the Assembly elections of 2011? Perhaps this happens in the case of a long drawn movement for self-rule, which always looks forward in a liberal democratic polity for securing the best deal out of a political bargain keeping pace with the upcoming political events. However, it needs to be judged very carefully whether such gestures make the self-rule movement attain the status of mere self-management or not? In fact, a cursory look at some of the distinctive provisions of the agreement may help us understand the problem in a much more comprehensive manner.

The Composition of GTA

Unlike the erstwhile arrangement of the DGHC (which was formed under the State Act) or the Bodoland Territorial Council (BTC was constituted under the Sixth Schedule of the Constitution of India), it is proposed that the Gorkhaland Territorial Administration (GTA) would be formed through direct election subject to a Bill to be introduced in the State Legislative Assembly for this purpose. So far as the composition of the GTA is concerned, it is having far more numerical strength of the electoral members than the erstwhile DGHC or even the BTC arrangement. Apart from the fifty members (out of which forty-five members would be elected and five would be nominated by the Governor), the GTA *Sabha* (Council) would be composed of seven *ex-officio* members (comprising of the three Hill MLAs, three Hill Municipality Chairpersons, and the single Member of Parliament of the district). Besides the GTA *Sabha*, there would be an Executive Body having fourteen members (to be nominated by the Chief out of the fifty *Sabha* members) headed by the Chief Executive, a Deputy Chief (to be nominated by the Chief out of the fourteen members), a Principal Secretary (the Chief would select him/her from a panel prepared by the State Government). The following layout presents a comparative picture of the composition of GTA.

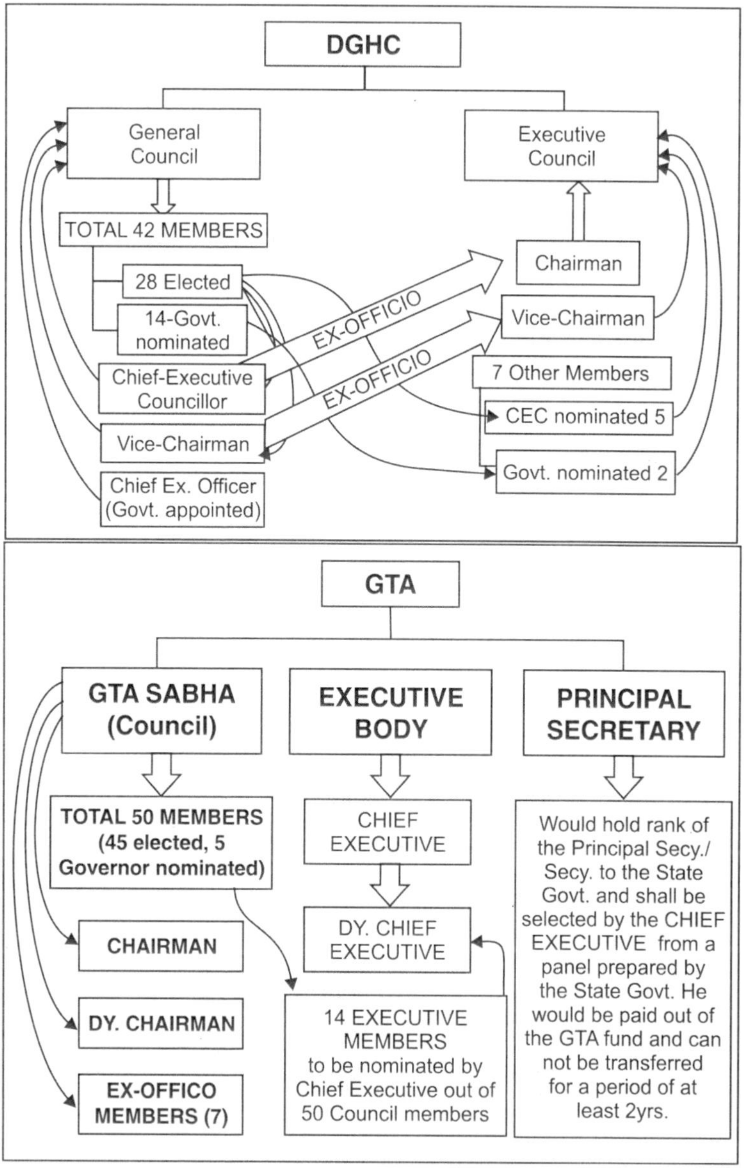

Fig. 6.1: The Composition: A Comparison between DGHC and GTA

It needs to be stressed that there is no specific clause in the agreement on the mode of selection of the Chief Executive. One cannot be very sure, even after reading the accord's clauses several times, as to how the Chief Executive would be appointed. Is the position an elected or a nominated one? Would he/she be the *ex-officio* head of the Executive body by dint of his/her capacity of being the Chairperson of the GTA *Sabha* (not to mention that this had been the arrangement the DGHC upheld)[3]? Moreover, no specification regarding the policy of reservation (for the women, Scheduled Castes, Scheduled Tribes, non-tribes, non-Gorkhas, religious minorities etc.) is there in the nine-page-long text of the Accord itself. The terms of office of the various elected members of the GTA, DGHC, and BTC are the same (five years in each case). Whereas the BTC Accord besides having specified the reservation policy also made suitable arrangements for the safeguard of the interests of the non-tribals, the GTA, even after its due ratification by both the State Assembly (on Septmeber 2, 2011) and the President (on March 7, 2012), still maintains some of these rather grey areas.

Power and Functions of GTA

A cursory look at the provisions of the Accord would help one to realise that both the GTA and DGHC are identical politico-administrative arrangements to execute power at the sub-State level. To return to the basic question whether the GTA or DGHC or any such arrangement is capable of reflecting the urge self-rule of the dissident group in any meaningful way, let us revise. Pared down, both were created on the pretext of a chaotic situation and as a strategic design to bring forth peace and normalcy in the troubled zone, albeit temporarily. Both the bodies are constituted as autonomous bodies although with no legislative powers. Pared down further, both the institutions emerged amidst the zig-zags of political compromise and compulsion: compromise to the so-called claim of a separate State *inter alia* self-rule and the compulsion to remain as a legitimate organising body of the sub-State level federal administration.

As pointed out earlier, the GTA has not been assigned with any legislative power. The agreement, however, affirms in clear terms that the powers to frame rules/regulations, under the State Acts, to control, regulate and administer the fifty-nine departments/offices and subjects transferred to the new body will be conferred upon the new body. The administrative, executive and financial powers in respect to the transferred subjects will be vested in such a manner that the GTA may function in an autonomous way. Compared to this, the DGHC was having only executive power (subject to the provisions of Central and State laws) over such subjects transferred to it. Besides having control over such important departments like education, agriculture, cottage and small scale industries, rural development and *Touzi* (which deals with land records of the tea gardens) as well as control over all unreserved forests in the region, the GTA will also have the power to create government jobs in the B, C, and D categories.

It deserves mention that the General Council of the DGHC was also having the power to appoint (with the prior approval of the State Government) officers and other employees as may be necessary for the due discharge of functions of the Council. Armed with such a clause, the Chairman of the DGHC had appointed thousands of casual employees more as a measure to quell the mass animosity towards the Council itself. This section of the casual workers finds a place in the new arrangement too, wherein it has been maintained that the GTA would not go for outright absorption of the huge number[4] of *ad hoc*, casual, daily-wage workers of the DGHC since it would go against the current position enunciated by the Supreme Court. However, the matter of regularising those employees who have ten years continuous work experience would be guided by the Finance Department Order of April 23, 2010. Those outside this ambit would be extended an enhancement in wages to a minimum of Rs. 5000 per month. As and when they would complete ten years of continuous service, they will be eligible for the full employment benefit. In essence what stands out is the fact that while the accord incorporated in it some juridically framed arrangements for promoting restricted power over the issue of recruitment, in effect it has the propensity to encourage the politics of recruitment to be accrued from the provision(s) of the accord itself.

Objectives of GTA

The GJM, while not dropping its demand for a separate State of Gorkhaland, has agreed to the setting up of an 'autonomous body' (empowered with administrative, financial and executive powers) for the overall development and restoration of peace and normalcy in the region. It is worth noting that both the State and Central Governments kept it on record that the GJM's aspiration for a separate State remains unabated even though a temporary truce has been reached; whereas the earlier DGHC agreement categorically maintained in the very first sentence that 'the GNLF has agreed to drop the demand for a separate State of Gorkhaland'. This is indeed a very significant departure in the way proposals of conflict containment were finalised in contemporary India. While in the case of the DGHC agreement the state appeared to be overpowering, in the case of the recent GTA Accord the contending parties seem to have more teeth than earlier. This does not, however, mean that the significance of the State has been diminished in a significant manner.

In fact, there is hardly any deviation in the approach of the state regarding the settlement of problems like that of the Darjeeling hills. Whether it is Gorkhaland, Bodoland or Telengana, the State looks into the problem more as an issue of law and order and the consequence of uneven development, or the lack of development. Such crucial issues like culture, self-respect, or self-rule are all clubbed together and considered as significant only when they are pitted against the discourse of development. This becomes crystal clear when one considers the way the objectives of the peace agreements are framed. For example, the major objective of the GTA, as the agreement upholds, is to establish ethnic identity of the Gorkhas by expediting all-round (socio-economic, infrastructural, educational, cultural, and linguistic) development of the people in the region. While comparing the situation with the DGHC we find that the major objective of the DGHC agreement was to guarantee the social, economic, educational and cultural advancement of the people residing in the hill areas of Darjeeling district. To no one's surprise similar is the case with the BTC Accord, whose objective was to fulfil economic, educational and linguistic aspirations and the preservation of land-rights, socio-cultural and ethnic identities of the Bodos; speed up the infrastructure development in the area through the creation of an autonomous self-governing body under the Sixth Schedule.

In fine, the issues of conflict containment and its empirical reference in present-day India have in fact equated the politics of peace with the politics of development. There is a general apprehension that development *per se* is the major problem that needs to be addressed in any discussion on ethnicity, despite the fact that such arguments appear to be paradoxical in the real sense of the term. That is because development has not only been treated, by such an approach, as the major stakeholder in the augmentation of ethnic conflict and movement but at the same time it is also being considered as the panacea which would surely mitigate the problem that the lack of it has instigated. The latest instance of the GTA in the case of the Darjeeling hills or for that matter the Srikrishna Commission Report in the context of Telengana are cases in point. Besides analysing some of the provisions of the GTA agreement let us now deal with the major potentially contentious issues incorporated in the agreement itself.

Provisions for Touzi Department in the New Arrangement

One such major issue is that of the *Touzi* Department which, according to the terms of the agreement, was handed over to the GTA. There is much hype surrounding the issue.[5] Those acclaiming it did treat it as a significant departure since it was not there in the DGHC, or even in the earlier draft proposal of the GAA. The *Touzi* Department is somewhat unique in the sense that it had been created by the colonial rulers primarily to look after the interests of the European planters, which was done by setting apart the tea plantations from the agricultural sector and thereby from the jurisdiction of the land revenue administration too. This possibly explains why the *Touzi* Department is having its existence till today only in the two tea producing districts of the State, namely Jalpaiguri and Darjeeling.

It is interesting to note that the *Touzi* Department did maintain the same colonial structure in those two districts even after the promulgation of the West Bengal Estate Acquisition Act (WBEAA), 1953 and West Bengal Land Reforms Act (WBLRA), 1955. Till today the Department enjoys its autonomous existence from the jurisdiction of the Land and Land Revenue Department and is headed by the District Collectorate. Effectively there has been none in between the tea gardens and the government, except the single-layered bureaucratic frame headed by the District Collectorate. Under these circumstances handing over of the responsibility of the *Touzi* Department to the GTA, without specifying the role of the District Collectorate, could possibly lead towards procedural complexities and create hurdles in the management of the tea gardens as the resources of the State. The significance of *Touzi* Department in matters of regulating issues like tea plantation land, particularly in the district of Darjeeling, can be ascertained from the following Table 6.2.

Table 6.2: Information on Land of Tea Gardens (in acres) in Darjeeling District

Total no. of Tea Gardens	144
Retained Area	141056.02
Area under Tea	74843.82
Area under Housing, etc.	12499.98
Unused Area	16308.93
Area under Forest	17217.27
Doubtful Area	20186.02

Source: http://darjeeling.gov.in/tea-garden.html (Retrieved on 6.8.2011).

The *Touzi* section deals with land matters of the tea gardens involving issues like lease of the tea garden land, renewal of the lease of the tea garden, collection of land revenue and Cess/*Salami*/ Penalty/fine etc. The *Touzi* Department also deals with giving NOC for development purpose, permission for uprooting and replanting/ felling of shed trees. The Department is also held responsible for the resumption[6] of the retained land of the tea garden. The tea garden lands are guided by the Estate Acquisition Rules, 1954 and Section 4 of the WBEAA and under Sub-Section (3) of Section 6 of the WBEAA along with Form-I Schedule F of the Lease Deed Agreement (all the terms and conditions for tea garden land were prescribed in the Lease Deed Agreement). The fixation of rent of the tea garden is done under Section 42(2) of the WBEAA.

Table 6.3: Status of Lease of Tea Gardens in Darjeeling Hills

Status of Tea Gardens	*Number*
Lease Renewed	34
Lease not yet Expired	10
Lease Expired	59
Total strength of tea gardens in the three hill subdivisions	**103**

Source: Data collected during fieldwork (June 2011) from the office records of the District Collectorate, Darjeeling.

Amongst the total 144 tea gardens 103 gardens are located in the three hill subdivisions of the district (Darjeeling 56, Kurseong 41, and Kalimpong 6) covering an area of 41,837.36 acres (out of the total area of 97,731.33 acres comprising the three hill subdivisions) generating a sum of Rs. 37,68,082 as land revenue and cess. These figures amply indicate why the *Touzi* Department can still be considered as very significant in the so-called tea economy of the region itself. All these also help us understand the concern of the GJM to have the responsibilities of the *Touzi* Department handed over to the GTA.

However, it needs to be remembered that the tea garden land is guided by the WBEAA 1953 along with Form-I, Schedule-F, of the Lease Deed Agreement. Under the Act, the Collector is empowered by the government to deal with the land matters of the tea gardens except the sanction of the renewal cases. As the GTA has no power to function as the Collectorate, it would be difficult to look into the land matters of the tea gardens of the hills. Moreover, in spheres like resumption of land, the authority of the State Government stands binding. Conspicuously, the text of the GTA agreement fails to draw attention to these rather inescapable administrative stipulations involved in the functioning of the *Touzi* Department. As it stands today, the *Touzi* Department runs on the dictates of the State Government in general, and the Collectorate in particular. Hence, the mere transfer of the *Touzi* Department would hardly yield anything unless the intricacies of its functioning *vis-à-vis* the authority of the GTA in the same is spelled out in some definitive terms. All these led the tea planters to have second thoughts over the issue of transferring *Touzi* to the new body. Newspaper reports also reveal that Morcha leaders recently started alleging that the tea planters were playing the game of 'double standard'.

Provisions for Panchayati Raj Institutions in the GTA

Even though the agreement handed over to the Department of Panchayats and Rural Development, including DRDA, to the GTA, the GJM leadership is yet to be free from the anxiety as to how it would function. Referring back to the earlier DGHC Act of 1988 one may recall that the said Act mentioned in clear terms that "there will be no *Zilla Parishad* in the district of Darjeeling. The Hill Council will be a substitute for the *Zilla Parishad* in the hill areas, the existing

HADC and the District Planning and Coordinating Council." And for the plains areas of the district there shall be the *Siliguri Mahakuma Parishad* as a substitute for the *Zilla Parishad*. According to the provisions of DGHC Act, the Darjeeling hills have enjoyed the atypical two-tier system of local governance; that too was opposed by Ghising and it ultimately ceased to exist from 2006. Currently in West Bengal there are 17 *Zilla Parishads*, 333 *Panchayat Samitis* and 3354 *Gram Panchayats*. In Darjeeling district, local governance comprises *Gram Panchayats* and Darjeeling Gorkha Hill Council (DGHC) in the hill Subdivisions of Darjeeling, Kalimpong and Kurseong and of *Gram Panchayat*, *Panchayat Samiti* and *Siliguri Mahakuma Parishad* in Siliguri Subdivision. In the hill Subdivisions of Darjeeling District there are no *Panchayat Samitis* for the eight blocks. Hence, in West Bengal there are 341 blocks but 333 *Panchayat Samitis* (Government of West Bengal, 2007: 9).

It is crucial to note that while the entire country has been enjoying the benefits of the 73rd Constitutional Amendment Act, particularly in terms of participation of the common masses in matters of grassroots level governance, the people of Darjeeling hills hardly had that scope. This was thanks to the Gorkhaland movement, which aimed at achieving self-rule at the cost rendering injustice to the common people and denied them the minimum opportunity to take part in the process of governance with whatever capacity they possess. As a matter of fact, the 73rd Amendment Act 1993, which emphasised empowerment of people at the grassroots level not only in the manner of exercising political rights but also to have a share in the process of governance, debarred the Darjeeling hills from enjoying these rights which are being practised in other parts of this country successfully. The 73rd Amendment Act promulgated a three-tier system of Panchayat in the entire country with the apex body at the district level. Since the Darjeeling hills have been divided into the DGHC and *Siliguri Mahakuma Parishad*, it is not possible to hold three-tier *Panchayati Raj* elections here. However, the single-tier system, which was in force since the last five years, now stands as a totally defunct body due to political reasons.

What stands out is again the crucial question of amendment. Because it is not feasible as per the strictures of the three-tier structure of the *Panchyati Raj* that a district would have two *Zila Parishads*. If we are to treat the *Siliguri Mahakuma Parishad* as a substitute to the *Zilla Parishad*, then setting up another *Zilla Parishad* for the hills would amount to contravention of law. Perhaps this led the government in terms of thinking of redrawing the administrative boundaries of the districts and also the GJM leadership to become vocal over the issue of bifurcating the Darjeeling district into two parts, besides constantly reminding the general masses that the issue of including the provisions for the three-tier *Panchayati Raj* structure in the new agreement is indeed a significant achievement.

The Idea of Development and the GTA

As pointed out earlier, the major objective of the GTA, as the agreement maintains, is to establish the ethnic identity of Gorkhas by expediting all-round (socio-economic, infrastructural, educational, cultural, and linguistic) development of the people in the region. Hence, an 'autonomous body' (empowered with administrative, financial and executive powers) is prescribed for the overall development and restoration of peace and normalcy in the region. It is crucial to note that the idea of development envisaged by the autonomous councils is equated with a process that would result in greater material production but seldom as a process of change that will lead to greater self-sufficiency.

In fact, within this borrowed idea of development in which there is hardly any scope either to ensure the involvement of the locals or to make the development agenda intertwined with local resources and local requirements one could hardly expect that the Council model of development could serve the interests of the community and thereby pave the way for inclusion in the larger society. In the absence of any self-reliant mode of development, the autonomous councils generally become a burden on the national and State budgets, and emerge as agencies which remain increasingly dependent on imported inputs. The experience of the Ladakh Autonomous Hill Development Council (LAHDC) and the earlier DGHC are pointers in this regard. There is thus considerable doubt whether the present GTA arrangement would be able to prove itself as an exception on this score.

The way development has been worked out in Darjeeling hills deserves further comments. After Independence Darjeeling's development no longer remained the "white man's burden".

However, this did not help the region to experience anything other than the same mode of 'civilisational' developmentality. The neo-Benthamites of Independent India are keen to offer 'greatest good' for the 'greatest number' by following the same top-down approach in which the same steel frame of bureaucracy is entrusted with the responsibility to formulate and execute policies to 'develop' and 'uplift' those who lagged behind according to a hard scientific socio-economic scale. In short, India's Independence has failed to usher in any significant paradigm shift in the praxis of development.

Economic development in the Darjeeling hills has, therefore, been unplanned, uneven and skewed, producing sharp cleavages between the richer and poorer and the rural and urban sections of the community (Chakrabarty, 1997:30). The development package outlined in the GTA arrangement would lead even a casual observer to conclude that the current fashion of development (under the terms of the GTA agreement) puts heavy emphasis on urban development in general and tourism in particular, while the concern of the village and the real issues of development of the rural population hardly get a proper place in the various (proposed) development schemes. In the urban-centric model of development the stagnation of the village economy and impoverishment of the rural poor are not addressed properly.

It is well known that the self-sufficiency of the hill economy largely depends upon its rural economy that helps restore the social, economic and ecological equilibrium of the hill social formation as a whole. The significance of the development strategy, particularly in the ecologically vulnerable zones like that of the Darjeeling hills, should be assessed in welfare terms rather than in productivity terms. This, however, is missing in the current fashion of development as worked out in the GTA Accord. In short, the GTA mode of development strategy could hardly enable the hills and her people to build up capacities that could help them attain liberation from the '*increased dependency*'[7] trap, which is, however, commonly attributable for the entire subcontinent.

Autonomous Council and the Notion of Community

The basic assumption of autonomous councils as they worked out either in Darjeeling or elsewhere in India is that they were thought of as an institution that works at the level of community. However, in State's consideration communities appear as merely a pre-given benign stock of population and not as dynamic sites which were constituted and even contested in the available wider networks of social relations structured in dominance (Beek, 1999: 446). In case of Darjeeling, the assumption of community and identity demands the erasure of West Bengal from the region. This indeed has a genealogy of its own which was elaborated in some detail earlier (in Chapter 3). Surprisingly most popular officials and even academic representations of the region effectively ignore this fact. In the imagination of the in-group, the presence of West Bengal generally appears as relative, and in most cases as a result of historical blunder, and is also depicted as a threat towards what is considered as their own property. Among the politically inclined authors terms such as neo-colonialism became handy to scrutinize the present situation of the hills.

The autonomy package offered through the District Council model is the by-product of a liberal logic that 'excludes' people of territorially concentrated and insulated cultural experiences while simultaneously 'including' them (read controlling) through the same initiative. Autonomy, in practice, is reflective of both the notions of 'democratic exclusion' that provided room for self-rule on the one hand and 'liberal inclusion' that made available the networks of power and control by the State on the other. The underlying assumption behind the arrangement autonomous regional council is that communities (be they the tribes, Gorkhas or the others) should be integrated but they should be allowed to preserve their own autonomy. Integration along with autonomy would also mean the respect for the plural identities of the communities. However, the paradigm of inclusive state as worked out through the autonomous regional councils actually treats community/tribe as a homogenous category and denies the difference actually existing in them. While on the other hand, the implementation of autonomy as a measure of inclusive governance has been made on the basis of the actually existing differences between the communities/tribes and the rest of the population of the concerned region undermining the heterogeneous and dynamic relationship that has long been maintained by the communities with each other. It is in this sense peace accords are seen as 'strategically deployed' means alongside force and coercion by the state in order to establish and perpetuate its 'domination' over the adversaries. 'Strategic deployment', therefore, involves an intelligent mix of force and coercion on the one hand and negotiation, consensus building on the other (Das, 2005:73). However, both these processes of domination-coercion and negotiation-consensus building are aimed at achieving the same goal of *status quo*. What is interesting is to note that all these issues and processes initiated before and after the finalisation of the peace accords, have ever tried to hit the basics. They hardly question the asymmetrical and iniquitous social formation and replaces instability by *status quo* (Singh, 1999).

This brief elaboration may help us appreciate that there is no easily identifiable 'community' waiting to be empowered in Darjeeling hills, in spite of decades of common struggle for autonomy and obvious cultural, linguistic, and geographical distinction from the rest of the state and indeed the country. This is how the State misreads the situation and makes arrangement in the GTA agreement for the Gorkhas only for consideration of Scheduled Tribe Status. This has evoked serious concerns amongst the already designated tribes like the Lepchas to raise voice in terms of having separate development council for the protection of their identity and interest (TEL: August 11, 2011). While the apparent homogeneity—at least on the surface—of Darjeeling hills helped activists to stake a claim for recognition and autonomy, and enabled it to be represented and accepted in public, official, and academic imagining as a unified 'natural' community worthy of special measures, its equally apparent real lack of cohesion, uniformity and identity illustrates the dangers inherent in assuming community to exist unproblematically (Beek, 1999:447). This assumption at the heart of present votaries of GTA becomes far more precarious when issues of including territories from Dooars and Terai come in.

Inclusion of Territories and the GTA

Gorkha Creed, a free Nepali Social Network site, in one of its recent postings maintained that the GJM has demanded 398 *mouzas* from Dooars and Terai (199 in each case) and eight wards of the Siliguri Municipal Corporation (SMC). The shaded parts of the current SMC Map (Fig. 6.2) are the wards GJM is demanding. The eight wards are plotted in the shaded part of the map according to their present location.

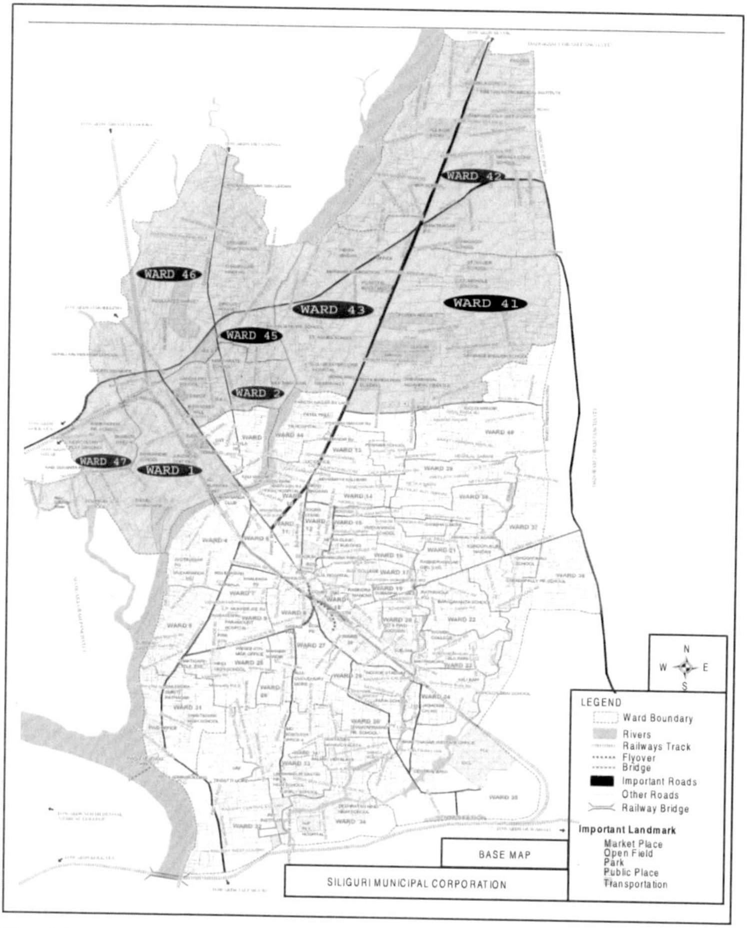

Fig. 6.2: Siliguri Municipal Corporation Map and the Wards claimed by the GJM

Source: Available at: http://www.siligurismc.com/(Accessed on 10.3.2011).

A High Powered Committee has already been formed to prepare a report on the issue of inclusion of territory. The Government stand over the issue as it is enshrined in the text of the treaty reads: "The committee will look into the question of identification of additional areas to the GTA with regard to their compactness, contiguity, homogeneity, ground level situation and other relevant factors" (for details *vide* the text of the agreement provided in Appendix II). The

GJM further proposed, although in a different context (on the issue of District bifurcation), "Only population cannot be the criteria for reorganization. Topography, backwardness of the area, available infrastructure has to be taken into consideration too" (Hindustan Times: August 3, 2011). The *Adivasi Vikash Parishad* is insisting on the year of 1950 as the cut of year and 1951 Census as the benchmark for counting heads before the things get settled. But the question that remained unaddressed is that: what then would be the criteria for determining a region. Is it only geographical factors, administrative permutations and combinations, census figures and head counts, or the notion of infrastructural and developmental status?

It needs to be stressed out that even though the claim over a territory often manifests itself in political terms, it is not merely a political issue. In fact, the politically charged emotive content of such issues are rooted in and routed through the cultural plane. Region as a social construct refers to historically contingent practices and discourses in which actors produce and give specific meanings to intersubjectively shared material and symbolic world, which lead towards the formation of a specific regional entity, if not an identity. One way of delving deep into such discourses is to put stress on the *cognitive, affective*, and *instrumental*[8] meanings people employ in relation to their selves' *vis-à-vis* the region in which they belong to. However, the relationship between individual self-identity and the collective regional identity is far from being clear-cut. In other words, the individual life histories and the histories of a region do not always share the common frames of reference. The present arrangement of GTA that emphasizes on the possibility of including new territories from the Terai-Dooars region has encouraged a politics of claim and counter-claim immersed in such touchy issues like ethnicity, history, regional identity, nationality, and even citizenry. The following map (Fig. 6.3) shows the areas the GJM has been demanding for inclusion and the GTA agreement has provisions for such an inclusion.

The risk involved in such political courses of action is that it attempts to superpose the domain of individual life histories over and above the histories of the region while in actuality both the domains share perhaps no common frames of reference at least in the Terai-Dooars region. The Gorkhas much like the *Adivasis, Bodos, Meches, Totos, Beharis, Marwaris, Rajbanshis* besides the Bengalis have

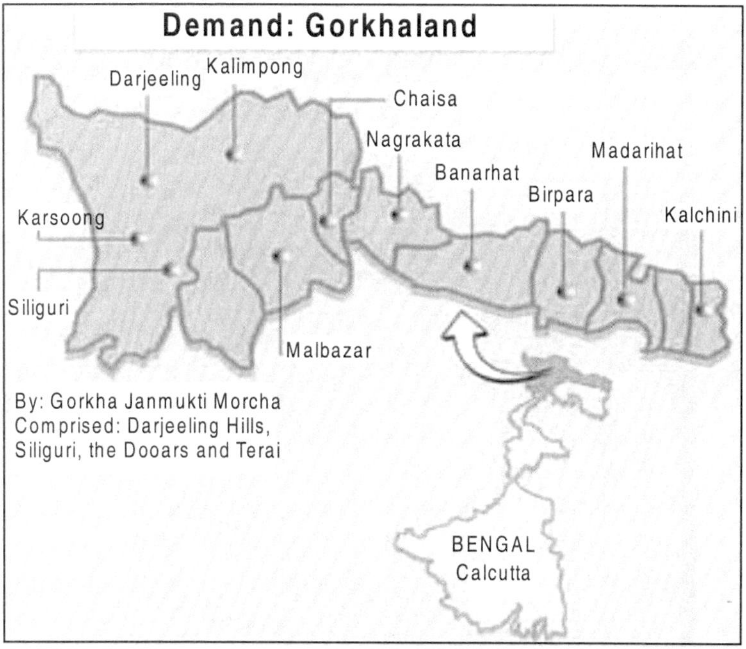

Fig. 6.3: Extended Map of Gorkhaland showing the areas claimed by the GJM

Source: Available at: http://himalnews.files.wordpress.com/2010/03/gorkhaland-map1.jpg (Accessed on 12.5.2011).

their respective narratives and the entire tract of *Dooars-Terai* acquires a true multicultural landscape coloured with the distinctive specificities of all these (and perhaps many others too, whom I could have missed to include) micro community histories. Besides these micro narratives, which in fact contributed towards the formation of a distinctive regional history, forces like colonialism, rule of the native king of Cooch Behar, Bhutan and above all the event of partition indicates the specificities of region formation in this tract. Hence, the tract though spatially located in two districts (Darjeeling and Jalpaiguri) of West Bengal, can hardly be thought of as a cultural region that is truly reflective of a Bengali identity. This does not however, help the area become a region of another community. Despite having numerical dominance and even sharing a contiguous settlement pattern distributed over several *mouzas* throughout the tract, neither the Gorkhas nor even the *Adivasis* can claim the status of being the proprietor of the region.

It is one thing to claim that people belong to a particular region (emphasis here is on individual life histories) but it is altogether a different assertion that a particular 'region belong to us' (this happens particularly when individual self identity and the collective regional identity congregates). Needless to mention that the Gorkha cause of being a claimant of territories of the *Dooars-Terai* tract to be included in the GTA is not tenable as far as the history, society and culture of the region is concerned. The recommendations of the so-called High Power Committee were grafted only on the pretext of head counts and the homogeneity, compactness and contiguity factors. Such an effort has in fact, the potentiality to transform the cultural boundaries, which existed historically between the micro histories of the different communities, into political one. At the ground level of everyday reality cultural boundaries are always easily penetrable and that is why they are tolerated as the mundane mechanism of recognizing difference, while political boundary is a formal arrangement of categorizing difference possibly by denouncing cultural reciprocity that occurs at the level of everyday life and/or replacing them by power relations. All this explains why the salience of Gorkha regional identity did fail to attain unanimous acceptance (like that of the hills) either in the Terai or in the Dooars region, despite the fact that these regions do contain a sizeable section of the Nepali speaking population in them.

There were several issues involved in the political battle of the Gorkhas to include Dooars and Terai in the proposed Gorkhaland *vis-á-vis* the struggle of the *Adivasis* and other communities to save the region from Gorkha invasion. What is really significant is to note that Gorkha leadership this time was rather forced to dilute the exclusivity of Gorkha ethnicity that it enjoyed hitherto. This was perhaps for the first time that State has been able to attack the exclusivity of Gorkha identity itself. By way of acceding to the demand of area inclusion raised by the GJM and inserting favourable provisions in the GTA treaty in this regard, the State in fact, encouraged the Gorkhas to come in terms with the *Adivasis*. In its recent revival we have seen that Gorkha agitation did not harp much on the Gorkha identity politics in Dooars (which followed a vertical ethnic line mobilizations in the hills) but on the politics of development and the required mobilization was activated on a horizontal plane so that reasonable space could be provided to the *Adivasis* and other non-Gorkhas for articulating their own interests and aspirations in the so-called 'politics of development'. In fact, the GJM was not in a position to have some political leverage in the Dooars-Terai region unless it corroborated to this idea of horizontal politics of development.

What is significant in the present context is that the social reality of the Dooars-Terai region reflects criss-crossing differentiation based on both ethnic and class line politics. There have been supporters of the Gorkha cause among the *Adivasis* and there were many Nepalis who believed in a common *Gorkha-Adivasi Pradesh* (the recently formed *Dooars Gorkha-Adivasi Welfare Society* is a case in point). The emergence of such political platforms as the *Garib Janata Samaj Seba Party* headed by a Gorkha president, and an *Adivasi* secretary is indeed a significant departure from the contra pools of ethno-political undercurrents that the region as a whole is experiencing for a couple of months now. These developments, in fact, invalidate the image of the Gorkhas and the *Adivasis* as ethnically antagonised warring groups. What is significant is the fact that Dooars-Terai region has historically maintained faith in a multicultural society where both the communities lived together rather peacefully until recently.

Let me share a significant experience gathered out of a short field trip in Dooars in the month of May 2012. While interviewing Anmol Prasad, a Behari youth of about 25 years of age running a *pan* shop at Birpara Bus stand, I asked him about his perception regarding the present political hara-kiri going on in the Dooars surrounding the issue of area inclusion in the proposed GTA territory. Anmol vehemently opposed the idea of area inclusion saying that '*it is not at all practically feasible. If the Gorkhas go on insisting on the area inclusion issue, Dooars would be blazed, bloodsheds would be inevitable*'. Although Anmol was aware that in Dooars and particularly in Birpara where a sizeable section of the Nepalis live in, he firmly believed that '*the mere presence of the Nepalis is not a sufficient condition of what they are demanding*'. Anmol went on saying '*Nepalis settle mostly in the other side of the railway track they don't have any significant presence in the market place or in the bus stand area of Birpara. People of Dooars would not tolerate such a politically motivated claim*'. Before he would have asserted in a much more emotionally charged way a Nepali young man asked Anmol '*Bhai! Sikhar (gutka) huncha*?' Anmol quickly replies '*Kati wara line*?' '*Dui ta*?' the man replied. Anmol again asked about change '*char rupiya chutta dinu hos*?' The man (who was neither known to Anmol nor even to me) took the required material after paying four rupee in coins and went away. Anmol just wanted to begin discussion with me but before he would have done that another lady (this time an Adivasi one) requested Anmol whether he was having cold drinks: '*Bhai thanda heik*?' the lady asked. Anmol replied '*Kitne ker leibe*?' the lady said '*Das rupiya kar de*?' The lady paid the required amount, picked up a chilled frooti (mango juice) and went back. I asked Anmol from where and how he has learnt all these languages? Encouraged Anmol said that he don't know how he actually learnt all these. '*Possibly*', he reasons, '*by way of growing up with the Adivasis and the Nepalis, playing and studying with them in the same Bengali medium school might have resulted in all these*'. Anmol also revealed that he could speak Bhojpuri and Marwari besides Bengali. I said good bye to Anmol and left the place thinking that Anmol's life experience was perhaps the best portrayal of contemporary Dooars where there was enough indication that bloody community clashes might erupt but at the level of everyday life people in Dooars did practice a multicultural way of life.

In fact, the evolution of Gorkha ethnicity in the hills and its recent political manoeuvring in the Dooars-Terai are not the same thing. It is true that the entire political process surrounding the issue of area inclusion in the GTA has resulted into the Gorkha-*Adivasi* joint political move that has gained some currency too. However, this new political gesture definitely has weakened the hill variety of Gorkha identity politics to flourish in the Dooars-Terai region. This is indeed a 'success' (if it can at all be called as 'success') and the credit of this success definitely goes to the ruling party of the present State Government. In fact, it is by way of incorporating the provision in the GTA treaty that additional areas may be included from the Dooars-Terai region, if the HPC so recommends the Government has encouraged the GJM to establish its political presence in the Dooars Terai region and in so doing, as we have seen, they were bound to concede the ethnic exclusivity that Gorkha identity inhered. In a certain sense Gorkhaland movement this time was directed towards such an end where there was no claimant for a separate state but there were many who could go for any length of discussion just to prove how much rational the claim of *mouza* inclusion was. This was indeed a win-win situation for the state in that the state has become able to reduce the movement of a separate state into a claim for certain *mouzas*.

NOTES

1. In September 2007 Prashant Tamang of Darjeeling won Indian Idol, a popular TV show much similar to its American or UK counterparts. Tamang's musical success has brought once again the political awakening of the Nepali speaking population of Darjeeling into limelight. The multi-racial Nepali community has united like never before not only in Darjeeling but elsewhere too. Bimal Gurung at this period of time used his position as the Chief Adviser to the Prashant Tamang Fan Club to garner support for the prospective Indian Idol by organising the numerous fan clubs that sprang up overnight in the Darjeeling hills and Sikkim. It is interesting to note that just after two weeks of Tamang's victory, Bimal Gurung formed the GJM in October 2007 and spearheaded the renewed political activism favouring the cause of Gorkhaland.
2. Among the political murders that took place during this renewed stir of the Gorkha agitation the AIGL Chief Madan Tamang's murder has been significant. The brutal daylight killing of Madan Tamang in May 2010 created political havoc in Darjeeling hills for some time. The GJM has been charged with such pernicious courses of action and eight GJM men were put behind bars. The Tamang murder case was handed over to the CBI following the direction of Calcutta High Court, although the decision is still pending.
3. Although there was no specification in the GTA Agreement regarding the appointment of the Chief Executive, the GTA Elections Rules 2012 published on March 15, 2012 in the Calcutta Gazette mentioned it that the Chief Executive would be elected by the Chairman of GTA *Sabha* in its very first meeting from among the elected members (GTA Elections Rules 2012: 37).
4. Although the GTA accord did not mention the actual figure of these casual workers created during DGHC regime, the newspaper estimates reveal that the figure is roughly around six thousand.
5. Darjeeling Tea Association initially felt that the transferring of the *Touzi* to the new body would solve lots of problems (Bengal Post 23.6.2011).
6. The proposal for resumption of land is placed before the District Land Advisory Committee after getting the NOC from the tea garden

management/application from the concerned applicant and report from the Block Land and Land Reforms Officer concerned. Thereafter, the proposal will be forwarded to the government through the Divisional Commissioner, Jalpaiguri for resumption of the land from the tea garden to the government *Khatian*. The settlement proposal of the said land will be finally initiated by the District Land and Land Reforms Officer.

7. While commenting on the paradoxical nature of mountain development Sankrityana (1997: 127) has located the existence of what he termed as *'increased-dependency trap'* in case of Darjeeling hills, which pitches the human resource component of the resource-system in such a way that development can only take place by increasing its dependence on the critical natural resource component.
8. While linking region, regional identity and political action Keating (1998: 86) has stressed on the cognitive, affective, and instrumental perspectives. By cognitive link he suggested that people must be aware of a region and its boundary so as to distinguish a region from other regions. The affective component involves the meaning: how people feel about a region as the principle framework for the formation of common collective identity. The instrumental linkage in Keating's framework hinges around those particular spheres where region has been used for political mobilization and collective action in pursuit of social, political and economic goals. For details *vide* Keating (1998).

7
In Lieu of a Conclusion

In fact, the experience of autonomous council model of governance operationalized through institutions such as the DGHC, BTC, LAHDC or others fail to address the problem the communities of those areas raised. Moreover, these autonomous councils reinstated the problematique that the liberal democratic state structure inheres. The formula of regional autonomy and its institutionalization hardly offers any fundamental shift in the ways through which fragmentary logic of representation of the communities were made, governmentality of the modern nation state structure was worked out, and the strategy of development has been grafted. While commenting on the state of affairs of the regional autonomous councils in India, based on a detailed study of Ladakh Autonomous Council, Beek maintains that, "autonomous councils are no panacea for the ailing of the national/developmentalist state, nor do such institutional arrangements address the causes that gave rise to regional disgruntlement" (Beek, 1999:452). A far more pessimistic diagnosis has been provided by Bethany Lacina (2009) who equated the functioning of autonomous councils in the local context as local autocracies and argues that these localized autocracies limit peaceful political competition. In the absence of institutionalized and rule based means of politics, changes to the local distribution of power lead to violence by challengers looking to seize control of resources or leaders seeking to reconsolidate dominance. Lacina is of the opinion that much like the North East contemporary Darjeeling especially demonstrates these dynamics.

A social forecasting has been attempted in the present text on the basis of a scrutiny of some significant provisions outlined in the text of the tripartite agreement. Findings and observations made by other scholars working in similar situations were also made use of to substantiate the rather 'book view' of the present problem. This chapter will deal with some concrete empirical information (gleaned out of people's opinion) which may help us estimate how the people actually assesses the present eventualities happening there in the Darjeeling hills. People's opinion was collected through a detailed questionnaire specially designed for the present study. The field trip was made at that period of time when GTA was just on its offing. As pointed out earlier that the universe for the present study was constituted of fifty-seven well educated, better placed members of present day Darjeeling.

Within such a crucial juncture it is quite significant to know how people have assessed the prospect of GTA that in fact marred the relevancy of the much hyped Gorkhaland at least for the time being in contemporary Darjeeling hills. It is interesting to note that among the fifty-seven highly educated respondents (who did share a great deal of civic engagement too) twenty-four respondents (42.11%) were not sure regarding what will be the situation of the hills in the years to come. However, a sizeable section of the respondents twenty-two in actual number (38.60%) did find a prosperous future lying ahead for Darjeeling hills. A little short of ten per cent of the respondents (4 in actual number, i.e. 7%) did say that a worse future is just waiting for the hills while 7 respondents (12.29%) believed no significant change is about to come whatever might be the strategy being employed by the government to handle Darjeeling situation.

Attempts were also made to consider people's perception regarding the role of the State as a whole *vis-à-vis* the situations in Darjeeling hills. What is the feeling of people regarding the country's authority structure (maintained by the Centre as well as by the state government)? Whether they agree that the State is genuinely concerned about what happens there in the hills? Or they disagree or not very sure about the same? These were some such questions asked to the same fifty-seven respondents. The responses gathered were fact revealing. 36.84 per cent of the respondents (21 in number) agreed that the country's authority structure is genuinely concerned about the hills while 35.09 per cent of the respondents (20 in actual number) strongly disagreed with such a proposition and 28.07 per cent of the respondents (16 in number) showed an ambivalent attitude.

Situated in such state of affairs when there is an above average estimation that the country's authority structure is not genuinely concerned about the region did they prefer then an outright restructuring of the present social order or favour some minor modifications to be made in the system or *status quo* as such? Questions of this sort were raised and people recorded their response mostly in favour of reform measures (54.39%) while 21 respondents (36.84%) recorded their urge for total transformation and 5 respondents (8.77%) are not very sure regarding what is to be done in the present context. It is very significant to note that none of the respondents do have favoured *status quo*. In that everyone was in favour of some sort of change be they radical or reformative in nature. However, it needs to be pointed out that those who were in favour of reform measures have assessed their viewpoints on the pretext of contemporary developments taken place in the region and those who favoured total transformation they did not, however, mean radical restructuring of the order in the sense of revolution but complete separation of the hills from the State of West Bengal in all respect.

What are the major problems of the region? How the Gorkhas did count them? The highly educated fifty-seven respondents pointed out several such factors which they considered as the major problems that the Gorkhas have faced over the decades. Interestingly enough majority of the respondents (43 out of 57, i.e. 75.43%) recorded problems of discrimination and exploitation related with citizenship identity as the major predicament of the Gorkhas while only 14.04 per cent of the respondents (8 in actual number) considered underdevelopment as the major problem, and very few respondents (2 in actual number, i.e. 3.51%) recorded the denial of self-rule as the major problem of the Gorkhas of the region. Four respondents (7.02%), however, abstained from registering any comments in this regard. Although the conventional wisdom situates the issue of ethnic movement along the spectrum of underdevelopment the reality in the Darjeeling can hardly be grasped under such an analytic frame. So far as the viewpoint of these fifty-seven respondents are concerned development was not being identified by them as the real issue of contestation but the issue of identity and the related perceptions of discrimination and exploitation encoded there in the grammar of identity were perhaps the substance of Gorkha aggrandizement.

It is by now almost a well known fact that the Gorkhas are agitating for self-rule in the form of a separate state for quite some time now but they are yet to be successful in achieving their long cherished dream of Gorkhaland. What then would be the possible factors that acted as major obstacle in the path of the movement's success? How does hill people chart out such factors those lead the movement towards failure repeatedly? Fifty-seven respondents did reveal variety of opinions in this regard. 56.14 per cent of the total fifty-seven respondents did consider war and attending lawlessness and arbitrariness and the silence of civil society are the major impediment in the path of achieving self-government while 21.05 per cent of the respondents considered that Gorkhaland movement now is backed by more competitors than actually dedicated stakeholder, which makes inter-party clashes as somewhat regular phenomena and all these beyond doubt will weaken the movement in the long run. Absence of any respectable figure with a national orientation and the lack of consensus among the local people on issues of importance are some such significant factors that 19.30 per cent of the total respondents considered as obstacles in the path achieving a separate state. Only two respondents (3.51%) mentioned that it is the porous border and the frequent incoming of Nepali subjects create the problem indeed. These findings also come closer to Chakrabarty's pessimistic prognosis regarding the functioning of the DGHC. Chakrabarty (2005) attempted to narrate the working of Darjeeling Gorkha Hill Council—that attempted to institutionalize autonomy in the local context—and the suspension of democracy thereafter. The complete civic silence has contributed to the malfunctioning of the DGHC on the one hand and the sudden death of democracy in the hills on the other.

Regarding the present strategy of conflict containment as devised by the government in the fashion of GTA opinion of the hill people was very critical. Among the fifty-seven respondents 17.54 per cent of the respondents (10 in number) were of the view that the present government strategy would ultimately result in DGHC form of governance. A sizeable section of the respondents 24.56 per cent (14 in actual number) of the total respondents were of the view that the GJM had no other option left but to surrender to the government by way of accepting the GTA. Highest proportion of the respondents (20 out of 57 or 35.09%) have considered that the acceptance of GTA is equal to an act of betrayal since by way of accepting this the GJM has reduced the scope of a national movement and transformed the same into a mere localized problem. Only a handful of the respondents (12.29%) were of the view that the present GTA arrangement has properly addressed the problem of Gorkha ethnicity while six respondents (i.e. 10.52% of the total 57 respondents) avoided making any comment in this regard. In fact, majority of the respondents did not, however, show a very greeting temperament for the new arrangement called GTA.

As pointed out earlier that in the renewed phase of present day Gorkha movement the Dooars-Terai region has appeared as the new citadel of Gorkha ethnicity and that the new brand of leadership this time left no options unused to capitalize on the situation. The GJM has harped so vociferously on the issue of area inclusion that the government was rather forced to incorporate provisions in the GTA treaty favouring such claims. What was people's consideration in this regard, did they favour such territorial inclusion, was the imagination of Gorkhaland having such an enlarged territory grafted only by the political elites for political gain or did the people in general have a similar feeling that the ethnic brethren of the Dooars-Terai region this time cannot be left out. Responses of the fifty-seven respondents were solicited and the results were fact revealing. While 5.26 per cent of the respondents (3 in actual number) believed that the issue of area inclusion has created more problems than opportunities, eight respondents (14.04%) were of the view that the demand of including Dooars-Terai in GTA is basically a strategy to gain a huge following and thereby to strengthen the ongoing movement. Only two respondents (3.51%) have castigated the necessity of such a strategy by saying that mere ethnic similarity does not necessarily help create regional fellow feeling. And two respondents (3.51%) avoided marking out any comment in this regard. However, the majority of the respondents (73.68%) were of the view that Gorkhaland is unacceptable without Dooars-Terai region since 'we cannot deny justice to our ethnic brethren located in that region repeatedly'. On the whole the analysis we made so far on the basis of fifty-seven responses of the people on several crucial issues of the contemporary phase of the movement it becomes crystal clear that the crave for Gorkhaland is germane to hill society in general and to individual life histories of the hill people in particular despite the very many differences that might have existed historically in the local society.

Attempts were also made to intervene in the domain of the subjective realm of the respondents by way of tracing out at what particular age they had heard about Gorkhaland, from whom they learnt about the very fact that a political struggle is being maintained by the Indian Nepalis for a separate state or that how did they situate themselves in the trajectory of the Gorkhaland movement in terms of their participation or contribution rendered to the same phenomenon. The respondents almost unequivocally maintained that they have learned about the movement at a very tender age and that from their childhood the more they got socialized the more they were brought closer to the movement called Gorkhaland. In a certain sense Gorkhaland at least for this fifty-seven well educated and better placed members of the hill society appear more as an 'existential reality'. The idea of Gorkhaland brings home a practical sense of honoured living and a set of dispositions (modes of perceptions, thinking, and behaviour) that generate particular attitudes and behaviours. The desire of Gorkhaland hence appears more like what Bordieu would call *habitus*. That is to say in other words that the imagination of Gorkhaland embodies the subjective component of cultural practices that the individuals employ in their day-to-day living. Individuals acquired particular *habitus*, or dispositions, as a result of their encounter with particular social *fields* (constituted of the definitive form of socialization, interactions in the cultural, economic, and political spheres). Viewing the Gorkha problem in this way one can be apprehensive of another side of Bourdieuan perspective that may suggest us appreciate that the movement was not always for material benefits or resources (this is also being reflected in our analysis of the questionnaire too) but had been directed towards acquiring 'cultural' and 'symbolic capital' (that incorporates issues like accumulated prestige, honour and recognition, which remain germane to the cause of Gorkhaland).

The significance of a Bourdieuan perspective becomes far clearer when we approached the respondents to locate themselves in the body of the movement itself. Gorkhaland as *habitus* appear significantly in the responses wherein all the respondents have situated themselves in the category of participants of the movement. There were differences of opinion in the way they self categorized themselves either as an activist (10 respondents, i.e. 17.55%), ideologue (1 respondent, i.e. 1.75%), passive supporter (43 respondents, i.e. 75.44%), or as a critical intellectual (1 respondent, i.e. 1.75%). However, none of them denounced the cause of Gorkhaland in any form, although two respondents (3.51%) avoided responding the questions. There was no difference of opinion when we tried to locate the motives of participation in the movement. Thirteen (22.80%) respondents mentioned that they participated in the movement willingly and twenty-two (38.60%) other respondents recorded that they have not participated yet but will not hesitate to do so if required while the rest of the respondents (i.e. 22 or 38.60%) reveal that they will not participate actively but cherish the dream of a Gorkha homeland always in their heart. Quite expectedly none of the respondents have ever said that they would avoid participation. Gorkhaland when viewed on the pretext of the questions raised so far describes the unconscious internalization of objective social structures which makes the movement appear as spontaneous and hence natural, but obviously these are socially constructed. The imagining of Gorkha homeland consists of a set of behaviours and cultural practices which were inculcated into a child as s/he learns about the movement.

The issue is that the efficacy of the GTA as a conflict containment strategy has to be assessed on the pretext of such a reading that we attempted to elaborate so far. Needless to mention that the entire idea of autonomous council (be it DGHC, GTA or anything else) in case of Darjeeling hills has failed to dissipate the claim for a separate state. But, as was hoped, it could play the role of an effective administrative structure that comes up more as a dual strategy of 'democratic exclusion' and 'control'. On the whole such an arrangement could hardly resolve the aspiration for self-rule merely by advocating that the new arrangement would secure overall development for the region through situating the council to work at the level of community. However, both the experiences of autonomous council and the praxis of development worked out through such sub-state level administrative arrangement in Darjeeling hills as also in other places largely suggest that they had been a very poor substitute of being a machinery of inclusion. In the liberal democratic body polity like that of ours own one can hardly expect for an inclusive arrangement (as mediated through the autonomous councils) through which the Gorkhas could feel at home. Perhaps that is why the Gorkha urge for self-rule remained unabated even after the implementation of autonomous council(s) in the region. It seemed to be quite imprecise that whether a separate state could guarantee the Gorkhas a status of 'settled community' and eradicate the Gorkha sense of 'homelessness'. The point is that unless the conventional national imaginary in India is radically altered, which has a profound bias 'towards one nation one state model' and therefore, towards a 'racial foundation', the problematique that Gorkha ethnicity raises can hardly be addressed properly.

Instead of writing up an epitaph of identity based movements the present chapter strongly proposes that any strategy/policy measures aimed at dismantling/controlling/resolving the identity based movements must have a resonance to the shifting identity claims that the movement upholds in the long run. This is, however, is missing in the otherwise scholarly analyses available in this field. Peace analysts and practitioners have an innate tendency to treat the identity issues as a static phenomenon. That is why in most cases peace initiatives fail to address the dynamics of identity delineation that goes on beyond the imagination of a statist approach. While negotiations of different identity positions keep on rolling peace keeping initiatives on the other hand keep its eyes fixed on reinforcing the war time logic of fixed ethnic boundaries. This process of negotiation always involves the risk in which dialogue takes place only between two groups the contending parties on the one hand and the stakeholders of authority on the other. This uncritical assumption of bipolarity simplifies the crucial processes involved in everyday life in which difference are accorded a normal social substance. That is to say in other words that the critical engagement of identity issues with the relations of power embedded in everyday life hardly gets the opportunity to have some place in the bipolar dialogic process of negotiation. The plea is not to deny the efficacy of a dialogic approach but that the dialogic approach should have to be framed properly so that multiple voices of identity issues can enjoy some breathing space in the discussions and deliberations which go on in the name of chalking out strategies of peace and tranquillity.

This has never been the case in Darjeeling hills so far as the question of state response to Gorkha movement is concerned. In state's imagination the problem of Gorkha ethnicity is having only one face all the time that gets reflected by a single party and its leader. Needless to mention such an approach comes closer to what we earlier elaborated as ME approach. As we have noticed earlier, the Gorkha movement appeared in state led negotiation process more as a property of the stakeholders like Dambar Singh Gurung and AIGL till the 1960s, Subhas Ghising and GNLF till late 2000, and Bimal Gurung and GJM till date. What happened in actuality is that the equally competent leadership who emphasised on the different versions of the movement grafted on some radical postures of identity discourse has been out rightly bypassed and ignored in the process of negotiation. Much in a similar vein Horowitz (1985: 597-600) has also pointed out that the weakness of such an approach lies in its assumption that as if each ethnic community will produce only one single set of leaders at a particular moment. When, instead, intra-ethnic competition develops, it is much more difficult for any factional leaders within the group to gain general acceptance of their policies (McGarry and O'Leary, 1993:37).

It needs to be emphasised that the rejuvenation of the Gorkha cause is led by the alternative leadership who felt dissatisfied with the state led project of negotiating the demands of a 'true Gorkha self'. The state felt relieved by the initial success of such negotiating gestures but the movement was far from being resolved and resurfaced again and again. Since Dambar Singh Gurung's time, who became the chief patroniser of inclusionist politics and was close to Congress leadership at the Centre, Rup Narayan Sinha and others spearheaded the exclusionist war path and revived the movement. Similar was the case with Subhas Ghising who signed the treaty of DGHC at that period of time when there existed a group of aggrieved leaders who despised the cause of autonomous council. The recent tripartite agreement of GTA which was signed by the present brand of leadership under the banner of GJM has reinstated the same issue. There are many contenders of the proposed GTA arrangement and the GJM leadership seems to be under pressure from both the direction the state on the one hand and the dissident groups on the other. The contemporary social political undercurrents in the hills have revealed enough indication of the resurfacing of the movement even after the signing of the so-called tripartite arrangement in which the State Government, Central Government and the GJM representatives were the only signatories.

Available literatures on social movement draw attention to the very fact that construction of identity in the context of social movement is indeed a dynamic process. That identity issues are both a prerequisite for and a consequence of mobilization (Melucci, 1996). This insight can help us understand the recent shift of stand that has taken place in the Dooars-Terai region with ABAVP's decision to join hands with the GJM to raise a demand of GATA instead of GTA. The politics of peace brought forth in the name of GTA has produced the urgency of strengthening the shared identity by making it a non-exclusive category. To put the matter in other words, the question of identity no longer remains an exclusive domain for the Gorkhas alone. Rather the present dynamics in Dooars-Terai region suggests that the scope of identity can get enlarged to such an extent in which the non-Gorkhas may be accommodated. The Gorkha-*Adivasi* joint move is undoubtedly a product of political convenience but it needs to be stressed out that such a dramatic turn is based on the mobilising efforts initiated by the state towards attaining peace and normalcy in the region. From another stand point, such mobilizations for peace activated by the state, in fact, attempt to polarize the movement in the long run. There lied also the potentiality of political chaos that can be instigated by such processes. Political dynamics of contemporary Dooars-Terai region is indicative of such issues. With the joining of hands by the *Adivasis* and Gorkhas to raise the demand of GATA several local political outfits started decrying against such a political move. Besides the *Amra Bangali* and *Jana Jagaran Samittee* the Kamtapur People's Party (KPP), the Greater Cooch Behar Democratic Party, the *Bodos, Meches, Totos* started raising resenting voice against such a design of political convenience that in fact decentred the exclusivity of Gorkha ethnicity. The point is that under such state of affairs, which went on in the name of mobilization for peace, neither the state nor even the contending parties are at all in a comfortable zone. Politics of peace this time yielded more costs than opportunities.

All said and done, the response of the state towards Gorkha movement has been piecemeal: to be non-responsive as long as the movement remained dormant, to use repressive measures when the movement turned violent, and to become accommodative at the last instance and reinstate the same accommodative stand with reprieve whenever group claims resurfaced. However, the present study of Gorkhaland movement *vis-à-vis* the state response has indicated that the dominant approach of the state towards issues like conflict resolution is based on the idea of 'liberal peace'—where peace is closely linked with the processes of democratisation on the one hand and free market development paradigm on the other. In this discourse there is hardly any chance for the engagement of ordinary people. It needs to be remembered that most violent conflicts are grounded in some form of popular grievances. It becomes necessary to listen to the deprived and the victims and to consider their complaints while building up policies for sustainable peace (Orjuela, 2008:25). Many peace practitioners have suggested the efficacy of a pyramidal approach (Lederach, 1997:39) that visualises how peace need to be built simultaneously and interconnectedly with the stakeholders of society at all levels: leaders at the top and at the middle and the masses at the bottom.

There exists an apparent hostility in the way the issue of conflict resolution has been thought of by the people in general and by the state in particular. While people think in terms of ethnic group loyalty first and have a tendency to view it as autonomous of the state and they subscribe to the viewpoint that the state should make necessary arrangements (in terms of structures and policies) that suit the variegated predispositions of identity claims, the state on the other hand superposes national loyalty above anything else and views ethnic loyalty as counterproductive towards the unified logic of a homogenous nation state. In matters of working out policy measures for restoring peace and normalcy in conflict zones the ethnic groups always remain at the receiving end and the state appears as the major stakeholder in the process, which in fact, transformed the linkage that actually exists between ethnic loyalty and national loyalty in dialectical terms. That is why the inclusionary measures which have been grafted in the name of conflict resolution measures have an innate tendency to reinforce forceful assimilation of the contending parties within the body of the liberal bourgeois democratic set up that the Indian nation state as a whole upholds. On the contrary, ethnic movements like Gorkhaland have in fact questioned the very foundational logic of liberal nation state that disapproves by and large the social cultural plurality of individual minds and souls.

As proposed earlier both the issues ethnic and national loyalty needs to be viewed as social processes in continual interaction in societies like India which have a richer cultural and civilizational heritage of a 'nation thing'—to use Spivak's (Spivak, 2010:13-4) attribution—rather than a politically cultivated nationalism. When viewed in this way ethnic movement appears basically as a process, a product of historical conjuncture of social forces through which the linkages between two types of loyalties are not only established or expanded but also discursively strengthened. Ethnicity in this sense reveals ethnic loyalty as a tendency inspired by its existence or as the aspiration to build up its own existence and in both way it hardly counters the predispositions of national loyalty. Unless these conceptual issues are appreciated beforehand any attempt to devise policy measures for conflict resolution is bound to be a failure. Conspicuously enough this perspective has been totally absent in the way Gorkhaland movement has been handled by the state over the years. Instead of disciplining and punishing those who superpose ethnic loyalty over national loyalty in a certain sense the state should take utmost care in making provisions—not merely in the form of liberal accommodation—so that the ethnic groups could have a reasonable space in order to get recognised in the eyes of the mainstream. The conflict resolution measures thus should not aim at advocating the ethos of forced assimilation but rather be worked out in such a manner so that the contending parties could find reasonable space in the larger body polity of the nation wherein their voices could be heard and recognised by the 'other'.

The study raises the argument that the claim of state's response to ethnic movements in general and Gorkhaland in particular to be inclusive is far from being unproblematic. In identity based violent conflicts (much like the Gorkhaland movement) the dichotomous positions of ethnic loyalty *versus* national loyalty poses the problem in the path of working out policies and measures for conflict resolution. Because within such a perspective both the sides see each other merely as enemies than anything else and reduces the scope for designing alternatives. The formula that the state wants to invest in the way it responds to ethnic situation is based on the liberal expectation that the 'us-them' divide would eventually become 'we' through the different mechanics of inclusion that the state has offered in the process of accommodating the conflicting claims. The point is that the formula 'us-them divide would become we' is neither simple nor even necessarily desirable. The execution of conflict resolution directed towards achieving the universal 'we' as an all inclusive identity (read national loyalty) actually resulted in the forced subjugation of the locally perceived hegemonic structures of dominance and subordination—a feeling that in fact breeds ethnicity. This is exemplified in the recurring process of peace building in which the state with all sincerity attempted to invoke the essence of national loyalty while the Gorkhas willy-nilly accepted the institutional mechanisms of inclusion with distrust and doubt.

It needs to be remembered that ethnic violence or ethnic hostility appears in the cognitive map of those who are involved in such courses of action, not as an 'intellectual question', one to be solved by a more informed, and thus assuredly more rational understanding (Hazleton, 1998:111). The expectation that the promotion of, what has been called as, 'confidence building measures' advocating changes in existing social, economic and political power arrangements to eliminate grievances, discrimination and to assume minority political participation will yield physical safety and cultural security to minority groups through power sharing arrangements, election or regional autonomy may not necessarily be treated as permanent solution to ethnic antagonism. That the problem is not merely of decreased contact or the lack of knowledge, skill or resources or of decaying interpersonal relations but of security and trust.

Peace initiatives framed by the state with the vision of homogenising the actually existing differences between the 'us and them' run the risk of submerging the rebel voice and reinstate the same hegemonic structure which in fact bred the problem. This has led towards the dilution of the 'security' and 'trust' components of Gorkha ethnicity whose lethal mixture aggravated the propensity of aggressive nationalism on the one hand and communal insecurity on the other. An alternative thus could be suggested favouring a policy that recognizes the different stakeholders of the ethnic cause. The alternative is basically about the approach which promotes the plurality of identities and thereby provides the space for a number of different voices and struggles. Such an approach may lead towards highlighting the shared identities and aim at strengthening ethnic identities and cultures. Peace efforts should not aim at homogenisation at the cost of local differences rather local cultural substances be allowed to enjoy a full blown growth in the so-called plural texture of Indian society. It is not a dichotomy that exists between ethnic and national loyalty rather it is by recognising the ethnic particularities that a national loyalty can possibly be achieved.

It needs to be stressed out that Gorkha ethnicity, which remained unambiguously vocal towards raising ethnic loyalty, never aspired for jettisoning the national loyalty. The claim of Gorkhaland is not unconstitutional. But such claims of self-determination were raised by the Gorkhas often by following extraconstitutional paths. The event structure of Gorkhaland movement gives enough indication that the movement hardly has followed an inverse 'U' curve trajectory as proposed by Kohli. In fact Gorkhaland movement defies the liberal expectancy of the political scientists who viewed heightened mobilisation of group identities are followed by negotiations, and eventually such movements decline as exhaustion sets in, some leaders are repressed, others are co-opted, and a modicum of genuine power-sharing and mutual accommodation between the movement and the Central and State authorities is reached. The state in fact, followed the same policy as suggested by Kohli but the strategy failed to yield similar result in case of Darjeeling hills. If we are to gauge the trajectory of Gorkhaland movement *vis-à-vis* state response to the same we have to conclude that it followed a curvilinear pattern of development in reality.

This has been the case when Gorkhaland movement of the 1980s was temporarily stalemated with the formation of a District Council (namely Darjeeling Gorkha Hill Council) in 1988 and resurfaced once again in the late 1990s and the process went on. It may seem that the state has become successful to convert the so-called turbulent Gorkha agitation for separate statehood into a conflict to achieve political power located there in the Council. However, such liberal expectations were soon belied. What happened in the 1990s is going to be repeated in contemporary period. The council model of governance (be it DGHC or GTA) or for that matter power-sharing and mutual accommodation of interests between the conflicting parties, State and Central Government has been proved to be counterproductive. This has been so because of the simple logic that these strategies of conflict containment have in fact reinstated the fault lines of liberal democracy.

Many Gorkha activists and their followers sincerely believe that they would be better off economically, more secure politically, and far happier socially and culturally on their own, or given the chance to govern their own destiny. When such is the reality, conflict resolution strategies aimed at bridging the cultural differences, eradicating specific grievances, and providing development doles will have little effect in the absence of communal security and mutual trust. Nor even the introduction of new administrative arrangements based on political concessions and economic subsidies will be capable of establishing consensus and cooperation. It is at this juncture the necessity of working out an alternative approach to peace and conflict resolution, that the study proposed, may appear as worthwhile.

Postscript

Gorkhaland Territorial Administration: Towards Implementation

Since March 2012 the political developments took place in the State of West Bengal (with regard to the issue of settling the Gorkha imbroglio) paved the way for the successful implementation of GTA arrangement. Although the GTA treaty has already been ratified by the West Bengal State Assembly on September 2, 2011, it took fairly long time of about six months to get the required assent of the President over the matter. Considering this procedural delay as 'unusual' the GJM in the intervening period started pressurizing the government with the claim that it would start afresh the movement for separate state from March 27, 2012, if GTA is not materialized by then (TOI: January 18, 2012). On the contrary the State Government started raising confidence regarding the fate of the GTA Bill to become an Act, which was finally realized soon it received the much awaited approval of the President on March 7, 2012.

Three particular provisions of the tripartite agreement on GTA signed on July 18, 2011 were of enormous significance. In fact, the later (since January 2012) courses of political development—be they the strategies of the state or the counter claims of the contending parties—revolved around these provisions. Let us consider them in some detail. The very first clause of the agreement upholds: "An Autonomous Body, which shall be called the Gorkhaland Territorial Administration (GTA), will be formed through direct election. A Bill for this purpose will be introduced in the West Bengal Legislative Assembly." What is significant in this clause is the provision that makes direct election mandatory for the formation of GTA. The issue of election has been insisted repeatedly both by the State and the Central Government during the period ranging from January to March 2012. GTA Bill after having received President's assent became an Act within a week on March 14, 2012. Accordingly the State Government began to initiate all-round efforts for the conduction of the first general election to the GTA Sabha.

The second significant provision of GTA treaty reads: "The area of the Gorkhaland Territorial Administration shall comprise the areas of the entire subdivisions of Darjeeling, Kalimpong with extended areas of Kurseong. In regard to transfer of additional areas of Siliguri *Terai* and *Dooars* to the new Body, a High-Powered Committee (HPC) will be formed comprising four representatives of GJM, three representatives of the State Government (one from the Home Department; the District Magistrate, Darjeeling; the District Magistrate, Jalpaiguri); the Director of Census Operations representing Government of India, apart from the Chairman of the Committee to be appointed by the State Government. The Chairperson of the Board of Administrators, DGHC will be the convener of this Committee. The Committee will look into the question of identification of additional areas in Siliguri Terai and Dooars that may be transferred to the new Body, having regard to their compactness, contiguity, homogeneity, ground level situation and other relevant factors. The Committee will be expected to give its recommendations within a short period, preferably within six months of its constitution" (Clause V). Although the HPC was formed according to the terms of the Tripartite Agreement on July 29, 2011[1], the Committee has failed to submit its recommendations within the stipulated six months (w.e.f. July 29, 2012) timeframe. This gave the GJM an opportunity to raise voice against the sincerity of the state led process of negotiation, which finally culminated in the demand of the GJM that the GTA election could not be held till the territorial jurisdiction of the GTA was finalized. It is on this pretext that the GJM in early January 2012 has raised the ultimatum of March 27, 2012 beyond which it would launch anew the move for a separate State. Before the GJM would have created much pressure upon the State Government another Gazette Notification was made on January 25, 2012 extending the term of the HPC for a further period of six months (w.e.f. January 29, 2012). However, the terms and conditions of the HPC remained as it was.

The outline of the third significant aspect of the tripartite agreement is provided in the clause six of the agreement that stipulates: "The work of this High-Powered Committee will run parallel to the electoral process which will be based on the existing area delimitation. However, the empowering statute will have a provision for transfer of the additional areas from Siliguri *Terai* and *Dooars* that may be agreed upon, based on the recommendation of this Committee". By dint of this clause the State Government went all out in stressing out the feasibility of the GTA election even amidst the severe opposition raised by the GJM. As noted earlier, the GJM since January 2012 has been consistently demanding the early submission of the HPC recommendations without which the GTA election, as it claimed, would not be possible. With the extension of tenure of the HPC for a further six months period the GJM strategically insisted that the GTA election would be rather impossible even though the State Government was firm in its decision to hold the GTA *Sabha* election at an early date. Accusing the State Government for having read the GTA agreement wrongly the GJM has insisted that the GTA *Sabha*, as per the provisions of the treaty (Clause 10), shall have to be constituted out of forty-five elected members. According to the provisions of the Agreement the State Government has also agreed upon the claim of transferring additional areas from Darjeeling Terai and Jalpaiguri Dooars to this new Body. However, the issue of transference of additional areas to the new Body entirely depended upon the recommendations of the HPC, which was supposed to be submitted by the end of June 2012. The GJM felt seriously concerned about the fate of its demand for the inclusion of *mouzas* from *Dooars-Terai* region. The GJM office bearers were also hopeful that the HPC recommendations would be favourable for its demand of area inclusion since four GJM men were already there in the ten member HPC. Under such circumstances the idea of conducting election of GTA *Sabha* would invite further complications if the HPC will recommend the inclusion of several *mouzas* to the new Body. Consequently, the people of the newly added territories would be very much a part of the GTA but they would not have any representation in the new Body if the election to the GTA *Sabha* was held prior to the submission of the HPC recommendations. This was how the GJM clarified its stand and attempted to persuade the public as to why it insisted that the conduction of the GTA *Sabha* election must not be held before the submission of the HPC recommendations. From January to March 2012 the GJM has mobilized this issue for creating political pressure and finally, on March 18, 2012 it directed the party MLAs to abstain from the Assembly proceedings until Gorkha dominated *mouzas* were included in the new hill set up (TEL: March 19, 2012).

After much political hue and cry regarding the issue of area inclusion *vis-à-vis* GTA election the State Government was successful in persuading the GJM leadership for discussion. A meeting was held on March 24, 2012 in the chamber of the Chief Minister with six office bearers of the GJM including its President and the General Secretary. The resolutions of the meeting were unanimously accepted by all the members. The decisions taken were fact revealing. It was decided in the meeting that both the State Government and the GJM would abide by the recommendations of the HPC. Both parties have also agreed upon the issue that the elections to the GTA *Sabha* would be held some time towards the end of June 2012 or in the early July 2012 irrespective of the fact whether the recommendations of the HPC were submitted or not by that time. Relieving the anxiety of the GJM as to what will happen if the HPC would recommend the inclusion of areas in the new Body the State Government clarified its position. It was thus decided that for the new area, if any, which may be included in the GTA on the basis of the recommendations of the HPC, the Government would nominate representatives from the new areas in consultations with the GJM. Considering that this was quite feasible as the GTA agreement contained provisions for nominations of five members by the State Government (Clause 10), the GJM willy-nilly agreed upon all the resolutions taken in the said meeting. Consequently, the GJM withdrew its earlier political programmes like the declaration of the ultimatum of March 27, 2012 and the boycott call by the GJM MLAs from attending Assembly proceedings. Peace and normalcy was restored in the hills, though temporarily. The GJM optimistically waited for the HPC Report, which the GJM presumed would yield favourable recommendations regarding the issue of area inclusion. The HPC submitted its recommendations on June 8, 2012 to the State Government and it has recommended the inclusion of only five *mouzas* from *Dooars-Terai* region to the GTA. This has created political uproar in the hills. The GJM felt betrayed by the recommendations of the HPC and went on demanding its immediate scrapping by the State Government. Political situation in the hills once again became tensed with the unwelcome attitude of the GJM to the HPC Report. Alleging that the recommendations were 'humiliating and one-sided' the GJM announced a number of agitation programmes including strikes and resignation of the party MLAs and even threatened to resurrect the Gorkhaland demand scrapping the GTA agreement. Aggrieved GJM leadership met the Chief Minister on June 16, 2012 to table their grievances against the HPC Report. A workable solution came out of the meeting in the form of a decision to constitute a three member fact finding committee to review the HPC recommendations (HT: June 17, 2012). Keeping in view the repercussions of the HPC Report it seems to be important to put some stress as to how the recommendations were framed? Were the allegations raised by the GJM do hold water? In order to have a handle over these rather controversial issues let us briefly examine the *modus operandi* of the Report itself.

High Power Committee (HPC) Report[2]: A Synoptic Overview

As noted earlier that the GJM had claimed an extended area covering several *mouzas* from Darjeeling *Terai* and Jalpaiguri *Dooars* for the inclusion in the GTA arrangement. As per the terms of GTA agreement the government appointed a high power committee to look into the question of identification of additional areas which may be transferred to the new body. The HPC has already submitted its recommendations in early June 2012. Out of the 158 pages of the lengthy and well documented Report 111 pages were spared for Annexure containing supportive documents mentioned in the Report. The HPC recommended total five *mouzas* (M.M. *Terai*, Gulmakhari and Purba Karaibari Chhat from Siliguri *Terai* and Samsing Tea Garden and Chalaoni Tea Garden from Jalpaiguri *Dooars*) for inclusion in the GTA territory and the criteria for such identification were decided upon as compactness, contiguity, homogeneity, ground level situation, and other relevant factors. Through a public notification (circulated through several news dailies on September 16, 2011) the government asked for petitions from persons/associations/councils etc. Such petitions were accepted till October 31, 2011, the last date of submission of petitions. Within this stipulated period as many as 723 petitions (512 from Jalpaiguri district, 208 from Darjeeling District, and 3 from Uttar Dinajpur district) were submitted. Majority of the petitions raised the demand for area inclusion while few petitions disfavoured such a claim[3]. After scrutiny majority of the petitions were disposed of on the ground that they did not match the criteria earmarked in the public notification. Only a handful of petitions (numbering 170) were taken into consideration along with the main demand raised by the GJM. For scrutiny the petitions were classified under several categories and decisions against each category of petitions were taken by the HPC on the basis of a thorough scrutiny of their contents. Table P1 can be helpful in understanding how the decisions were taken by the HPC.

The main demand of the GJM (which has been referred to in the Report several times) was submitted to the Government on June 7, 2011 in the form of a memorandum including a list of *mouzas* from Darjeeling *Terai* and Jalpaiguri *Dooars* to be included in the new arrangement. The basis of such a claim to include areas from *Dooars-Terai* region was based on the understanding that the proposed *mouzas* did contain preponderance of Gorkha population. The number of *mouzas* (falling under different Blocks and *Gram Panchayats* of *Dooars-Terai* region) claimed by the GJM were as follows (vide Table P2).

The Criteria of Area Identification Followed by the HPC

As noted earlier that the GJM has claimed 398 *mouzas* for inclusion in the GTA arrangement while the HPC after scrutiny recommended only five *mouzas* for such an inclusion. What seems relevant at this point is to examine how the decision of area inclusion was taken? What were the criteria considered for such a recommendation? How the HPC interpreted those criteria? What was the stand point of the GJM regarding those criteria (since GJM was aware of these matters as the criteria were already mentioned in the public notification of September 16, 2011)? What was the approach of the HPC while applying these criteria for scrutinizing the petitions? Let us consider these issues in some detail. The five-fold criteria (as per the GTA Agreement and also the Notification) being followed by the HPC were compactness, contiguity, homogeneity, ground level situation, and other relevant factors.

Table P1: Classification of 723 petitions as per their contents and decisions taken thereof by the HPC

No of petitions (N = 723)	*Petitions submitted from*	*Reason/Criteria (as per the Notification) stated in the content of the petitions*	*Decision*
369	Jal.-319 Darj.-50	No criteria/reason (as per Notification) in support of submission was spelled out	**Disposed of**
38	Jal.-35 Darj.-3	Reason mentioned in the petitions ('Non-development') did not come under the criteria mentioned in Notification	**Disposed of**
95	Jalpaiguri	Petitions argued in favour of '*status quo*'. No need of area altercation was sought	**Disposed of**
60	Jal.-23 Darj.-37	Claimed majority of Gorkha population in the *Dooars-Terai* area	**Disposed of** The petitions will abide by the decision to be made with regard to the main petition of the GJM
77	Jal.-11 Darj.-66	Stated some criteria in favour of area inclusion in the GTA	**Disposed of** These matters will abide by the decision to be taken with regard to the main petition of the GJM
30	Jal.-6 Darj.-24	Demanded vote-on-account in favour of area inclusion in the GTA. No criteria have been mentioned for area inclusion	**Disposed of**
04	Jalpaiguri	Expressed 'whole hearted support' in favour of inclusion of areas claimed by the GJM but no criteria/reason have been furnished as required under Notification	**Disposed of**

(*Contd.*)

Table P1: (*Contd.*)

No of petitions (N = 723)	*Petitions submitted from*	*Reason/Criteria (as per the Notification) stated in the content of the petitions*	*Decision*
04	Jal.-01 Darj.-03	No English version was available as it was mandatory and stated clearly in the Notification	**Disposed of**
09	Darjeeling	'No-objection' regarding area inclusion but no criteria/reason have been furnished	**Disposed of**
04	Darjeeling DGHC area	Claimed inclusion of Gangajalghati *Mouza* into the GTA. The area fall under DGHC area and under the present territory specified for the GTA	**Disposed of**
06	Jal.-01 Darj.-05	Petition for inclusion of the area into GTA	**These petitions will be considered and disposed of along with the decisions to be given in the main matter**
20	Jal.-10 Darj.-07 N. Din.-03	Expressed stand against area inclusion	**These petitions will be considered and disposed of along with the decisions to be given in the main matter**
07	Jalpaiguri	Opposed the formation of GTA but agreeing support towards the formation of GATA	**These petitions will be considered and disposed of along with the decisions to be given in the main matter**

Note: Jal., Darj. and N. Din. stand for Jalpaiguri, Darjeeling and North Dinajpur districts respectively.

Source: The necessary data and interpretations were compiled from the HPC Report.

Table P2: List of *Mouzas* claimed by the GJM from *Dooars-Terai* Region

Block	*Police Station/Gram Panchayat*	*No. of Mouzas claimed*
	Dooars Jalpaiguri District	
Mal	Mal	30
Maitali	Maitali	17
Nagarkata	Nagarkata	19
Dhupguri	Banarhat	21
Madarihat-Birpara	Birpara	21
Madarihat-Birpara	Madarihat	29
Kalchini	Jaigaon	19
Kalchini	Kalchini	24
Kumargram	Kumargram	16
Rajganj	Dabgram	03
Total Mouzas claimed from Jalpaiguri Dooars		**199**
	Terai Darjeeling District	
Matigara	Champasari GP	27
Matigara	Patharghata GP	22
Matigara	Matigara-I GP	05
Matigara	Matigara-II GP	04
Matigara	Atharakhai GP	04
Naxalbari	Upper Bagdogra GP	13
Naxalbari	Lower Bagdogra GP	04
Naxalbari	Naxalbari GP	10
Naxalbari	Gosainpur GP	06
Naxalbari	Hatighisa GP	13
Naxalbari	Moniram GP	22
Khoribari	Upper Raniganj Panisali GP	12
Khoribari	Upper Binnabari GP	07
Khoribari	Upper Buraganj GP	19
Phansidewa	Phansidewa GP	31
Total Mouzas claimed from Darjeeling Terai		**199**
	TOTAL MOUZAS CLAIMED (199 + 199) = 398	

Source: HPC Report Annexure 'C'.

Although the five-fold criteria were having their reference in the GTA agreement as well as in the public Notification but nowhere it was clearly spelled out as to what they actually mean. Nor even the HPC Report did maintain any clear emphasis on these rather crucial issues. However, based on a close reading of the HPC Report the following details were culled out from the assorted interpretations available in the Report itself. The following details may provide some clue in understanding how the recommendation of only five *mouzas* was made.

I. Compactness

The essence of compactness was derived out of 'book view'. That is to say no field visits were made so as to ascertain the demographic composition in reality but census data were considered as suitable for determining the compactness on the basis of demographic composition of each *mouzas*. Needless to mention that ethnic classification of population data was not considered (this may be because of the fact that since India's Independence Census Bureau do not furnish community-wise population data) rather compactness was defined on the basis of linguistic data available in the 2001 Census report. A *mouza* was presumed to be compact if it was found that more than fifty per cent of its population uses Nepali as their mother-tongue. The GJM on the other hand interpreted the idea of compactness in a different fashion. The GJM did not feel concerned with Census based demographic data nor even its linguistic classification, what it considered significant was perhaps the agglomeration of population (no matter what language they spoke or what ethnic community they belonged to) who ever have supported their claim of area inclusion will contribute towards the compactness of the respective *mouzas*. Hence, it is quite understandable why the GJM has insisted that 'the word compactness is needed to be taken in the liberal way because population in Siliguri *Terai* and Jalpaiguri *Dooars* does not have one single community. It's a mixture of *Adivasi* communities. They live side by side (HPC Report 2012: 17). In fact, GJM was aware that the Gorkhas or the Nepali speaking population hardly constituted the majority in all the *mouzas* it demanded[4]. They would constitute a majority if the *Adivasi* population was considered in unison with the Nepali speaking population. Perhaps this explains why the GJM has brought the *Adivasis* of *Dooars-Terai* region in the centre stage of contemporary Gorkha movement. This *Adivasi*-Gorkha nexus was further emphasized in the way GJM interpreted the other criteria earmarked in the Notification.

II. Contiguity

Contiguity was determined on the basis of contiguous geographical location of the claimed *mouzas* with the existing DGHC/GTA area. The contiguous areas so identified were classified according to two options: (i) Indo-Aryan and (ii) Tibeto-Burman plus Nepali speaking people. After having considered both the options a common broad based basis has been followed and sixty *mouzas* have been considered. After having identified the sixty *mouzas* they were further considered on the basis of their compactness (i.e. on the basis of more than 50 per cent Nepali speaking population criteria). Accordingly, ten *mouzas* of *Dooars* and eleven *mouzas* of *Terai* have been identified on the basis of *prima facie* satisfaction as contiguous to DGHC/GTA area. *Mouzas* identified as such were further taken into consideration if they can be recommended for inclusion on the basis of other criteria mentioned in the tripartite agreement and the Notification. GJM's emphasis on the contiguity principle was somewhat different. As per their submission they insisted that the parameter of contiguity should be area and not community, as nowhere (either in the said Agreement or in the Notification) any community had been mentioned. The GJM also insisted that the forest falling in between inhabitant area should be treated as the linkage and deep joining to the populated area in all respect. Regarding the issue of forest and as to whether the forest be considered as a divider or a linkage the HPC maintained that the worth of forest in relation to the contiguity criteria would be considered on the basis of location, and nature of forest, and if there is a way/passage/road in-between the forest that connects the *mouza* with the DGHC/GTA area.

III. Homogeneity

Homogeneity was defined by the HPC through such factors like uniformity in lifestyle, language, food habits, all of which are seen as typical of any language group. Language has been taken as an indication and surrogate of homogeneity amongst a diverse group. It may be noted that the use of a particular language (i.e. Nepali) by the inhabitants of the claimed *mouzas* has been a very important factor in the consideration of the HPC. The GJM on the other hand considered the homogeneity criteria rather lightly. The parameter homogeneity, as claimed by the GJM, should be related to population of the area seeking inclusion or non-inclusion within the GTA. GJM has in fact considered the issue of homogeneity more in political terms as if it was an agitational agenda. The more unified the voice for area inclusion the more homogenous the claim would be. But the factors on the basis of which the HPC endeavoured to identify homogeneity amongst the claimed *mouzas* were certainly far more complex. Although these factors appear to be apparently apolitical but the way they were placed in the decision making process was certainly a calculated step. In fact, if homogeneity has to be decided on the basis of such factors like uniformity in lifestyle, language, food habits etc. then possibly the entire DGHC/GTA area would appear as a conglomeration of heterogeneous *mouzas*.

IV. Ground Level Situation

Under Ground level situation the HPC has considered such issues like the road connectivity, access to GP headquarters, schools, hospitals in respect of the areas under their jurisdiction. It can be well presumed that there was every possibility that several of the *mouzas* would be left without the above facilities if they were recommended for inclusion. It is interesting to note the GJM has considered the ground level situation in the light of its political programmes again. Though the GJM has considered ground level situation criteria as very significant but the way they realized its significance was not at par with HPC's consideration. While the HPC considered ground level situation more in terms of the availability/unavailability of development institutions the GJM has considered the same in respect of the recent political manoeuvring initiated by it. Hence the GJM has claimed that the agreement between the *Adivasis* and Gorkhas for area inclusion in the GTA should be considered as the most important factor in the present situation (HPC Report 2012:17).

V. Other Relevant Factors

By other relevant factors the HPC meant those factors whose consideration and non-consideration thereof may create difficulty or cause hazard from practical and administrative standpoint. It also appeared from the HPC Report that the necessary data indicating other relevant factors were supplied from the report submitted by the two district magistrates to the HPC. In such reports the migratory background of the population, particularly of the Nepali speaking population was considered. By other relevant factors the GJM wanted to mean those factors which were mentioned in the various petitions submitted by the different bodies, organizations, associations favouring the cause of inclusion. GJM has requested the HPC to consider the submissions and the grounds mentioned in them as other relevant factors.

Approach

Much like the variation in interpretation regarding the five-fold criteria the approach of the GJM and the HPC with respect to the issue as to how these five-fold criteria were to be applied while formulating the recommendations also varied. The HPC Report clearly mentioned that 'all such conditions are required to be fulfilled as one is related to other and cannot be looked in isolation. Compactness cannot be taken into account if the area concerned does not fulfil the condition of contiguity to DGHC/GTA area as the same may involve administrative and other complications. Similarly, the criteria mentioned in the Notification are required to be looked into from the standpoint of ground level situation so that it may not cause any problem from the practical standpoint' (HPC Report 2012: 38). While the HPC has considered the five-fold criteria in a conjunctive manner the GJM considered them following a disjunctive approach. It deserves mention that neither the Tripartite Agreement nor even the Notification did mention how these five-fold criteria will be considered by the HPC. This gave the HPC a free hand in executing these criteria to arrive at a desired outcome. This vagueness of approach on the other hand did confuse and puzzle the GJM leadership who finally failed to realize the ploys of the State. The GJM instead considered the HPC and the entire negotiation process as favourable for the fulfilment of its political agenda. In a certain sense, the GJM was pretty sure that the HPC would submit sympathetic recommendations particularly when four of its party men (out of ten members) acted as GJM representatives in the said Committee. Perhaps this presumption led the GJM to insist on its growing political ascendancy in the *Dooars-Terai* region articulated through the alliance with the *Adivasis*. This is why the GJM has repeatedly insisted on the Gorkha-*Adivasi* nexus while establishing its own stand on the five-fold criteria and their operationalization. This would be interesting to consider the submission of Mr. S.N. Pradhan, the member representative of the HPC, in this regard. Mr. Pradhan in the eighth meeting of the HPC (held on May 29, 2012) has submitted that 'the GJM from the table of signing the Tripartite Agreement is demanding additional areas of Siliguri *Terai* and *Dooars* for inclusion in GTA by which they are keenly desirous to form an ethnic group of people along with *Adivasi* group of people along the road of NH 31 of the area' (HPC Report 2012: Annexure E). The HPC, however, ruled out the possibility that Gorkha-*Adivasi* nexus could constitute a single ethnic group and accordingly such a claim did not find the required attention in the decision making process, despite the insistence of the GJM representatives. Regarding the contention of the GJM that they constituted majority with the support of John Barla faction of *Adivasis* the HPC maintained that 'such a claim is not tenable and the same has no basis as Mr. Barla cannot claim to represent ABAVP and he and his supporters were expelled from the organization by the State Committee' (HPC Report 2012: 38). The HPC also noted that John Barla initially submitted a petition opposing the claim of the GJM and that he cannot be permitted to blow hot and cold at the same time. Subsequent application which is contradictory to his original stand was made on the letter-head of ABAVP, which he was not entitled to do since he was expelled from the said organization.

The HPC after having considered the already scrutinized 170 petitions (which fulfilled at least one of the above said five criteria) through following the conjunctive approach finally recommended total five *mouzas* (which fulfilled all the five criteria at once) for incorporation in the GTA. Three among these five *mouzas* fall under Darjeeling *Terai* part (namely Gulmakhari, Purba Karaibari Chhat under Matigara Block, and M.M. *Terai* under Naxalbari Block) and the remaining two falls under Maitali Block of Jalpaiguri District namely Chalauni Tea Garden, and Samsing Tea Garden. It can be well said that there existed a qualitative difference between the way HPC considered the issues related with the claim of area inclusion and the way the GJM has realized them. It is thus quite understandable why the recommendations of the HPC have displeased the GJM. It was also true that four of its representatives actively participated in the overall functioning of the HPC but did not submit note of dissent. Hence, the claim the GJM has raised that the report was one sided and prepared by keeping its representatives in complete darkness, seems to be unconvincing. It is in order to ascertain what has actually happened and what was the actual mode of participation of the GJM representatives in the HPC, some emphasis on the functioning of the HPC is warranted.

Functioning of the HPC

Let us begin with the fact that the HPC has conducted altogether eight meetings during its one year tenure and each of the meetings was attended by the member representatives of the GJM. It was only in the third meeting (held on December 15, 2011) Kitap Singh Rai (one among the four GJM representatives) remained absent while S.N. Pradhan (another GJM representative) was absent twice in the sixth and seventh meetings (held on March 16, 2012 and April 20, 2012 respectively). Although it was true that the Chairman of the HPC has given final shape to the recommendations but the HPC did not function in an autocratic way. All the members of the ten-member HPC have played significant role and actively participated in the serious discussions held during the hearings (in which the petitioners were called on) and submitted their valuable observations as and when necessary.

In the very first meeting of the HPC (held on August 30, 2011) regulations and procedures of functioning of the HPC were worked out. Needless to mention all the ten members of the HPC were present and all the resolutions regarding the regulations and procedures related with the functioning of the HPC were unanimously accepted. One particular regulation passed in the first meeting was of enormous significance. Clause XVI of the regulations reads: 'Any petition after examination in office shall be submitted to Chairman who shall finally decide to place the same before the Committee for disposal' (HPC Report 2012: Annexure E). Thus one can be apprehensive of the very fact that the functioning of the HPC from the very beginning has made it amply clear that the Chairman was exclusively entitled to take final decisions in matters of working out the recommendations. In the second meeting of the HPC (held on November 29, 2011) this provision was amended and some further additions and deletions were also made. As per the decisions of the second meeting of the HPC the said provision (XVI) of the regulation was deleted and an amended arrangement of the same was added as XVI-A, which reads: 'Any petition after examination in office shall be submitted to the Chairman who shall finally decide if the same be placed before the Committee or be disposed of by himself. However, if the Chairman on perusal of the petition is of the opinion that the petition does not disclose any ground or is not in compliance with clause XI[5] mentioned herein above, the Chairman may reject the said petition inlimine or he may in appropriate cases give opportunity to the petitioners to disclose the ground by submitting further petition which may be treated as supplementary to the original petition' (HPC Report 2012: Annexure E). With this amendment the exclusive entitlement of the Chairman in the decision-making process of the HPC was firmly established. Although all the four representatives of the GJM were present in the second meeting but none of them have raised any dissenting voice. The amendment was thus unanimously accepted even though it curtailed down significantly the power of the members to influence the decision making process.

In the second meeting another noteworthy addition was made (as clause XX-A) in the rules and functioning of the HPC as decided in the first meeting. The newly added clause XX-A maintains: 'For the purpose of rendering complete justice, parties who are also members of the Committee and whose interests are likely to be involved in any dispute on their petitions or otherwise may make submissions in that matter but shall not take part in deliberation and decision making process' (HPC Report 2012: Annexure E). A careful reading of this additional clause makes it amply clear that it speaks in favour statutory exclusion from the decision making process of those members whose interests are supposed to be involved in the functioning of the HPC. It can be well presumed who these targeted members were. It is interesting to note that all the GJM representatives in the HPC did not submit note of dissent even though the said additional clause had the potentiality of formally excluding them from the decision making process. It is not only that such an addition was unanimously approved in the second meeting of the HPC attended by all the four GJM members, Mr. S.N. Pradhan has also submitted an appeal for the rectification in the number of *mouzas* submitted by the GJM on an earlier occasion. Such a step by the GJM representative is an indication of contentment with the additional clause (which in fact aimed at their exclusion from the decision making process) and that is perhaps why they felt it justified to submit a further petition (Mr. Pradhan's submission of rectification is a case in point) as it was permissible according to the provision of the said additional clause.

Besides these procedural arrangements the HPC has also rendered several responsibilities to its members. Kitap Singh Rai, for example, was assigned with the responsibility to scrutinize the submissions made by several organizations opposing the demand of area inclusion and to prepare a report thereof. Mr. S.N. Pradhan likewise was entrusted with the responsibility of preparing a report out of the scrutiny of the submissions made by the Left Front and RSP. Both the GJM representatives submitted the required reports to the HPC in its fifth meeting held on February 24, 2012. While the District Magistrates of Jalpaiguri and Darjeeling districts submitted reports on Ground Level Situation the other Government official members furnished desired information including facts, figures and statistics as was required by the HPC Chairman. In the eighth meeting of the HPC (held on May 29, 2012) another major decision was taken at the imitative of Mr. Basudev Banerjee, Principal Secretary, Home Department, Government of West Bengal and a member of the HPC, that Government Official members of the Committee will not take part in any of the decision-making process and finding (HPC Report 2012: Annexure E). Among the ten members of the HPC there were five such Government Official members and GJM representatives were four in number besides there was the Chairman. It is interesting to note that as per the unanimously approved additional clause of XX-A the GJM members were already excluded from the decision-making process again it was further decided in the last meeting of the HPC that the Government Officials will not take part in formulating the recommendations of the HPC. To no one's surprise what stands out then is the fact that the Chairman would remain solely responsible in finalizing the recommendations of the HPC. Hence the claim of the GJM that the HPC recommendations were one-sided and that its representative members were completely ignorant as to how the decisions were taken is not tenable.

What is surprising is to note that the State Government has entertained such a politically motivated claim of the GJM and agreed to constitute a three-member fact finding committee to scrutinize the recommendations of the HPC. Apparently it may seem that the present State Government has been too much accommodative to the burgeoning claims of the GJM. On closer scrutiny it appears that such a course of action was perhaps a blend of accommodation on the surface with control and pressure at the core. The HPC

Report has helped the State Government to pacify the anxiety of the people of *Dooars-Terai* tract and to dissipate the political hue and cry surrounding the issue of area inclusion and finally to propagate the message with more political pronouncement than earlier that Bengal is not going to be divided (*'Bangla Bhag Hacchena'*). On the other hand by acceding to the demand of the GJM and by constituting the fact finding committee the state has become able to convince the disappointed GJM office bearers that there is still some scope to redress their grievances and also left the indirect message that for the moment they should feel contented with the new arrangement and join hand with the state to form the GTA.

The government went exerting its pressure tactics upon the GJM from all possible directions. There was the pressure of GTA election to be initiated at the earliest possible occasion. With the declaration of election cumulative political pressure was exerted upon the GJM. Overriding political pressure did ensue with the recent decision of establishing Trinamool Congress local branches in the hills[6] on the one hand and with the opening up of North Bengal unit of JMM in collaboration with the Barla faction of the ABAVP[7] on the other. Pressure did also crop up from the step taken by Subhas Ghising to file up a case on June 14, 2012 in the Calcutta High Court questioning the constitutional validity of the GTA. Public mood in the hills was also desirous to know the achievement of the GJM particularly after the submission of the HPC Report. The GJM was really in trap. It cannot outrightly overrule the machinery of the present State Government which has already provided enough space for ventilating its aggrandizement besides relieving huge financial overdue already and assuring further economic subsidies and development packages for socio-economic uplift of the region to be accrued in future. Nor even it was possible for the GJM to organize a fierce battle of separate state once again within a war fatigue hill society. It was in such a crucial situation the GJM was left with no other option but to come to terms with the state. Consequently, it started preparing the grounds for the much awaited election of the GTA *Sabha* and thereby paved the way for the formation of GTA and not Gorkhaland.

GTA Sabha Election

The election notification was made public on June 25, 2012 wherein it was stipulated that the last date of filing nominations was July 9, 2012, the last date of withdrawal of nominations was July 12, 2012, date of poll was scheduled on July 29, 2012 and the counting of votes would be held on August 2, 2012. It was also mentioned in the said notification that in any case the election procedure shall have to be completed on or before August 10, 2012. Needless to mention that the declaration of election has enabled the state to enjoy an upper hand over the contending parties who had been a bit hesitant to go for the elections. Although studies have shown that electoral competition can reduce as well as precipitate ethnic conflicts (Chandra, 2004: 237), the expansion of electoral space in Darjeeling hills did not take place at the cost of the separatist sentiment and politics.

In fact, sentiments of ethnic separatism remained intact in Darjeeling hills and the insistence on electoral politics hardly have transformed even the minuscule of such political idioms. In fact, the legitimization of the mainstream electoral politics has been possible in the contemporary hills perhaps because there was no contradiction between the separatist and mainstream politics and people were not forced to make a choice between the two. Rather the two domains of politics this time appeared more as the two sides of the same coin. At the one side we have politics of governance (to be maintained by the conflicting parties) and on the other side we have politics of conflict containment (this would be the neat outcome for the state for which it insisted on the invocation of mainstream electoral politics). The history elections in the hills suggest that the hill political parties have sought to restrict the scope of mainstream electoral politics to the issues related to 'governance'. In contrast to the larger political realities of the state, these parties acknowledge the widely prevalent sentiments of ethnic separatism as the most viable resource for manoeuvring. In no way such performances of the hill political parties did reveal that the mere extension of electoral space would result in the shrinking of separatist space.

The parallel existence of the two kinds of politics reflects a complexity that exists at the ground level, generated both by the change in the dynamics of the separatist politics, and the nature of popular responses (Chowdhary, 2009: § 22). In the absence of militant politics, popular politics in the hills during the past few decades has been highlighted through the assertion of ethnic separatism. Hence, the growing emphasis on the consolidation of mainstream politics in the hills has increased the necessity to localize the hill politics itself. All these make the hill politics an intricate sphere where both mainstream political processes and the assertion of ethnic separatism alternate. In fact, the history of hill politics has been the history of fluctuation of these two political tendencies. The abrupt political changes those have taken place in the recent past on the pretext of GTA *Sabha* elections are to be assessed keeping on view the above posed unpredictable predispositions of hill politics.

Despite repeated insistence of the State Government on the free and fair election to the GTA *Sabha* the election that was held on July 27, 2012 resulted in a walk over victory for the GJM. All the major hill political parties like ABGL, CPRM, GNLF, and GNLF(C) did not even file the nominations. They virtually shunned the GTA election treating it as an act of approving the denial of Gorkhaland. GTA *Sabha* would consist of 45 elected members and for that purpose 45 GTA constituencies were identified from within the three hill sub-divisions. Within the last date of filing nominations (July 9, 2012) the GJM has submitted nominations for all the 45 constituencies, Trinamool Congress submitted nominations for 18 constituencies (withdrawal of one candidate has also happened), CPI (M) for 13 constituencies and 46 nominations were submitted by the Independent candidates. The fate of GTA election was almost decided by the last date of withdrawal of candidature (July 12, 2012). On the date of scrutiny (July 10, 2012) candidature of 19 candidates (all of whom were Independent candidates) were rejected. By July 12, 2012 (the last date of withdrawal of nominations) 40 candidates (among whom 27 Independent candidates were there) withdrew their nominations. It is remarkable to note that all the 13 CPI (M) candidates have withdrawn their candidature accusing that they were forced to do so (Chattopadhyay, 2012). Consequently, out of the 45 seats GJM secured 28 seats without any contest. And elections were held only in 17 constituencies. Among these 17 constituencies 4 were distributed in Darjeeling, 4 in Kursong and the remaining 9 were in Kalimpong. Elections were held in 292 polling booths spread out among the said 17 constituencies and 74.13 per cent of votes were polled in all these constituencies. A more detailed and vivid picture of the GTA *Sabha* election can be ascertained through the following Table P3:

Table P3 : GTA *Sabha* Elections 2012 Result

Sub-div.	No. and Name of GTA Constituencies	GJM Candidate (Votes secured)	TMC Candidate (Votes secured)	IND Candidate (Votes secured)	Total Voter	Valid Votes
Darjeeling	1 Rimbick-Lodhoma	Prakash Gurung **(Uncontested)**			13213	
	2 Relling-Kaijalia	Satish Sharma **(Uncontested)**			11140	
	3 Pul Bijanbari-Goke	Kajiman Lohagun **(Uncontested)**			14686	
	4 Bloomfield-Rishihat	Binoy Tamang **(Uncontested)**			10138	
	5 Tukver	Bimal Gurung **(Uncontested)**			13420	
	6 Lebong Badamtam	Deo Prakash Pradhan **(Uncontested)**			13605	
	7 Phoobsering-Pandam	Bhupendra Pradhan, **(Uncontested)**			10814	
	8 Darjeeling-I	Asha Gurung **(Uncontested)**			11181	
	9 Darjeeling-II	Urmila Rumba **(Uncontested)**			13465	
	10 Darjeeling-III	Shanti Thapa **(Uncontested)**			14694	
	11 Darjeeling-IV	Taranga Pandit **(6384)**	Gopal Singh Chhetri (790)		11088	7174

(Contd.)

Table P3 (*Contd.*)

Sub-div.	No. and Name of GTA Constituencies	GJM Candidate (Votes secured)	TMC Candidate (Votes secured)	IND Candidate (Votes secured)	Total Voter	Valid Votes
Darjeeling	12 Ghoom Jorebunglow	Pemba Tshering Bhutia **(9712)**	Milan Dukpa (957)		14864	10669
	13 Chongtong Tamsang	Tilak Chand Roka **(9228)**	Manjit Subba (237)		13436	9867
	14 Sukhia Maney Bhanjyang	Uday Dewan **(Uncontested)**			17279	
	15 Pokhriabong Chamung	Dipen Malay **(8573)**	Dhan Bahadur Mukhia (237)		10416	8810
	16 Nagari Dhajia	Jyoti Kumar Rai **(Uncontested)**			10889	
	17 Rungbull Dhotria	Rabindra Lama **(Uncontested)**			13123	
	18 Sonada Pacheyang	Mahendra Pradhan **(Uncontested)**			13280	
	19 Takdah Glenburn	Sanjay Rai **(Uncontested)**			13070	
	20 Takling Peshok	Ramesh Lama **(Uncontested)**			12911	
	21 Takdah Teesta Valley	Narbu Lama **(Uncontested)**			17727	
	22 Mungpoo Labdah	Ratan Kr Thapa **(Uncontested)**			13895	
Total					**288334**	**36520**

(*Contd.*)

Table P3 (*Contd.*)

Sub-div.	No. and Name of GTA Constituencies	GJM Candidate (Votes secured)	TMC Candidate (Votes secured)	IND Candidate (Votes secured)	Total Voter	Valid Votes
Kurseong	23 Seeyok Gopaldhara Okaity	Phoebe Rai **(8259)**	Anil Chhetri (477)		11662	8736
	24 Mirik Thurbo Duptin	Arun Tamang **(6918)**	Brihas Subba (715)		10208	7633
	25 Soureni	Arun Singhji **(8992)**	Rajesh Chhetri (1706)		14790	10698
	26 Sukna Panighata	Champa Bivar **(9836)**	Rajen Mukhia (1526)		16018	11362
	27 Tung St. Mary's	Anus Kumar Thapa **(Uncontested)**			14885	
	28 Kurseong Town Deorali I	Yogendra Rai **(Uncontested)**			12366	
	29 Kurseong Giddapahar	Anit Kumar Thapa **(Uncontested)**			14271	
	30 Pankhabari Ambootia Longview	Pranoy Thapa **(Uncontested)**			14432	
	31 Mahanadi Tindharia	Prabha Chettri **(Uncontested)**			15172	
	32 Sittong Latpanchar	Roshan Giri **(Uncontested)**			12827	
Total					**136631**	**38429**

(*Contd.*)

Table P3 (*Contd.*)

Sub-div.	No. and Name of GTA Constituencies	GJM Candidate (Votes secured)	TMC Candidate (Votes secured)	IND Candidate (Votes secured)	Total Voter	Valid Votes
Kalimpong	33 ChiboTashiding	Kajem Bhutia **(7578)**	Mahendra Gajmer (923)		13413	8501
	34 Homes Bhalukhop	Neema Tamang **(Uncontested)**			15977	
	35 Bong Durpin	Sunil Ch. Pradhan **(Uncontested)**			15055	
	36 Dungra Pudung	Ramesh Allay **(Uncontested)**			15019	
	37 Algarah Dalapchand	Kalpana Tamang **(8353)**	Suk Bahadur Subba (896)		13228	9249
	38 Lava Lingsay	Chandra Prasad Sharma **(5943)**	Chandra Prakash Sharma (343)		8589	6286
	39 Rongpo Munsong	Gopal Ruchal **(Uncontested)**			10196	
	40 Pedong	Dawa Lepcha **(7737)**	Chewang Lendup Bhutia (324)		10196	8061
	41 Gitdabling Nimbong	Kalyan Kumar Dewan **(4095)**	Bruno Lepcha (264)	Sanchbir Subba (3418)	10561	7777

Table P3 (*Contd.*)

Sub-div.	No. and Name of GTA Constituencies	GJM Candidate (Votes secured)	TMC Candidate (Votes secured)	IND Candidate (Votes secured)	Total Voter	Valid Votes
Kalimpong	42 Relli Santhar	Ram Bahadur Bhujel, **(9620)**	Micheal Lingdamo (600)		13713	10220
	43 Gorubathan	Chandra Kumar Tamang **(14242)**	Prem Bahadur Adhikary (1057)		19239	15229
	44 Samsing Kumai	Samuel Gurung **(6258)**	Ugen Sherpa (382)		8960	6667
	45 Rongo Today Jaldhaka	Lopsong Rai **(8773)**	Pema Dorjay Moktan (413)		11744	9186
Total					165890	81176
Grand Total					590855	136125

Source: (i) Information Booklet 2012: 39 and (ii) GTA Elections 2012 (online resource).

In fact, the charm of election was absent in the hills as it was almost decided before the elections were held that the GJM would form the GTA *Sabha* almost without contest. Though the Trinamool Congress, the ruling party of the State, initially declared that it will contest the GTA election from all the constituencies, it filed nominations only against 17 constituencies out of 45. Again as a measure of political gimmick the Trinamool Congress Chief *vis-à-vis* the Chief Minister Ms. Mamata Banerjee has directed her party candidates not to contest the election just nine days after the date of withdrawal of nominations was over (*Hindu*, July 21, 2012). Such a step though was directed towards the maintenance of an amicable relationship with the GJM, virtually transformed the Trinamool Congress candidates as 'dummy' candidates and resulted in a pre-poll assurance of uncontested victory for the GJM party men. The emergence of Trinamool local branches in the hills has been a very recent phenomenon evolved just at the eve of GTA *Sabha* elections as a pressure tactics. However, the filing of nominations for the 17 constituencies and the quick fix decision of not contesting the election, for whatever reason it might be, amply proved that the party was yet to consolidate its presence in the hill politics and its mere presence hardly yielded anything for the return of 'substantial' democracy in the hills.

On the contrary what was interesting is to note that a dissident GJM leader Mr. Sanchbir Subba, the President of GJM's Nimbong unit decided to contest the election after he was denied a party ticket for the GTA *Sabha* election. Mr. Subba contested the Gitadabling Nimbong constituency against the GJM official candidate Mr. Kalyan Diwan, the Vice-President of GJM's Kalimpong Sub-divisional Committee. There was also a Trinamool Congress 'dummy' candidate Mr. Bruno Lepcha for the same constituency. Although the constituency was having 10,561 voters in total and Mr. Subba was able to fetch 3418 votes (out of 7777 valid votes) resulting in the victory of Mr. Dewan (with a margin of 677 votes only), but Mr. Subba's decision to contest the election against the party verdict has in fact challenged the contention of Bimal Gurung that GJM will secure all the 45 seats without any contest. It is also interesting to note that Mr. Subba, who was neither expelled nor suspended, before the counting of votes were over declared that he has been a loyal soldier of the GJM and will work under the direction of the GJM chief if he becomes successful in securing the public mandate in his favour. However, the GJM chief announced, on the other hand, that Mr. Subba will not be brought to GTA *Sabha* even if he wins. GJM will include Mr. Dewan as one among the five nominated candidates, in case of his failure (Stat.: August 2, 2012). Keeping in view all these it can be well maintained that Mr. Subba's failure in the GTA election was perhaps the single most important event that in fact, questioned the GJM hegemony on the one hand and showed some rays of hope—though operated merely at individual level—for the return of 'substantial' democracy in the hills, on the other.

Formation of GTA

Just after two days of the counting of votes (August 2, 2012) the GTA *Sabha* was constituted out of the 45 members (among whom 17 were elected members and 28 were uncontested candidates) and in the swearing-in ceremony graced by the Chief Minister, and the Governor of West Bengal besides the Union Home Minister Mr. Sushil Kumar Shinde the fourteen Executive members took the oath of office on August 4, 2012[8]. In its very first meeting held (on August 3, 2012) at Gorkha Rangamanch Bhavan in Darjeeling, GTA *Sabha* Chairman and Deputy Chairman were chosen from among the 45 members while Mr. Soumitra Mohan, the District Magistrate of Darjeeling (who was also a member of the HPC) was selected as the Principal Secretary of the GTA. Gorkha Janmukti Morcha vice-president Mr. Bhupendra Pradhan (popularly known as Pradip Pradhan) was selected the Chairman. Members also selected Lopsang Yolmo (who represented the Rongo-Today-Jaldhaka constituency) as the Deputy Chairman of the GTA *Sabha*. Bimal Gurung, the President of the GJM, was sworn in as the Chief Executive Mr. Roshan Giri, the General Secretary of the GJM, was allotted with the Department of School Education. Lt. Col. (Retd.) Ramesh Alley, the Head of the Gorkhaland Personnel (GLP), was nominated by the Chief Executive as the Deputy Chief Executive and was allotted with the Departments of Sports, Youth Welfare and District Sainik Board. The Chief Executive has kept as many as 11 Departments under his control. The distribution of offices to these 14 members of the Executive Body was made according to the following order presented in Table P4.

As per the Tripartite Agreement the GTA *Sabha* would have to be constituted of 50 members. Besides the elected 45 members there

Table P4: Executive Body Members of the GTA and the distribution of portfolio

Name	*Designation*	*Allotted departments*
Bimal Gurung	**Chief Executive**	Land and Land Revenue, Panchayat and Rural Development, *Touzi*, Food and Civil Supplies, Consumer Affairs, Tourism, Relief and Rehabilitation Management, Disaster Management, Planning, and Development, Finance, Weights and Measures
Lt. Col. (Retd.) Ramesh Alley	**Deputy Chief Executive**	Sports and Youth Welfare, District Sainik Board
Roshan Giri	Member	School Education (Primary, Secondary, Vocational, Physical Education, Govt. Schools)
Ratan Thapa	Member	Management of Forest
Jyoti Kumar Rai	Member	Transport and RTO
Dr. R.B. Bhujel	Member	College Education, Library Services
Binay Tamang	Member	Information and Cultural Affairs
Urmila Rumba	Member	Social Welfare (including SC, ST Development)
Ramesh Lama	Member	Animal Husbandry and Veterinary
Kalyan Dewan	Member	Agriculture (including Agricultural Education and Research)
Prabha Chhetri	Member	Woman and Child Development and Social Welfare
Phubi Rai	Member	Small-Scale and Cottage Industries
Samuel Gurung	Member	Cinchona Plantation
Asha Gurung	Member	Health and Family Welfare, Registration of Births and Deaths
Anit Thapa	Member	PHE

Source: Himalaya Darpan, August 11, 2012.

were provisions for five nominated members whose names would be proposed by the Governor. Politics of pressure and counter pressure surrounding the issue of nominated members took place even before the counting of votes. While the GJM stressed on the inclusion of people from *Dooars* particularly John Barla, the match maker of Gorkha-*Adivasi* nexus, the State Government disagreed with such a proposal of including nominated members from *Dooars* on the grounds that much of the *Dooars* has been left out of the present territory of the GTA. In a meeting took place on July 31, 2012 between Chief Minister and GJM President and General Secretary it was decided that the Government will nominate three members from the hills whereas the GJM was left with the option of nominating two members (HIM DAR: August 2, 2012). The contentious issue of inclusion of nominated members either from *Dooars* or *Terai* was temporarily resolved. The three nominated members from the State Government's side were Durga Kharel, Milan Dukpa and Satish Kumar Thing while the GJM nominated members were Sabitri Rai and Birkhu Bhujel. It is worth recalling here that Mr. Milan Dukpa has contested the GTA *Sabha* election as a Trinamool Congress candidate against Pemba Tsering Bhutia of GJM from Ghoom Jorebunglow constituency and secured only 957 votes.

Just after the four days of formation of GTA Executive Body the GTA *Sabha* members adopted a strange resolution in a meeting held on August 8, 2012 at Lalkothi, Darjeeling for including 10 invitee members to the GTA. The invitee members list included John Barla, Saraswati Pradhan and Asok Lama from the *Dooars*, Praveen Singh, Dina Chettri and P. Arjun from the *Terai*, Sabitri Chettri from Kurseong and Tshering Tamang, Latika Sinha and Bandana Yonzon from Kalimpong (HT: August 9, 2012). It was claimed that the powers and functions of these invitee members will purely be ceremonial in nature and as invitee members they were expected to provide suggestions on various issues, which will, however, not be considered as binding nor even would they have any power either of veto or of endorsement. It is not out of place to mention that there was no such provision of 'invitee members' neither in the GTA agreement nor even in the GTA Act. Hence the decision that the newly formed GTA *Sabha* has taken runs short of statutory of provisions. The point is that if the arrangement of invitee members has to stand as valid with whatever qualification it may be, an amendment in the GTA Act in this regard is mandatory. The entire issue would again require President's ratification since the GTA Act was primarily based on a Tripartite Agreement in which the Central Government has been a party. It is interesting to note that the State Government although being well aware of these rather illegitimate and unauthorized developments preferred to remain silent. In fact, the idea of 'invitee members' as worked by the GJM has revealed that it was an act of appeasing both the dissident leaders of the GJM and the *Adivasis* from the *Dooars-Terai* tract. Such apprehensions gain grounds of reality when we see that the Bimal Gurung, the GTA Chief Executive, has very recently announced that the GJM will go for a joint political move with the *Adivasis* in order to secure a better deal in the forthcoming *Panchayat* elections of *Dooars-Terai* tract (HT: August 21, 2012).

Let us conclude by making some comments on a recent write-up of Mr. Saumitra Mohan, the District Magistrate of Darjeeling and also the Principal Secretary of the GTA. The write-up was published as a lead article in the post-editorial section of a leading national daily (*The Statesman*) very recently in which he submitted some positive nods and suggested an outline of a 'new model' of development which may be operationalized through the GTA (Mohan, 2012). He stressed on two significant aspects of what he calls as the 'new model of development'. Firstly, the GTA should act as a platform for the execution of a participatory model of development, which ensures stakeholder's involvement at different stages. Secondly, that GTA should act as an instrument to realize the end of development and should not be treated as an end in itself. While the first domain of the 'new development' model puts stress on the process through which rebels may become stakeholders—a usual endgame and not an optimal solution to the rather hydra headed problem of identity and self-determination, the second aspect, in fact, emphasizes the necessity of coordination and integration of the GTA with other already existing development agencies like the district administration, municipality or the *Panchayati Raj* Bodies, an issue that is easy to identify but very complex and problematic to execute. In fact, much of earlier DGHC's operational aberrations were marred with such procedural bottlenecks.

Though peace has restored in the hills, neither the claim of Gorkhaland is stalemated nor are even the GJM adversaries sitting idle. Amidst such a topsy-turvy situation the formation and the successful functioning of the GTA *Sabha* is the only hope that came out of the recent negotiation took place between the state and the GJM, the bidder of Gorkha cause this time. With all the assurances of easy flow of required funds to execute the prioritized development projects hill people may feel assured of the capacity of the GTA as a development agency. However, one should not become overenthusiastic[9] by the declaration of yearly financial entitlement of Rs. 200 crore to be accrued there from the Central exchequer. Since such an entitlement—as was categorically mentioned in the Triapartite Agreement—would sustain only for the three years. Let us hope the negotiated Gorkha ethnicity this time would become successful in restoring peace and normalcy in everyday life and in engaging the rebels as the stakeholders of development *vis-à-vis* governance beyond 2015.

NOTES

1. As per the Gazette Notification dated July 29, 2011 the HPC was constituted with the following ten members: Hon. (Retd.) Justice Shayamal Kumar Sen (Chairman), Basudev Banerjee, Home Secretary to the Govt. of West Bengal (Member), Anil Verma, Chairperson Board of Administrators, DGHC (Member as well as the Convenor of the HPC), Dr. R.C. Sethi, Director of Census Operation, West Bengal (Member, who acted as the representative of the Government of India), L.B. Pariyar (Member, who acted as the representative of the GJM), S.N. Pradhan (Member, representative of the GJM), Kitap Singh Rai (Member, representative of the GJM), Shankar Adhikari (Member, representative of the GJM), Soumitra Mohan, D.M. Darjeeling (Member), Smt. Smaraki Mahapatra, D.M. Jalpaiguri (Member).
2. The HPC Report is available in three parts in the State Government website. This section and virtually the entire 'Postscript' have been prepared on the basis of a careful reading of the HPC Report itself.
3. Petitions favouring inclusion of *mouzas* in the GTA were submitted mainly by the several local units of the GJM and ABAVP (Barla faction) while the petitions those objected area inclusion were submitted by the Jalpaiguri and Darjeeling District units of several political parties like CPI(M), CPI, AIFB, RSP, CITU, and KPP. Petitions of objection were also submitted by Bangla-O-Bangla Bhasa Bachao Committee, Jana Jagaran (Mal unit), ABAVP (Tirkey faction),

and Bodo People's Forum. Petitions of objection were also submitted by several cultural organizations/associations like Indo Indigenous People's Organisation, All India Mahila Association, SC/ST & BC Social Welfare Forum, Dooars *Adivasi* Utthan Kala Aur Sanskriti Sangathan, North Bengal Tribal Development Centre and Kartik Oraon Memorial Academic & *Adivasis* Cultural Centre. Petitions of objection were also submitted by some individuals in person like Sri Biswa Ranjan Das and Tamal Kanti Dey.

4. Perhaps this perception led the GJM representative Mr. S.N. Pradhan to submit in the eighth meeting of the HPC (held on May 29, 2012) that the majority of a language speaking population should considered as 30 per cent of single language speakers on the basis of the population of a *mouza*. However, HPC has decided to use the widely accepted concept of majority of numbers in excess of 50 per cent.
5. Clause XI maintains: 'Every representation must be useful for, or relevant to the subject matter to be examined by the Committee and it must not contain any offensive or scandalous matters/remarks' (HPC Report 2012: Annexure E).
6. Trinamool Congress has floated a separate hills unit on June 11, 2012 and roped in some former leaders of Gorkha National Liberation Front (GNLF), Gorkha Janmukti Morcha (GJM) and All India Gorkha League (AIGL) to begin with (HT: June 18, 2012).
7. The John Barla-led *Adivasis* joined hands with the Jharkhand Mukti Morcha and formed the north Bengal branch of Shibu Soren's party, asserting that they would strive for a separate State—Darjeeling Terai Dooars Gorkha *Adivasi* Pradesh—if the Government failed to bring more plains *mouzas* under the hill set-up (TEL: June 16, 2012).
8. Restlessness still loomed large surrounding the issue of formation of GTA. Anti Gorkhaland pressure group, *Bangla O Bangla Bhasa Bachao Committee* (BOBBBC) activists have embarked on a two day relay hunger strike from August 3, 2012 in Siliguri as a protest demonstration against the formation of GTA *Sabha* and the swerving-in ceremony held on August 4, 2012. While the youth unit of CPRM has organized a *dharna* on August 8, 2012 in Delhi demanding the formation of the separate State of Gorkhaland instead of the GTA.
9. The GTA Chief has already announced, before the GTA has started functioning officially, the sanction of Rs. 1,02,98,000 for the maiden GTA project, a 10-bed hospital in the remote Tukling area in Darjeeling subdivision (HT: August 8, 2012). On August 19, GTA Chief has further sanctioned Rs. 1 crore to Darjeeling Municipality for the renovation of roads (HIM DAR: August 20, 2012).

Appendices

Appendix I
Chronology of Gorkhaland Movement

PRE-INDEPENDENCE PHASE

Sl. No.	*Year*	*Existing Administrative Status*	*Protagonists*	*Issues raised*	*Area earmarked for exclusion/ separation/ inclusion*	*Precipitating factor(s)*
1.	1907	Scheduled District	Leaders of Hill people	Separate Administrative arrangement outside Bengal	Hill areas of the district	Post-Partition Territorial/ Administrative rearrangement, possibility of Darjeeling's inclusion in the Morley-Minto Reforms Act, 1909.
2.	1917 (8.11.1917)	Scheduled District	Representative of hill people (eight signatories)	(a) Separate unit outside Bengal (b) North Eastern Frontier Province	(a) Darjeeling District and portion of Jalpaiguri District annexed from Bhutan (b) Darjeeling district, the Assam Dooars and territories lying east of Bhutan	Colonisers' trepidation regarding the implications if Darjeeling remains amenable to the provisions of Government of India Act, 1919.

(*Contd.*)

Appendix I *(Contd.)*

Sl. No.	*Year*	*Existing Administrative Status*	*Protagonists*	*Issues raised*	*Area earmarked for exclusion/ separation/ inclusion*	*Precipitating factor(s)*
3.	1921 (12.8.1921)	Backward Tract	Peoples Association of Darjeeling, Kursong and Kalimpong Samittee (eighty signatories)	Inclusion in Bengal for attaining the full benefit of the 1919 Reform Scheme	The whole Darjeeling district to be a part of Bengal	Hill peoples' apprehension of the implications of the Government of India Act 1919, if Darjeeling remained within Bengal.
4.	1930 (25.10.1930)	Backward Tract	Hillmen's Association of Kalimpong & Darjeeling, Gurkha Officer's Association, Kursong Gurkha Library (five signatories)	Independent Administrative Unit outside Bengal with Dy. Commissioner as an administrator and One Electoral seat for the Gorkhas only in the Imperial Legislature as recommended for Excluded Areas by the Simon Commission	The District of Darjeeling as a whole, in general and the Gorkha dominated areas of the District, in particular to be excluded from Bengal and be treated as an independent administrative unit.	Hill peoples' apprehension of the implications of the Simon Commission. Particularly the protectionist measures in matters of job and for political representation meant for the minorities in a province as mentioned in the provisions of the Simon Commission.

(Contd.)

Appendix I *(Contd.)*

Sl. No.	*Year*	*Existing Administrative Status*	*Protagonists*	*Issues raised*	*Area earmarked for exclusion/ separation/ inclusion*	*Precipitating factor(s)*
5.	1934 (6.8.1934)	Backward Tract	Hillmen's Association Darjeeling (three signatories)	(a) The district may remain within Bengal only after the provisions for the safeguard and protection of hill people in matters of job, education, allocation of funds, electoral representation etc. are laid down in clear terms. (b) The district of Darjeeling may totally be excluded from Bengal by creation of independent Administrative Unit and be taken care of by the Governor General himself.	Darjeeling district as a whole; no further addition of adjacent areas/territories of Dooars or of Assam was demanded.	Apprehension of the opportunity to participate in the 1934 Central Legislative Assembly Election having definite protectionist measures for the 'minority' Gorkhas so that the leaders of the hill people may get an opportunity to insert adequate provisions in the Statute Book for the protection of the interest of the hill people.

(Contd.)

Appendix I *(Contd.)*

Sl. No.	*Year*	*Existing Administrative Status*	*Protagonists*	*Issues raised*	*Area earmarked for exclusion/ separation/ inclusion*	*Precipitating factor(s)*
6.	1938 (11.12.1938)	Partially Excluded Area	Hill Men's Association, Rai Sahib Hari Prasad Pradhan (President)	The drawbacks of the existing arrangement which might lead towards the breakdown of social solidarity, dependency on Bengal for welfare activities, assurance of military security throughout the length and breadth of the proposed province.	Separate province in the style of North Eastern Frontier Province constituted of the sub-Himalayan regions ranging from the eastern frontier of Nepal to Assam.	Denial of any access in the statutory and legal apparatuses of Bengal Assembly and the helplessness of the hill people as a whole for not being able to register their voice in any form in the Bengal Assembly.
7.	1943 (12.8.1943)	Partially Excluded Area	AIGL	Gorkhas should be recognised as a (minority) community in order to realise the benefits of Cripps Mission and to safeguard their interest in the future federation of India, permission for organising mass meetings and to initiate a Nepali Journal as the mouthpiece of League.	Nothing specifically was spelled out regarding separation from or inclusion of Darjeeling with Bengal. Grave concerns regarding the future political status of the Gorkhas was registered.	Realisation of the benefit(s) of Cripps Mission and safeguard the interest of the Gorkhas in the future federation of India.

(Contd.)

Appendix I *(Contd.)*

Sl. No.	*Year*	*Existing Administrative Status*	*Protagonists*	*Issues raised*	*Area earmarked for exclusion/ separation/ inclusion*	*Precipitating factor(s)*
8.	1947 (6.4.1947)	Partially Excluded Area	Darjeeling District Committee of (the undivided) CPI	Establishment of Gorkhasthan the homeland of the Gorkhas.	Gorkhasthan should be constituted of three contiguous areas of Darjeeling District, Southern Sikkim, and Nepal.	The idea of Gorkhasthan was the outcome of the Communists' endeavour to apply without much modification (at least in the initial years) the Soviet model of self-rule of the nationalities on the basis of right to self-determination in Indian situation. The revision was clearly spelled out in the Party Programme of 1951 which put emphasis on the issue of complete regional autonomy and regional development for national minorities in India instead of right to self-determination.

(Contd.)

Appendix I *(Contd.)*

Sl. No.	*Year*	*Existing Administrative Status*	*Protagonists*	*Issues raised*	*Area earmarked for exclusion/ separation/ inclusion*	*Precipitating factor(s)*
POST-INDEPENDENCE PHASE						
9.	1949 (30.11.1949)	District under Presidency Division	AIGL (radical group), people of Sikkim and Cooch Behar	Formation of Uttarakhand Pradesh on the basis of racial characteristics, geographical affinity and historical association.	Uttarakhand Pradesh would comprise Sikkim, Darjeeling, Jalpaiguri, and Cooch Behar Districts.	The AIGL firebrands' idea was to enliven the project of segregation in the post-independence situation too. To act more as a pressure group of Eastern Indian body polity and also to emerge as a faction from within the AIGL, the single most important political platform of the hill people that favoured the cause of integration under the leadership of Dambar Singh Gurung.

(Contd.)

Appendix I *(Contd.)*

Sl. No.	*Year*	*Existing Administrative Status*	*Protagonists*	*Issues raised*	*Area earmarked for exclusion/ separation/ inclusion*	*Precipitating factor(s)*
10.	1952 (29.4.1952)	District under Presidency Division	AIGL (undersigned by N.B. Gurung as President)	(a) Separate Administrative Unit directly administered by the Centre (b) Separate state of Darjeeling (c) Inclusion of Darjeeling in the state of Assam.	The separate state would comprise Darjeeling District along with the neighbouring areas; the inclusion of Darjeeling District along with some portions of Jalpaiguri District should be included in Assam.	Assuming that the post independent political firmament is that opportune moment in which the best possible alternative for Darjeeling may be carved out. Not to mention the Memorandum was submitted just at the eve of first General Election of the Nation, and at that juncture when it was finally decided that SRC would start formulating its prescription for the reorganisation of states on linguistic basis.

(Contd.)

Appendix I *(Contd.)*

Sl. No.	*Year*	*Existing Administrative Status*	*Protagonists*	*Issues raised*	*Area earmarked for exclusion/ separation/ inclusion*	*Precipitating factor(s)*
11.	1953 (11.11.1953)	District under Presidency Division	CPI, Darjeeling District Committee	Regional Autonomy for the district of Darjeeling, besides there were 26 other demands mostly related with a descent social living both in the tea plantation areas as well as in the non-plantation areas of the hills.	Regional Autonomy for the District as a whole	The amended party stand regarding the issue of self-determination was reflected in the concept of regional autonomy which the (undivided) CPI had made use of for gaining political leverage in the hill political scenario.
12.	1958 February	District under Presidency Division	AIGL MLA Deo Prakash Rai	Autonomous District Council	Autonomous District Council status for the entire District	The increasing popularity of the Communists by dint of the political manoeuvring on the issue of regional autonomy led the League leaders consider the political capacity of the concept with due seriousness. Much like the undivided CPI the AIGL has started insisting on the issue of regional autonomy, with a new nomenclature, for the realisation of political stronghold in hill politics.

(Contd.)

Appendix I *(Contd.)*

Sl. No.	*Year*	*Existing Administrative Status*	*Protagonists*	*Issues raised*	*Area earmarked for exclusion/ separation/ inclusion*	*Precipitating factor(s)*
13.	1968 (25.8.1968)	District under Presidency Division	Congress, Darjeeling District Committee	Autonomous Administrative Set-up for the hill areas of the District of Darjeeling.	Darjeeling, Kalimpong, Kurseong these three hill subdivisions of the District will form one administrative district within West Bengal while Siliguri subdivision with some contiguous areas will form another administrative district within West Bengal.	Following the instances of undivided CPI and the AIGL the Congress was rather forced to accept the principle of regional autonomy as the key to emerge as a burgeoning political force to be reckoned with. Regional autonomy and its different nuances made popular by different political parties in the hills appeared as an issue of *realpolitik*.
14.	1980 (2.4.1980)	District under Presidency Division	Prantiya Morcha (Subhas Ghising as Chairman)	Separate State of Gorkhaland	Separate State of Gorkhaland be carved out from the State of West Bengal	The emergence of Sikkim as a Separate State in 1975, having lesser population and lesser areas than the District of Darjeeling was the major impetus to hard press the demand of separate State of Gorkhaland.

(Contd.)

Appendix I *(Contd.)*

Sl. No.	*Year*	*Existing Administrative Status*	*Protagonists*	*Issues raised*	*Area earmarked for exclusion/ separation/ inclusion*	*Precipitating factor(s)*
15.	1980 (2.8.1980) Telegram to Prime Minister of India	District under Presidency Division	Gorkha National Liberation Front (GNLF)	Gorkhaland State	Darjeeling District	Experiencing the lack of dedicated party workers within Prantiya Morcha, on the one hand and the growing ascendancy of the Pranta Parishad, on the other Subhas Ghising initiated the GNLF led Gorkhaland movement since 5th April, 1980.
16.	1981 (9.9.1981), 1982 (4.1.1982), 1984 (6.12.1984)	District under Presidency Division	Pranta Parishad	Separate State of Darjeeling	The proposed separate state would be constituted of the District of Darjeeling as a whole.	Overpoliticisation of regional autonomy issue by all the leading political parties of the region and the sterility of the concept to fulfil the aspiration of self-rule, to reflect the numerical dominance of the hill people in general and the Gorkhas, in particular in all possible spheres of everyday life (like decision-making, governance, resource

(Contd.)

Appendix I *(Contd.)*

Sl. No.	*Year*	*Existing Administrative Status*	*Protagonists*	*Issues raised*	*Area earmarked for exclusion/ separation/ inclusion*	*Precipitating factor(s)*
						competition, a share and say in the development cake etc.) created utter frustration within the hill politics and paved the way for the emergence of newer political fronts having faith only in the demand of separate state.
17.	1981 (9.4.1981) Telegram to CM West Bengal	District under Presidency Division	Gorkha National Liberation Front (GNLF)	To take back the prison –administration of Bengal within six months	Darjeeling district	Ghising started flexing his muscles and went ahead by branding the Bengal administration as an alien rule and showed little faith in parliamentary form of democracy.

(Contd.)

Appendix I *(Contd.)*

Sl. No.	*Year*	*Existing Administrative Status*	*Protagonists*	*Issues raised*	*Area earmarked for exclusion/ separation/ inclusion*	*Precipitating factor(s)*
18.	1983 (23.12. 1983)	District under Presidency Division	Gorkha National Liberation Front (GNLF)	Appeal to King of Nepal for the abrogation of the 1950 Indo-Nepal Peace Treaty for the permanent political settlement of the issue of citizenship. The copy of the letter was forwarded to the Heads of other foreign countries like USSR, UK, USA, France, China, Pakistan, Bangladesh, Sri Lanka, Bhutan and the Secretary General of the UNO.	Gorkhas of Darjeeling in general, and the Nepali speaking population of the whole India.	For the first time the issue of identity and the ambiguity of citizenship of the Nepalese of Indian origin was made an issue of political mobilization, which was needed not only to justify his distinctive position over the other contemporaneous political leaders and political parties while raising the same claim of a separate State.

(Contd.)

Appendix I *(Contd.)*

Sl. No.	*Year*	*Existing Administrative Status*	*Protagonists*	*Issues raised*	*Area earmarked for exclusion/ separation/ inclusion*	*Precipitating factor(s)*
19.	1984 (3.12.1984)	District under Presidency Division	Gorkha National Liberation Front (GNLF)	Telegram to Rajiv Gandhi, the then Prime Minister of India, to take immediate action for the creation of a separate State of Gorkhaland for the sake of political status and Indian identity of the whole destitute Gorkhas.	District of Darjeeling as a whole	The Telegram was sent just at the eve of Parliamentary Election of 1984 to garner maximum political pressure upon the Central Government and thereby to expedite the move towards the attainment of a separate State of Gorkhaland.
20.	1986 (5.7.1986) Letter to Prime Minister of India, copy to the King of Nepal	District under Presidency Division	Gorkha National Liberation Front (GNLF)	(a) Demand of separate State of Gorkhaland as legal right; (b) Abrogation of Indo-Nepal Peace Treaty of 1950, in general and the deletion of Clause VII of the said Treaty, in particular.	Darjeeling District as a whole	The concern of abrogation of Indo-Nepal Peace Treaty emerged as politically the most potential issue since it at the same time harped on the three crucial problems: citizenship, identity, and the legality of the claim of Gorkhaland.

(Contd.)

Appendix I *(Contd.)*

Sl. No.	*Year*	*Existing Administrative Status*	*Protagonists*	*Issues raised*	*Area earmarked for exclusion/ separation/ inclusion*	*Precipitating factor(s)*
21.	1987 (26.3.1987) Telegram to Prime Minister of India	District under Presidency Division	Gorkha National Liberation Front (GNLF)	Demand for a separate State of Gorkhaland within the framework of Indian Constitution within thirty days w.e.f. 23rd March, 1987.	Darjeeling District and Dooars	It seems that the telegram was more a justifycation as to why the GNLF has boycotted the State Assembly Election of 23rd March, 1987 and to suggest that the 450 empty ballot boxes are the proof of a referendum of the Gorkhas and if their demands were not fulfilled they would be bound to initiate another spell of mass movement.
22.	1991 (26.7.1991)	District under Presidency Division	Gorkha National Liberation Front (GNLF)	Greater Nepal hoax	Darjeeling, Sikkim, Bhutan	Reiterating the security perspective Ghising insisted on the need of forming Gorkhaland. The major issue was to exploit politically the Gorkha cause to the furthest possible extent as he apprehended that the Government of India showing gestures to include Nepali in the Eighth

(Contd.)

Appendix I *(Contd.)*

Sl. No.	*Year*	*Existing Administrative Status*	*Protagonists*	*Issues raised*	*Area earmarked for exclusion/ separation/ inclusion*	*Precipitating factor(s)*
						Schedule of the Constitution of India. Not to mention that Ghising was not at the centre stage of Nepali language movement at that period of time.
23.	1992 (12.1.1992)	District under Presidency Division	Gorkha National Liberation Front (GNLF)	Legal status of Darjeeling region was disputed; Darjeeling is a 'No Man's Land'.	Darjeeling included portions of Dooars and the entire tract of Kalimpong was referred to as 'No Man's Land'.	Ghising was no longer treated as the undisputed leader of the Gorkhas. This necessitated the employment of newer substances for political manoeuvring. The problematique of 'No Man's Land' emerged on this pretext more as a strategy to survive in the power game. GNLF boycotted the Panchayat Election of 1994 more as a threat and to secure the fate of Indian Gorkhas within the separate State of West Bengal.

(Contd.)

Appendix I *(Contd.)*

Sl. No.	*Year*	*Existing Administrative Status*	*Protagonists*	*Issues raised*	*Area earmarked for exclusion/ separation/ inclusion*	*Precipitating factor(s)*
24.	1996 (6.11.1996)	District under Presidency Division	Gorkha National Liberation Front (GNLF)	Immediate upgradation of DGHC into a full-fledged State of Gorkhaland.	DGHC Areas	The memorandum was placed on the pretext of H.D. Deve Gowda's (the then PM of India) sudden announcement of the possibility of Uttarakhand State in his Independence Day speech. It began new kind political activism in which other political parties of the hills joined hands.
25.	1997 (25.8.1997) Memo submitted to the Speaker and all the MLAs of WB Legislative Assembly	District under Presidency Division	Communist Party of Revolutionary Marxists (CPRM)	Demand of a separate state as the only solution to do away with the discriminatory arrangement which will allow the underdeveloped and developing nationalities with its own peculiarities to determine its own fate by themselves and amongst themselves.	Darjeeling hills, Terai and Dooars	After the announcement of the favourable statement made by the Prime Minister on the Independence Day (1996) in regard to the formation of Uttarakhand State, demand for Gorkhaland has turned into a major battle cry even for the CPRM, besides the GDF, Pranta

(Contd.)

Appendix I *(Contd.)*

Sl. No.	*Year*	*Existing Administrative Status*	*Protagonists*	*Issues raised*	*Area earmarked for exclusion/ separation/ inclusion*	*Precipitating factor(s)*
						Parishad, AIGL, Cong. I, BJP (all clubbed together under a single platform Gorkhaland Peoples' Front).
26.	2000 (May)	District under Presidency Division	Gorkha National Liberation Front (GNLF)	Demand for a separate State of Gorkhaland was reiterated	Darjeeling hills	The revival of the demand of separate state was, in a certain sense the pre-poll (Gram Panchayat Poll was scheduled to be held on 21st May 2000) stunt, which worked well and resulted into the sweeping victory for the GNLF.

(Contd.)

Appendix I *(Contd.)*

Sl. No.	*Year*	*Existing Administrative Status*	*Protagonists*	*Issues raised*	*Area earmarked for exclusion/ separation/ inclusion*	*Precipitating factor(s)*
27.	2000 (17.8.2000) Ghising's Independence Day Speech	District under Presidency Division	Gorkha National Liberation Front (GNLF)	Instead of Separate State for the first time the demand for bringing DGHC areas within the purview of sixth schedule was raised.	DGHC Areas	In order to persuade over his adversaries and to work out the best possible political bargain out of the politically unstable hill situation and particularly to reinstate the GNLF hegemony the desire to include DGHC under the provisions of Sixth Schedule and the following courses of action subsumed in the overall process of tribalisation of the entire hill folk were played out more in a manner of 'politics of expediency'.

Appendix II

Text of the Memorandum of Agreement Gorkhaland Territorial Administration (GTA)

Whereas the Gorkha Janamukti Morcha (GJM) has been demanding for quite some time past a separate State of Gorkhaland for the hill areas of Darjeeling district including some areas of Siliguri Terai and Dooars (hereinafter referred to as the Region);

And

Whereas both the Government of India and the Government of West Bengal have repeatedly emphasized the need for keeping the region as an integral part of the State of West Bengal;

And

Whereas after several rounds of tripartite meetings at the ministerial and at the official levels, the GJM, while not dropping their demand for a separate State of Gorkhaland, has agreed to the setting up of an autonomous Body (hereinafter referred to as the new Body) empowered with administrative, financial and executive powers in regard to various subjects to be transferred to the said Body for the development of the region and restoration of peace and normalcy there at;

And

Whereas the objective of this Agreement is to establish an autonomous self-governing Body to administer the region so that the socio-economic, infrastructural, educational, cultural, and linguistic, development is expedited and the ethnic identity of Gorkhas established, thereby achieving all-round development of the people of the region ;

And

Whereas all issues including issues relating to transfer of subjects to the new Body have been agreed in various tripartite meetings at the official level;

And

Whereas after several rounds of Tripartite discussions between the Government of India, the Government of West Bengal and the GJM, an agreement was reached in respect of all the issues; Now, therefore, the Government of India, the Government of West Bengal and the GJM, keeping on record the demand of the GJM for a separate State of Gorkhaland, agree as follows:—

(1) An autonomous Body, which shall be called the Gorkhaland Territorial Administration (GTA), will be formed through direct election. A Bill for this purpose will be introduced in the West Bengal Legislative Assembly;

(2) While under the provisions of the Constitution transfer of legislative powers to the new Body is not possible, the power to frame rules / regulations under the State Acts to control, regulate and administer the departments/offices and subjects transferred to the new Body will be conferred upon the new Body ;

(3) The administrative, executive and financial powers in respect of the subjects transferred will be vested in such a way that the new Body may function in an autonomous and effective way;

(4) The subjects along with all Departments/Offices to be transferred to the new Body is appended as Annexure – 'A'.

(5) The area of the Gorkhaland Territorial Administration shall comprise the areas of the entire subdivisions of Darjeeling, Kalimpong with extended areas of Kurseong. In regard to transfer of additional areas of Siliguri Terai and Dooars to the new Body, a High-Powered Committee will be formed comprising four representatives of GJM, three representatives of the State Government (one from the Home Department; the District Magistrate, Darjeeling; the District Magistrate, Jalpaiguri); the Director of Census Operations representing Government of India, apart from the Chairman of the Committee to be appointed by the State Government. The

Chairperson of the Board of Administrators, DGHC will be the convener of this Committee. The Committee will look into the question of identification of additional areas in Siliguri Terai and Dooars that may be transferred to the new Body, having regard to their compactness, contiguity, homogeneity, ground level situation and other relevant factors. The Committee will be expected to give its recommendations within a short period, preferably within six months of its constitution.

(6) The work of this High-Powered Committee will run parallel to the electoral process which will be based on the existing area delimitation. However, the empowering statute will have a provision for transfer of the additional areas from Siliguri Terai and Dooars that may be agreed upon, based on the recommendation of this Committee.

(7) In regard to transfer of all forests including reserved forest, it was agreed that the State Government will make a reference to the Central Government on the issue of reserved forest as the power delegated to the State Government under the Central Statute cannot be delegated to any other authority straightaway. However, all offices catering to the unreserved forests under the jurisdiction of GTA would also be transferred to GTA.

(8) Regarding Tribal status to Gorkhas except the Scheduled Castes, the GJM or any organisation representing the Gorkhas will make an application to the Backward Classes Welfare Department of the State Government, which is the authority to process such claims. The Department, upon receiving such application supported by necessary documents will conduct a study through the Cultural Research Institute, Kolkata. After examination by the Department, the matter will be referred to the National Commission for Scheduled Tribes. The recommendations already submitted to the National Commission will be followed up by the State Government. The Government of India will consider for granting ST status to all the Gorkhas excepting SC.

(9) In regard to regularization of all *ad-hoc*, casual, daily wage workers of DGHC, regularization by way of outright absorption is not feasible due to the current legal position as

enunciated by the Hon'ble Supreme Court. However, those employees who have put in 10 years of continuous service would be guided by the Finance Department's order of 23rd April, 2010. Those outside this ambit would be extended an enhancement in wages. This would be equivalent to 75 per cent of the remuneration admissible under the order of the Finance Department subject to a minimum of 5,000 per month for those who have not completed 10 years of continuous service. As and when they complete 10 years of continuous service, they will be eligible for the full benefit in terms of the order of 23rd April, 2010. The employees will, however, have the liberty to apply for normal recruitment to any other posts of State Government. It was also agreed that the State Government will make necessary financial provisions for bearing the additional non-plan expenditure for this purpose.

(10) There shall be a GTA Sabha for the GTA. There shall be a Chairman and Deputy Chairman to conduct the business of Council. The GTA Sabha shall consist of forty-five elected members and five members to be nominated by the Governor to give representation to members of SC, ST, women, and minority communities. The M.Ps, M.L.As, and Chairpersons of municipality(s) of the region shall be *Ex-officio* Members to this GTA Sabha. The term of the GTA shall be five years.

(11) The Executive Body shall consist of a Chief Executive who will nominate fourteen members out of the elected/nominated members as Executive Members. One of them shall be the Deputy Chief to be nominated by the Chief Executive.

(12) Every member of the GTA shall before taking seat make and subscribe before the Governor or one of the elected members appointed in that behalf by him an oath or affirmation. The Chief Executive shall be administered an oath or affirmation by the Governor.

(13) There shall be a Principal Secretary of the GTA, who shall be of the rank of the Principal Secretary/Secretary to the State Government and who shall be selected by the Chief Executive from the panel sent by the State Government and shall be paid from the GTA Fund such salaries and

allowances as may be fixed by the State Government. The Principal Secretary once deputed to the GTA shall not be transferred for a period of at least two years without the consent of the GTA.

(14) The Government of India and the Government of West Bengal will provide all possible assistance to the GTA for the overall development of the region. The Government of India will provide financial assistance of Rs. 200 crore (Rupees Two Hundred Crore) per annum for 3 years for projects to develop the socio-economic infrastructure in GTA over and above the normal plan assistance to the State of West Bengal. A list of projects which may be considered to be taken up by the GTA is at Annexure 'B1'. List of projects to be separately taken up by the GTA with the State/Central Government is at 'B2'.

(15) The Government of India/State Government will provide one time financial assistance required for development of administrative infrastructure, *viz.*, GTA Sabha House, Secretariat Complex and the residential quarters for the elected members of GTA and the senior officers.

(16) The allocation sanctioned in the budget of GTA and all funds sanctioned by the State or the Union Government which remain unspent at the close of the financial year shall be taken into account for the purpose of providing additional resources in the Budget of the following year or years and the fund requirements will be met on a yearly basis.

(17) The Government of West Bengal shall provide formula based plan fund with 60 per cent weightage on population and the balance weightage on area backwardness, hill areas and border areas in two equal installments every year for executing development works.

(18) The Government of West Bengal shall provide Non-plan grant including provisions for bearing the additional Non-plan expenditure for existing employees payable in two installments in respect of the offices/departments transferred to GTA.

(19) The fund received from the Government of India shall not be diverted and the State Government shall release the fund in time.

(20) The GTA will have the power of creating Group B, C and D posts with the approval of Governor. The recruitment to Group B, C and D posts will be through a Subordinate Service Selection Board to be set up for this purpose.

(21) The State Public Service Commission shall be consulted for the recruitment of Group 'A' officers.

(22) The State Government will set-up a separate School Service Commission, College Service Commission; open an office of the Regional Pension and Provident Directorate; and set up an office for Registration of land, building etc., marriage, society etc. in the GTA area, subject to extant rules and regulations.

(23) The Governor of West Bengal shall obtain a report on the functioning of the GTA and cause that report to be laid on the table of the West Bengal Legislative Assembly annually.

(24) The Government of West Bengal will initiate action to re-organize/re-constitute the territorial jurisdictions of sub-divisions and blocks.

(25) The GTA, once established, will separately take up the issues relating to grant of incentives, subsidies, waiver of taxes and tariff and other benefits as appropriate to the region's backwardness, with the Central and State Governments.

(26) A three-tier Panchayat will be constituted by elections in the GTA region, subject to the provisions of Part IX of the Constitution of India. Notwithstanding anything contained in the West Bengal Panchayat Act, 1973, or the West Bengal Municipal Act, 1993, the GTA shall exercise general powers of supervision over the Panchayats and the Municipalities.

(27) Since the formation of new authority will take some time and since the developmental works in the hills, which have already suffered badly, cannot be allowed to suffer further, there will be a Board of Administrators in DGHC which would be fully empowered to exercise all the powers and functions of the Chief Executive Councilor under the DGHC Act, 1988 and to decide on the much needed developmental works in the hills. The Board of Administrators will comprise MLA, Darjeeling; MLA, Kurseong; MLA, Kalimpong; District Magistrate, Darjeeling and Administrator, DGHC in keeping with the provisions of the sub-section (1) of Section 17 of the

DGHC Act as amended *vide* Kolkata Gazette Notification of 22nd March, 2005.

(28) The GJM agrees to ensure that peace and normalcy will be maintained in the region.

(29) A review will be done by the State Government of all the cases registered under various laws against persons involved in the GJM agitation. Steps will be taken in the light of the review, not to proceed with prosecution in all cases except those charged with murder. Release of persons in custody will follow the withdrawal of cases.

(30) The GTA youth would be considered for recruitment in the Police, Army and Para Military Forces subject to their suitability for such appointment.

(31) The implementation of the provision of the Memorandum of Agreement shall be periodically reviewed by a committee representing the Government of India, Government of West Bengal and GJM.

(32) The Government of West Bengal shall repeal the DGHC Act, 1988 along with formation of GTA to be constituted by an Act of the legislature.

Signed on 18th July, 2011 at Darjeeling in the presence of Shri P. Chidambaram, Hon'ble Union Home Minister and Mamata Banerjee, Hon'ble Chief Minister, West Bengal.

Signatories
(Dr. G.D. Gautama)
Additional Chief Secretary,
Home & Hill Affairs Department, for and on behalf of the
Government of West Bengal

(Shri Rooshan Giri)
General Secretary,
Gorkha Janmukti Morcha, for and on behalf of the Gorkha
Janmukti Morcha

(Shri K.K. Pathak)
Joint Secreatry to the Government of India, Ministry of Home
Affairs for and on behalf of the Government of India

Annexure 'A'

List of Subjects to be Transferred to the GTA

(1) Agriculture, including agricultural education and research protecting against pest and prevention of plants diseases; Horticulture, Floriculture and Food processing;
(2) Animal Husbandry and Veterinary, that is to say preservation, protection and improvement of stock and prevention of animal diseases, veterinary training and practices, cattle pounds; Dairy development;
(3) Cooperation;
(4) Information and Cultural Affairs;
(5) School Education including primary education, secondary education, higher secondary education (including vocational training); Physical Education; Government Schools.
(6) College Education including Agricultural and Technical Colleges; Local Management of Government sponsored Colleges; Mass Education and Physical Education; Engineering, Medical, Management, and Information Technology with Government and Government sponsored colleges for which wings/cells shall have to be created by the GTA for the area under its jurisdiction;
(7) Adult Education and Library Services;
(8) Fisheries;
(9) Irrigation, drainage and embankments, floods and landslide protection;
(10) Food and Civil Supplies; Consumer Affairs;
(11) Management of any forest, not being Reserved Forest;

[Explanation – 'Reserved Forest' shall mean a reserved forest as constituted under Indian Forest Act, 1927 (16 of 1927)];

(12) Cottage & Small Scale Industries including sericulture, handloom and textiles; handicrafts and Khadi and Village industries;

(13) Cinchona plantation and settlement of land in possession of the plantation inhabitants; management of lease of cinchona lands etc. under it.

(14) Woman and Child Development and Social Welfare;

(15) District Sainik Board;

(16) "Health including Public Health and Family Welfare" including hospitals, dispensaries, health centres and sanatoriums, establishing a Nurses Training School;

(17) Intoxicating liquors, opium derivatives subject to the provisions of Entry 84 of List I of the Seventh Schedule; distilleries – control and regulation; Bonded House and Raising of Revenue;

(18) Irrigation;

(19) Water Resources Investigation and Minor Irrigation;

(20) Labour and Employment;

(21) Land & Land Revenue including allotment, occupation or use, setting apart of land other than land with reserved forest for the purposes of agriculture or grazing or for residential or other non-agricultural purposes to promote interest of the people;

(22) Library services (financed and controlled by the State Government);

(23) Lotteries (subject to the provisions of the Entry 40 of the List I of the Seventh Schedule);

(24) Theatre, dramatic performances and cinemas (subject to the provisions of the Entry 60 of List I of the Seventh Schedule); Sports; entertainment and amusements;

(25) Markets and fairs;

(26) Municipal corporation, improvement of trust, district boards and other local authorities; Fire Services;

(27) Museum and archaeology institutions controlled or financed by the State, ancient and historical monuments and records other than those declared by or under any Law made by Parliament to be of national importance;

(28) Panchayat and Rural Development including District Rural Development Agency (DRDA);
(29) Planning and Development;
(30) Printing and Stationery;
(31) Public Health Engineering; Public Works Department including work relating to State Highways as well as the responsibility discharged by the State Government for maintenance of National Highways within the jurisdiction of GTA;
(33) Publicity and Public Relations including Regulation of Media – both Print and Electronic media;
(34) Registration of births and deaths;
(35) Relief and Rehabilitation, establishing a branch of disaster management in consultation with NDMA under the extant laws/rules.
(36) Sericulture;
(37) Small, cottage and rural industry subject to the provisions of Entries 7 and 52 of List I of the Seventh Schedule;
(38) Social Welfare; including part of SC & ST Development and Finance Corporation under GTA area;
(39) Soil conservation;
(40) Sports and Youth Welfare;
(41) Statistics;
(42) Tourism: Tourism infrastructure within the jurisdiction of the GTA catering to the area of GTA would be transferred to GTA. However, GTA may set up its own wing of Tourism Development Corporation for the area under its jurisdiction;
(43) Transport (roads, bridges, ferries and other means of communication not specified in List I of the Seventh Schedule, municipal tramways, ropeways, inland waterways and traffic thereon, subject to the provision of Entry 40 of List I and List III of the Seventh Schedule with regard to such waterways, vehicles and other mechanically propelled vehicles);
(44) The State Government will consider opening an RTO Office in the GTA area, however, powers vested with the DM at present would remain with him only.
(45) Tribal research institution controlled and financed by the State Government;

(46) Urban development – town and country planning;
(47) Weights and measures subject to the provisions of Entry 50 of List I of the Seventh Schedule;
(48) Welfare of plain tribes and backward classes subject to the area being under GTA only;
(49) Welfare of the Scheduled Castes and Scheduled Tribes and Other Backward Classes;
(50) Welfare of Minorities;
(51) Management and settlement of land including markets and market sheds controlled by the Darjeeling Improvement Fund;
(52) Minor Minerals and Mineral development (subject to the provisions of Entry 23 of List II of the Seventh Schedule);
(53) Rural electrification;
(54) Renewable sources of energy including water-power (subject to Entry 56 of List I and Entry 38 of List III of the Seventh Schedule);
(55) Sharing electricity with GTA subject to evolving a mutually agreeable formula with the State Government;
(56) Pounds and prevention of cattle trespass;
(57) Management of burial grounds and cremation grounds;
(58) Regulation of Cable channels; to the extent the powers of Central Act, i.e. the Cable Television Network (Regulation) Amendment Act, 2002 vests with the State Government;
(59) Tauzi: Tauzi Department of the Collectorate.

Annexure 'B1'

List of Projects to be Undertaken by the GTA to Develop the Physical and Social Infrastructure in the GTA Area in Order to Accelerate the Development of the Region

1. Comprehensive water supply system in the new body area;
2. Multi-super speciality Medical College and Hospital;
3. Establishment of Hospitality and Tourism Management Institute;
4. Establishment of a College of Nursing;
5. Establishment of a Gorkha House at New Delhi;
6. Establishment of an Institute for Research and Development of the Nepali Language;
7. Establishment of a Cultural Institute to preserve, promote and develop culture, tradition, heritage of the people of the region;

8. Establishment of Research and Development Institute for Tea and Cinchona;
9. Research and Development Institute for Horticulture, Floriculture;
10. Balasan Drinking Water Project to be taken up by the Union Government and be declared as a National Project;
11. Sidrabong Hydro Project has been declared a National Heritage but neglected. Funds for its maintenance and upkeep;
12. Food processing, agro-processing complex and cold storage;
13. Creation and development of the IT industry in this region;
14. A new bridge connecting Dooars to be constructed over the Teesta River as the only Coronation Bridge has become very old and it may collapse any time;
15. Mini and Micro Hydro Projects in GTA;
16. Establishment of Eight Multidisciplinary College in different areas of the Region;
17. Establishment of Veterinary Hospitals;
18. High School/Higher Secondary School for every twenty-five villages;
19. Processing plants for Cinchona at Mungpoo;
20. Establishment of Polytechnics for all subdivisions;
21. 2 ITIs/Vocational Institutes in each subdivision
22. Construction of Multistoried Car Parking at Darjeeling, Kurseong and Kalimpong;
23. Construction of Circular Road connecting Darjeeling Town-Lebong-Pandam-Jorebunglow-Darjeeling Town;
24. Construction of Ropeway at Kalimpong (Delo-Relly), at Darjeeling (Tukvar-Singla) and (Batasia-Roack Garden), at Mirik (Mirik-Kurseong), at Kurseong (Giddeypahar-Rohini);
25. Special Fund for the construction of Super-speciality Hospitals in every Sub-Division;
26. Creation of an Industrial zone in an area of at least 1000 acres in the plain areas of the proposed GTA and to be accorded status of special economic zone;
27. Institute of Capacity Building & Livelihood School.

Annexure 'B2'

List of Project Proposals which GTA may Take up with the State/Central Government

1. Establish a Central Institute of Technology;
2. Establishment of a Central University;
3. National Institute of Technology (NIT) including IT and Bio-technology;
4. Construction of an alternative National Highway from Siliguri *via* Mirik along Balasan River to Darjeeling;
5. Establishment of a Fashion Technology Institute;
6. Establishment of a Sainik School;
7. Establishment of National Games and Sports Academy;
8. Establishment of a Tea Auction Centre at Darjeeling;
9. Darjeeling Himalayan Railway to be revitalized for boosting Tourism sector;
10. To establish a Broadgauge Railway Terminal Station at Sukna;
11. Strengthening and Widening of National Highway 55 and 31A;
12. Central Government Engineering College funded by GoI;
13. Revival of Trade route to Tibet *via* Jelepla from Kalimpong;
14. Reservation of seats for students of this region in College/ Institution of higher education including Engineering, Technical, Medical and Management etc. all over India.

Appendix III

Gorkhaland Territorial Administration (GTA) & Darjeeling Gorkha Hill Council (DGHC): A Comparative Analysis

ITEM	*GTA (18.7.2011)*	*DGHC (22.8.1988)*
Nomenclature	The new arrangement of 'autonomous self-governing Body' would be called Gorkhaland Territorial Administration.	The new arrangement was an autonomous Hill Council called as Darjeeling Gorkha Hill Council.
Formation	GTA would be formed through direct election subject to a Bill to be introduced in the State Legislative Assembly for this purpose.	DGHC was formed under the State Act.
Objective	Establish ethnic identity of Gorkhas through expediting all-round (socio-economic, infrastructural, educational, cultural, and linguistic) development of the people in the region.	The major objective of the agreement was to guarantee the social, economic, educational and cultural advancement of the people residing in the hill areas of Darjeeling district.
Demand for Gorkhaland	Without dropping the demand of Gorkhaland the GJM, State Govt., and Central Govt. have agreed to set up the new arrangement. The term Gorkhaland appears in the nomenclature of the new arrangement itself.	GNLF agreed to drop the demand for a separate State of Gorkhaland. Unlike GTA the term Gorkhaland never appeared in the DGHC agreement.

(Contd.)

Appendix III (*Contd.*)

ITEM	*GTA (18.7.2011)*	*DGHC (22.8.1988)*
Area	GTA shall comprise of the three hill subdivisions and *extended areas of Kurseong*. Additional areas of Siliguri Terai and Duars will be transferred on the basis of the recommendations of the High-Powered Committee to be submitted preferably within the six months of its constitution.	The Council covered the three hill subdivisions of Darjeeling district along with the 13 Mouzas of Siliguri Subdivision were added to Kurseong (this constituted the *extended areas of Kurseong*).
Power	Administrative, executive & financial powers in respect of 59 departments transferred to the new Body. There shall be no legislative power for the Body however, it can frame rules/regulations under State Acts to control, regulate & administer the departments/offices/subjects transferred to it.	The Council had enjoyed only executive power (subject to the provisions of Central & State Laws) over such subjects/offices/departments transferred to it.
Functioning	The administrative, executive & financial powers in respect to the transferred subjects will be vested in such a way that the new Body may function in an autonomous way.	There was no provision as such in this regard, although it was agreed to have an autonomous Hill Council to be set up under a State Act.
Restoration of normalcy	(i) GJM agrees to ensure peace & normalcy in the region; (ii) State Govt. will make a review of all the cases registered against persons involved in GJM led agitation and accordingly decide not to proceed with prosecution in all cases except murder cases; (iii) GTA youth would be considered for recruitment in	(i) It was agreed that a review will be done by the State Govt. of all cases registered against persons, under various laws, involved in the GNLF agitation & action will be taken, on the basis of the review, not to proceed with prosecution in all cases excepting the murder cases. This review will be completed within 15

(*Contd.*)

Appendix III (*Contd.*)

ITEM	*GTA (18.7.2011)*	*DGHC (22.8.1988)*
	the Police, Army & Para Military Forces subject to their suitability for such appointment.	days of signing of the agreement; (ii) Govt. agreed not to take disciplinary action against govt. employees in the context of agitation; (iii) GNLF agreed to make arrangement for unauthorized arms surrender by its cadres without the fear of prosecution; (iv) GNLF agreed to withdraw all agitational activities & to extend full cooperation for bringing in peace & normalcy in the hill areas of Darjeeling district.

Appendix IV

Gorkhaland Territorial Administration and Bodoland Territorial Council (BTC): A Comparative Analysis

Items/ Issues	*GTA*	*BTC*
Status	GTA would be formed through direct election subject to a Bill to be introduced in the State Legislative Assembly for this purpose.	Formed under the provisions of Sixth Schedule of Constitution of India. Suitable modifications were made to Safeguard the interests of the non-tribals
Objective	Establish ethnic identity of Gorkhas through expediting all-round (socio-economic, infrastructural, educational, cultural, & linguistic) development of the people in the region.	Fulfil economic, educational and linguistic aspirations and the preservation of land-rights, socio-cultural and ethnic identity of the Bodos; speed up the infrastructure development in the area through creating an autonomous self-governing body under the Sixth Schedule.
Composition	*GTA Sabha Members:* 50 (45 elected members, 5 Governor nominated) *Ex-officio Members:* 7 (3 MLAs, 3 Municipality Chairper-son, 1 MP) *Executive Body:* Chief Executive, 14 members (to be nominated by the Chief out of above 50), Deputy Chief (to be nominated by the Chief out of the 14) *Principal Secretary:* Chief would select from a panel prepared by the State Government.	*Total Members:* 46 (30 tribal, 5 general, 5 open, 6 Governor nominated among whom 2 would be women) *Executive Council:* 12 members maximum including Chief & Deputy Chief *Principal Secretary:* Appointed by the State Government *Term of elected members:* 5 years

(Contd.)

Appendix IV (*Contd.*)

Items/ Issues	*GTA*	*BTC*
	Term of elected members: 5 years	
Power	Administrative, executive & financial powers in respect of 59 departments transferred to it.	Legislative, executive, administrative, financial powers in respect of 40 transferred subjects.
Recruitment	Endowed with the power of creating Group B, C & D posts with the approval of Governor. The recruitment to Group B, C & D posts will be through a Subordinate Service Selection Board to be set up. Recruitment of Group A officers would be made through State Public Service Commission.	Shall be competent to make appointments for all posts (except APSC recruited posts) under its control in accordance with the rules of appointment followed by the Government of Assam. May constitute a Selection Board for appointments to be made by it and may also make rules, with the approval of the Governor to regulate appointments.
Development Agency	A three-tier Panchayat will be constituted by elections in the GTA region, subject to the provisions of Part IX of the Constitution of India. Notwithstanding anything contained in the West Bengal Panchayat Act, 1973, or the West Bengal Municipal Act, 1993, the GTA shall exercise general powers of supervision over the Panchayats and the Municipalities	Development functions and bodies within the competence of BTC shall be transferred to BTC. In respect of DRDA, concurrence of Government of India will be obtained. Full control over the officers and staff working in the BTC area and shall be competent to transfer the staffs/ officers within BTC area.
Financial Package	Central Government assistance of Rs. 200 crore per annum for 3 years for socio-economic infrastructure development. State plan grant, non-plan grant. One time financial assistance for the development of administrative infrastructure. Funds received from Centre shall not be diverted and be released in time by the State Government in time.	Central Government assistance of Rs. 100 crore per annum for 5 years for socio-economic infrastructure development. State plan grant, non-plan grant. One time financial assistance for developing administrative infrastructure. Suitable mechanism to ensure timely transfer of funds on a regular basis.

Appendix V

A Comparative Analysis of Allocated Departments/Subjects/Offices under the DGHC, GAA, GTA, and BTC

DGHC	*GAA*	*GTA*	*BTC*
The allotment, occupation or use, or setting apart, of land other than reserved forest, for the purpose of agriculture or grazing, or for residential or other non-agriculatural purposes, or for any other purpose likely to promote the interest of the inhabitants of any village, locality or town;	Land & Land Revenue including allotment, occupation or use, setting apart of land other than any land which is a reserved forest.	Land & Land Revenue including allotment, occupation or use, setting apart of land other than land with reserved forest for the purposes of agriculture or grazing or for residential or other non-agricultural purposes to promote interest of the people	Land & revenue
The management of any forest, not being a Reserved Forest.	Management of any forest, not being a Reserved Forest	Management of any forest, not being Reserved Forest	Forest
	Irrigation; Irrigation, drainage & embankments, floods & landslide protection; Water resources investigation & minor irrigation	Irrigation ; Irrigation, drainage and embankments, floods and landslide protection; Water Resources Investigation & Minor Irrigation	Irrigation; Flood control

(Contd.)

Appendix V (*Contd.*)

DGHC	*GAA*	*GTA*	*BTC*
Agriculture	Agriculture, including agricultural education and research, protecting against pest and prevention of plants diseases;	Agriculture, including agricultural education and research, protecting against pest & prevention of plants diseases; Horticulture, Floriculture & Food processing	Agriculture
Public health & sanitation, hospitals & dispensaries	Health & Family welfare	Health including Public Health & Family welfare including hospitals, dispensaries, health centres & sanatoriums, establishing a Nurses Training School;	Health & family welfare
Tourism	Tourism	Tourism infrastructure within the jurisdiction of the GTA catering to the area of GTA would be transferred to GTA. Separate wing of Tourism Development Corporation for the area under its jurisdiction to be set up	Tourism
Education-Primary, Secondary and Higher Secondary; Vocational training	School education (primary, secondary, vocational training); College education (agricultural & technical colleges, except Govt. & Govt. sponsored colleges; Adult education & library services,	School education (primary, secondary, vocational, physical education, Govt. schools); College education (agricultural & technical colleges, local management of Govt. sponsored colleges, Separate branch for engineering, medical,	Education [primary, higher secondary, vocational, adult, college (general)]

(Contd.)

Appendix V (*Contd.*)

DGHC	*GAA*	*GTA*	*BTC*
		management, IT with Govt. & Govt. sponsored colleges); Adult education & library services,	
Public works - Development and planning	Planning & development	Planning & development	Planning & development
Construction & maintenance of all roads except national highways and state highways	PWD	PWD including work relating to State Highways as well as the responsibility discharged by the State Government for maintenance of National Highways within the jurisdiction of GTA	PWD
Transport and development of transport	Transport (roads, bridges, ferries, municipal tramways, ropeways, inland waterways & traffic)	Transport (roads, bridges, ferries & other means of communication, municipal tramways, ropeways, inland waterways and traffic thereon; waterways, vehicles & other mechanically propelled vehicles);	Transport
Management of burials & burial grounds, cremation & cremation grounds	Management of burial & cremation grounds	Management of burial grounds & cremation grounds	No provision as such

(Contd.)

Appendix V (*Contd.*)

DGHC	*GAA*	*GTA*	*BTC*
Preservation, protection & improvement of livestock & prevention of animal diseases, veterinary training & practice.	Animal husbandry & veterinary (preservation, protection & improvement of stock & prevention of animal diseases, veterinary training & practice, cattle pounds)	Animal Husbandry and Veterinary, that is to say preservation, protection and improvement of stock and prevention of animal diseases, veterinary training and practices, cattle pounds; Dairy development	Animal husbandry & veterinary
Pounds & prevention of cattle trespass	Pounds & prevention of cattle trespass	Pounds & prevention of cattle trespass	No provision as such
Fisheries	Fisheries	Fisheries	Fisheries
Management of markets & fairs, not managed by Municipalities or PRIs	Markets & fairs	Markets & fairs	Markets & fairs
Works, Lands and Buildings vested in or in the possession of the General Council	Management & settlement of land including markets & market sheds controlled by the Darjeeling Improvement Fund	Management & settlement of land including markets & market sheds controlled by the Darjeeling Improvement Fund	No provision as such
Small-Scale & Cottage Industries	Small-Scale & Cottage Industries	Small-Scale & Cottage Industries	Small-Scale & Cottage Industries
No provision as such	Cooperation	Cooperation	Cooperation
No provision as such	Information & cultural affairs	Information & cultural affairs	Cultural affairs
No provision as such	Food & civil supply	Food & civil supplies, consumer affairs	Food & civil supply

(*Contd.*)

Appendix V (*Contd.*)

DGHC	*GAA*	*GTA*	*BTC*
No provision as such	Cottage & small scale industries including sericulture, handloom textile, handicrafts, Khadi & village industries	Cottage & small scale industries including sericulture, handloom textile, handicrafts, Khadi & village industries	Small cottage & rural industry
No provision as such	Intoxicating liquors, opium & derivatives	Intoxicating liquors, opium & derivatives	Intoxicating liquors, opium & derivatives
No provision as such	Labour & employment	Labour & employment	Labour & employment
No provision as such	Library services (financed & controlled by the State Govt.)	Library services (financed & controlled by the State Govt.)	Library services
No provision as such	Lotteries; Theatres, dramatic performances & cinema	Lotteries; Theatres, dramatic performances & cinema	Lotteries; Theatres, dramatic performances & cinema
No provision as such	Municipal corporation, improvement trust, district boards & other local authorities	Municipal corporation, improvement trust, district boards & other local authorities, fire services	Municipal corporation, improvement trust, district boards & other local authorities
No provision as such	Panchayat & Rural Development	Panchayat & Rural Development including DRDA	Panchayat & Rural Development
No provision as such	Museum and archaeology institutions controlled and financed by the State	Museum and archaeology institutions controlled and financed by the State	Museum and archaeology
No provision as such	Planning and Development	Planning and Development	Planning and Development
No provision as such	Printing & stationary	Printing & stationary	Printing & stationary

(*Contd.*)

Appendix V (*Contd.*)

DGHC	*GAA*	*GTA*	*BTC*
No provision as such	PHE	PHE	PHE
No provision as such	Publicity & public relations	Publicity & public relations including regulation of print & electronic media	Publicity & public relations
No provision as such	Registration of births and deaths	Registration of births and deaths	Registration of births and deaths
No provision as such	Relief & rehabilitation	Relief & rehabilitation, new branch of disaster management be set up	Relief & rehabilitation
No provision as such	Sericulture	Sericulture	Sericulture
No provision as such	Social welfare	Social welfare including a part of SC, ST development	Social welfare
No provision as such	Soil conservation	Soil conservation	Soil conservation
No provision as such	Sports & youth welfare	Sports & youth welfare	Sports & youth welfare
No provision as such	Statistics	Statistics	Statistics
No provision as such	Tribal research institute controlled & financed by the State Government	Tribal research institute controlled & financed by the State Government	Tribal research institute
No provision as such	Urban development-town & country planning	Urban development-town & country planning	Urban development-town & country planning
No provision as such	Welfare of plan tribes & backward classes	Welfare of plan tribes & backward classes	Welfare of plan tribes & backward classes
No provision as such	Weights & measures	Weights & measures	Weights & measures

(*Contd.*)

Appendix V (*Contd.*)

DGHC	*GAA*	*GTA*	*BTC*
No provision as such	Welfare of plan tribes & backward classes	Welfare of plan tribes & backward classes	Welfare of plan tribes & backward classes
No provision as such	Welfare of minorities	Welfare of minorities	No provision as such
No provision as such	Minor minerals & mineral developments	Minor minerals & mineral developments	No provision as such
No provision as such	Rural electrification	Rural electrification	No provision as such
No provision as such	Renewable sources of energy including water power	Renewable sources of energy including water power	No provision as such
No provision as such	Woman & child development & social welfare	Woman & child development & social welfare	No provision as such
No provision as such	No provision as such	Regulation of cable channels	No provision as such
No provision as such	No provision as such	Sharing electricity with GTA subject to evolve a mutually agreeable formula with the State Govt.	No provision as such
No provision as such	No provision as such	RTO to be set up with powers vested in the hands of the DM	No provision as such
No provision as such	No provision as such	District Sainik Board	No provision as such
No provision as such	No provision as such	Cinchona plantation, settlement of land in possession of plantation inhabitants, management of lease of cinchona lands	No provision as such
No provision as such	No provision as such	*Tauzi* department of the collectorate	No provision as such

Bibliography

Newspapers

Ananda Bazar Patrika (ABP), Kolkata.
Himalaya Darpan (HIM DAR), Siliguri
Hindustan Times (HT), Kolkata.
Sikkim Express (SE), Gangtok.
Telegraph (TEL), Siliguri.
The Bengal Post (BP), Siliguri.
The Sentinel (SENT).
The Statesman (STAT), Siliguri.
The Times of India (TOI), Kolkata.

Books and Articles

Appadurai, Arjun. 1993. "Number in the Colonial Imagination" in Carol A. Breckenridge and Peter van der Veer, (eds.): *Orientalislm and the Postcolonial Predicament: Perspectives on South Asia*. Philadelphia: University of Pennsylvania Press.

Balibar, Etienne. 1988. 'Propositions on Citizenship', *Ethics*, 98(4): 723-738.

Baruah, Sanjib (Ed.). 2009. *Beyond Counterinsurgency*. New Delhi: Oxford University Press.

Baruah, Sanjib (Ed.). 2010. *Ethnonationalism in India: A Reader*. New Delhi: Oxford University Press.

Benedikter, Thomas (Ed.). 2009. *Solving Ethnic Conflict through Self-Government: A Short Guide to Autonomy in South Asia and Europe*. Italy: EURAC Research, Institute of Minority Rights.

Beek, Martin van. 1999. 'Hill Councils, Development, and Democracy:

Assumptions and Experiences from Ladakh', *Alternatives,* 24(4): 435-460.

Bermeo, N. 2002. 'The Import of Institutions', *Journal of Democracy,* 13(2): 96–110.

Bhaba, Homi K. 1994. *The Location of Culture.* London: Routledge.

Bhowmik, Sharit. 2011. 'Wages and Ethnic Conflicts in Bengal's Tea Industry', *Economic and Political Weekly,* XLVI (32): 26-29.

Black, Donald. (Ed.). 1984. *Towards a General theory of Social Control.* Vol. I. Fundamentals Orlando, FL: Academic Press.

Bonta, Bruce D. 1996. 'Conflict Resolution among Peaceful Societies: The Culture of Peacefulness', *Journal of Peace Research,* 33(4): 403 – 420.

Byrne, Sean. 2001. 'Consociational and Civic Society Approaches to Peace Building in Northern Ireland', *Journal of Peace Research,* 38(3): 327-352.

Chakrabarty, Debabrata. 1997. 'Community Development Alternatives to the Rural Crisis: A Study in Three Tea-Villages of Darjeeling', *Himalayan Paryavaran,* 5: 28-36.

Chakrabarty, Subhas Ranjan. 2005. 'Silence under Freedom: The Strange Story of Democracy in the Darjeeling Hills', in Ranabir Samaddar (ed.): *The Politics of Autonomy: Indian Experiences.* New Delhi: Sage Publications.

Chandra, Kanchan. 2004. *Why Ethnic Parties Succeed: Patronage and Ethnic Head Counts in India.* Cambridge: Cambridge University Press.

Chattopadhyay, Suhrid Shankar. 2012. 'Walkover in the Hills', *Frontline.* 29 (15) July 28 – August 10 [Online Resource] Available at: http://www.flonnet.com/fl2915/stories/20120810291503600.htm (Accessed on August 2, 2012).

Chaudhuri, Kalyan. 1996. 'Reviving a Threat: Demand for Gorkhaland', *Frontline,* 13(20): 43-44.

Chima, Jugdep S. 2010. *The Sikh Separatist Insurgency in India: Patterns of Internationalization.* New Delhi: Sage.

Chowdhary, Rekha. 2009. 'Electoral Politics in the context of Separatism and Political Divergence: An Analysis of 2009 Parliamentary Elections in Jammu & Kashmir', *South Asia Multidisciplinary Academic Journal,* Thematic Issue - No. 3, Contests in Context: Indian Elections 2009. [On-line Resource] Available at: http://samaj.revues.org/index2785.html (Accessed on August 2, 2012).

Coakley, John. 1992. 'The Resolution of Ethnic Conflict: Towards a Typology', *International Political Science Review,* 13(4): 343-358.

Coakley, John. 1994. 'Approaches to the Resolution of Ethnic Conflict: The Strategy of Non-territorial Autonomy', *International Political Science Review,* 15(3): 297-314.

Cohen, F.S. 1997. 'Proportional versus Majoritarian Ethnic Conflict

Management in Democracies', *Comparative Political Studies,* 30(5): 607–30.

Cordell, Karl & Stefan Wolff. 2010. *Ethnic Conflict: Causes – Consequences – Responses*. Cambridge UK: Polity Press.

Darjeeling Times.com 21.6.2010. 'Supporting the issue of Darjeeling Sikkim unification is suicidal: G. M. Rai'. [On-line resource] Available at: http://www.darjeelingtimes.com/main-news/98-citizen-news/913-supporting-the-issue-of-darjeeling-sikkim-unification-is-suicidal-g-m-rai.html (Accessed on January 16, 2011).

Darjeeling Times.com. 21.9.2010. 'AIGL feels integration with Sikkim as solution for Darjeeling'. [Online resource] Available at: http://www.darjeelingtimes.com/main-news/politics/1472-aigl-feels-integration-with-sikkim-as-solution-for-darjeeling.html_(Accessed on January 15, 2011).

Das, Samir Kumar. 2005. 'Where Do the Autonomous Institutions Come From?', in Ranabir Samaddar (ed.): *The Politics of Autonomy: Indian Experiences.* New Delhi: Sage.

Datta, P. S. 1995. *Ethnic Peace Accords in India*. New Delhi: Vikas Publishing House Pvt. Ltd.

De, Koustav. 2009. 'Gorkhaland and Lalgarh: Dialogues, Parallels and a Challenge to Mainstream Parties', *Frontier,* March 21. [On-line resource] Available at: http://sanhati.com/excerpted/1294 (Accessed on January 2, 2012).

District Census Handbook: Darjeeling, Census 1961. Calcutta: Government Printing.

Dixit, Kanak Mani. 1993. 'Looking for Greater Nepal', *Himal,* 6(2): 15-19.

Dube, S.C.1997. 'Ethnicity: Myth History, Politics', in A.M. Shah, B.S. Baviskar and E.A. Ramaswamy (eds.): *Social Structure and Change.* Vol. IV. New Delhi: Sage.

Foweraker, Joe. 1995. *Theorizing Social Movements*. London: Pluto Press.

Ganguly, Rajat. 2009. 'Democracy and Ethnic Conflict', in Sumit Ganguly, in Larry Diamond & Marc F. Plattner (eds.): The State of India's Democracy. New Delhi: Oxford University Press.

Ghosh, Partha S. 1998. 'Ethnic Conflict and Conflict Management: The Indian Case', in Iftekaruzzaman (ed.): *Ethnicity and Constitutional Reform in India*. New Delhi: Manohar.

Government of West Bengal. 2007. *Strategy & Action Plan for Capacity Building of Panchayats & Municipalities in 11 Districts of West Bengal under Backward Regions Grant Fund 2006-07*. Panchayats & Rural Development Department.

GTA Elections 2012 [On-line resource] Available at: http://darjeeling.gov.in/GTAelected_candidates.html (Accessed on August 8, 2012).

GTA Elections Rules, 2012. The Kolkata Gazette Extraordinary, March 12, 2012.

Gupta, Dipankar. 1996. *The Context of Ethnicity: Sikh Identity in a Comparative Perspective*. Delhi: Oxford University Press.

Gurr, T.R. 1993. *Minorities at Risk: A Global View of Ethnopolitical Conflicts*. Washington, D.C.: United States Institute of Peace Press.

Gurung, Nar Bahadur. 1971. *Darjeeling*. (In Nepali). Kalimpong.

Harff, B. and Gurr, T.R. 2004. *Ethnic Conflict in World Politics*. Boulder, CO: Westview Press.

Hazleton, William A. 1998. 'Ending Violent Ethnic Conflicts: Separation or Sharing as Options for Negotiation', *Nationalism and Ethnic Politics,* 4 (3): 102-119.

Heraclides, Alexis. 1989. 'Conflict Resolution, Ethnonationalism and the Middle East Impasse', *Journal of Peace Research,* 26(2): 197-212.

(HPC Report). High Power Committee for Determination of Territorial Jurisdiction of GTA Report. June 8, 2012. [On-line resource] Available at: http://westbengal.gov.in/portal/banglarMukh/whatsNew (Accessed on August 2, 2012).

Horowitz, Donald L. [1985] 2000. *Ethnic Groups in Conflict*. Berkeley: University of California Press.

Horowitz, Donald L. 1990. 'Ethnic Conflict Management for Policy Makers', in J. V. Montville (ed.): *Conflict and Peacemaking in Multiethnic Societies*. Lexington, MA: Lexington Books.

Horowitz, Donald L. 2003. 'Electoral Systems and their goals: a primer for decision-makers', *Journal of Democracy*, 14(4): 115-127.

Horowitz, Donald L. 2004. 'The Alternate Vote and interethnic moderation: a reply to Fraenkel and Grofman', *Public Choice,* 121(3-4): 507-517.

Huntington, Samuel P. 1997. *Clash of Civilizations and the Remaking of World Order*. New Delhi: Penguin.

Information Booklet: Gorkhaland Territorial Administration Sabha Election 2012. Government of West Bengal, Office of the Election Officer & District Magistrate: Darjeeling.

Interim Report of the Excluded and Partially Excluded Areas (Other than Assam) Sub-Committee of the Advisory Committee (Constituent Assembly of India), Annexure III (Appendix D) Constituent Assembly of India Debates (Proceedings) Vol. VII. (On-line resource) Available at: http://164.100.47.132/LssNew/constituent/vol7p1.html (Accessed on 28.12.2011).

Jalali, Rita and S. M. Lipset. 1992-93. "Racial and Ethnic Conflicts: A Global Perspective", *Political Science Quarterly,* 107(4):585–606.

Kar, Chiranjib Kumar. 1999. *Darjeeling Himalaya in Flames*. Darjeeling: Jetsun Publishing House.

Keating, M. 1998. *The New Regionalism in Western Europe*. Cheltenham: Elgar.

King, R.D. 1997. *Nehru and the Language Politics of India*. New Delhi: Oxford University Press.

Kohli, Atul. 1997. 'Can Democracies Accommodate Ethnic Nationalism? Rise and Decline of Self-Determination Movements in India', *The Journal of Asian Studies*, 56(2): 325-344.

Lacina, Bethany. 2009. 'The Problem of Political Stability in North East India', *Asian Survey*, 49(6): 998-1020.

Lake, David A. and Donald Rothchild. 1996. 'Containing Fear: The Origin and Management of Ethnic Conflict', *International Security*, 21(2): 41-75.

Lama, Mahendra P. 1996. *Gorkhaland Movement: Quest for an Identity*. Darjeeling: Department of Information and Cultural Affairs (DGHC).

Lederach, John Paul. 1997. *Building Peace: Sustainable Reconciliation in Divided Societies*. Washington DC: United States Institute of Peace Press.

Lijphart, Arend. 1968a. 'Typologies of Democratic Systems', *Comparative Political Studies*, 1(1): 3-44.

Lijphart, Arend. 1968b. *The Politics of Accommodation: Pluralism and Democracy in The Netherlands*. Berkeley, CA: University of California Press.

Lijphart, Arend. 1977. *Democracy in Plural Societies*. New Haven, CT: Yale University Press.

Lijphart, Arend. 1984. *Democracies, Patterns of Majoritarian and Consensus Government in Twenty-One Countries*. New Haven, CT/ London: Yale University Press.

Lijphart, Arend. 1996a. 'The Framework Documents on Northern Ireland and the Theory of Power Sharing', *Government and Opposition*, 31(3): 267-275.

Lijphart, Arend. 1996b. 'The Puzzle of Indian Democracy: A Consociational Interpretation', *The American Political Science Review*, 90(2): 258-268.

Majeed, Akhtar 2003. 'The Changing Politics of States' Reorganisation', *Publius: The Journal of Federalism*, 33(4): 83-98.

McGarry, John and Brendan O'Leary. 1993. 'Introduction: The macro-political regulation of ethnic conflict', in John Mc Garry and Brendan O'Leary (eds): *The Politics of Ethnic Conflict Regulation*. London: Routledge.

McGarry, John and Brendan O'Leary. 1994. 'The Political regulation of National and Ethnic Conflict', *Parliamentary Affairs*, 47(1): 94-115.

McGarry, John and B. O'Leary. 2004. *The Northern Ireland Conflict: Consociational Engagements*. Oxford: Oxford University Press.

Melucci, Alberto. 1996. *Challenging Codes: Collective Action in the Information Age*. Cambridge: Cambridge University Press.

Misra, Amalendu. 2001. 'The Politics of Secessionist Conflict Management in India', *Contemporary Security Policy,* 22(2): 49-68.

Mitra, Subrata K. 1997. 'Legitimacy, governance and political Institutions in India after Independence', in Subrata K. Mitra & Dietmar Rothermund (eds.): *Legitimacy and Conflict in South Asia*. New Delhi: Manohar.

Mohan, Saumitra. 2012. 'Territory within State: A New Model of Development in Darjeeling', Post-Editorial Article, *The Statesman,* August 4, Saturday.

Nordlinger, Eric A. 1972. *Conflict Regulation in Divided Societies*. Cambridge, MA: Centre for International Relations, Harvard University.

Oberschall, Anthony. 2007. *Conflict and Peace Building in Divided Societies: Responses to Ethnic Violence.* London: Routledge.

Oommen, T. K. 1990. *Protest and Change: Studies in Social Movements*. New Delhi: Sage Publications.

Orjuela, Camilla. 2008. *The Identity Politics of Peace Building: Civil Society in War-torn Sri Lanka.* New Delhi: Sage.

Parliamentary Proceedings (Lok Sabha): USQ No. 3853, August 22, 1991.

Parliamentary Proceedings (Lok Sabha): USQ Nos. 262 & 4677, February 26, 1992 & March 26, 1992.

Pradhan, R.M. 1996. *Continuous political struggle for a separate constitutional status of ceded land of Darjeeling and leasehold land of Kalimpong*. Darjeeling: Department of Information & Cultural Affairs (DGHC).

Rabushka, A. and Shepsle, K. 1972. *Politics in Plural Societies: A Theory of Democratic Instability*. Columbus, OH: Merrill.

Rawat, Bhagirath 1996. *Bas Salkirahecha*. (In Nepali), 2nd edition. Darjeeling: Gorkha Parbatya Parishad.

Reilly, Benjamin. 2004. *Democracy in Divided Societies: Electoral Engineering for Conflict Management.* Cambridge UK: Cambridge University Press.

Roeder, Philip & Donald Rothchild (eds.) 2005. Sustainable Peace: Power and Democracy after Civil Wars. Ithaca, NY: Cornell University Press.

Ross, M. Howard. 2010. 'Creating the conditions for peacemaking: theories of practice in ethnic conflict resolution', *Ethnic and Racial Studies,* 23(6): 1002-1034.

Rothchild, Donald. 1986. 'Interethnic conflict and policy analysis in Africa', *Ethnic and Racial Studies,* 9(1): 66-86.

Roy, Sanjay K. 2011. 'The Liberal Democracy and the Struggle of the Adivasis in the Dooars and Terai for a Self', in Biswajit Ghosh (Ed.): *Interrogating Development*. New Delhi: Rawat Publications.

Saideman, S.M. *et. al,* 2002. 'Democratization, Political Institutions, and

Ethnic Conflict: A Pooled Time-Series Analysis, 1985–1998', *Comparative Political Studies*, 35(1): 103–29.

Samanta, Amiya K. 2000. *Gorkhaland Movement: A Study in Ethnic Separatism*. New Delhi: APH Publishing Corporation.

Sankrityayana, Jeta. 1997. 'Land-use and Forests: The Mountain Development Paradox in Darjeeling', *Himalayan Paryavaran*, 5: 121-129.

Sarkar, Jibesh. 2004. *Darjeeling Jelar Communist Andolan Prasange*. Vol. I. (in Bengali). Siliguri: Ratanlal Brahman Memorial Trust.

Schneckener, U. 2002. 'Making Power Sharing Work: Lessons from Successes and Failures in Ethnic Conflict Regulation', *Journal of Peace Research*, 39(2): 203–28.

Sengupta, Nitish. 2007. *Bengal Divided: The Unmaking of a Nation (1905-1971)*. New Delhi: Penguin.

Singh, Kumar Sanjay. 1999. 'Naga Accords: An Instance of Domination through Negotiation', *Mimeographed*.

Singh, Yogendra. 1988. 'Social Processes and Dimensions of Indian Nationalism', *Third I.P. Desai Memorial Lecture*. Surat: Centre for Social Studies.

Sisk, Timothy D. 1996. *Power Sharing and International Mediation in Ethnic Conflict*. Washington DC: United States Institute of Peace Press.

Sonntag, Selma K. 199. 'Autonomous Councils in India: Contesting the Liberal Nation State', *Alternatives*, 24(4): 415-434.

Smooha, Sammy and Theodore Harf. 1992. 'The Diverse Modes of Conflict Resolution in Deeply Divided Societies', *International Journal of Comparative Sociology*, 33(1-2): 26-47.

Spivak, Gayatri Chakravorty. 2010. *Nationalism and the Imagination*. Calcutta: Seagaull Books.

Srinivas, M.N. (1962)1998. *Caste in Modern India and Other Essays*. Reprinted. Bombay: Media Promoters and Publishers Pvt. Ltd.

Subba, T.B. 1992. *Ethnicity, State and Development: A Case Study of Gorkhaland Movement in Darjeeling Hills*. New Delhi: Har-Anand Publications in association with Vikash Publishing House Pvt. Ltd.

Swatantra Manchko Bulletin. 1985. 1 (6), 5th October.

Timsina, S.R. 1992. *Nepali Community in India*. Delhi: Manak Publicaions Pvt. Ltd.

Todosijeviæ, Bojan. 2001. 'Macro-Political Means of Ethnic Conflict Management in Southeast Europe: A Critical Examination', *Southeast European Politics*, 2(2): 77-93.

Varshney, Asutosh. 2002. *Ethnic Conflict and Civic Life: Hindus and Muslims in India*. New Delhi: Oxford University Press.

West Bengal Human Development Report. 2004. Government of West Bengal: Development and Planning Department.

West Bengal Legislative Assembly Proceedings (WBLAP) 1954. Assembly Proceedings (Official Report). 10(1): 271-276.

Why Gorkhaland? 1986. Darjeeling: Pranta Parishad.

Wimmer, Andreas. 2003. 'Democracy and ethno-religious conflict in Iraq', *Survival,* 45(4): 111-134.

Wolff, Stefan. 2010. 'Approaches to Conflict Resolution in Divided Societies: The Many Uses of Territorial Self-Governance', *Ethnopolitics Papers No. 5*. University of Exeter, UK: Exeter Centre for Ethno-Political Studies. (On-line resource) Stable URL: http://centres.exeter.ac.uk/exceps/resources/papers.htm (Accessed on January 12, 2012).

Wolf, Stefan. 2011. 'Managing ethno-national conflict: towards an analytical framework', *Commonwealth and Comparative Politics,* 49(2): 162-195.

Woods, E. Taylor. *et. al* 2011. 'Ethno-national Conflict resolution and its management', *Commonwealth and Comparative Politics,* 49(2): 153-161.

Wright, Frank. 1987. *Northern Ireland: A Comparative Analysis*. Dublin: Gill & Macmillan.

Zaid, A.M. and S.G. Zaid. (Eds.). 1981. *The Encyclopaedia of Indian National Congress*. Vol. 12: 1939-1946. New Delhi: S. Chand & Company.

Index